101 Great Tramps

IN NEW ZEALAND

Mark Pickering
&
Rodney Smith

REED

This book should not be used as the sole reference to the routes it describes. People planning to venture along these routes are advised to consult and use the relevant topographical maps.

Published by Reed Books, a division of Reed Publishing (NZ) Ltd, 39 Rawene Rd, Birkenhead, Auckland. Associated companies, branches and representatives throughout the world.

ISBN 0 7900 0637 5

Text © 1991, 1998 Mark Pickering and Rodney Smith
All photographs by Mark Pickering
Cover and text designed by Sunny H. Yang

Originally published as 75 *Great Tramps for New Zealanders* in 1986
Reprinted 1987
Revised and expanded as *101 Great Tramps in New Zealand* in 1988
Reprinted 1989
Fully revised 1991
Reprinted 1992
Fully revised 1993
Reprinted 1994
Fully revised 1998
Printed in Australia

Contents

Authors' note   6
Acknowledgements   7
Introduction   8

North Island

The Far North, Auckland and Coromandel
1 Cape Reinga Walkway   28
2 Whatipu Coast   31
3 Great Barrier Island   33
4 The Pinnacles   36

Kaimai Range and Mount Pirongia
5 Waitawheta Tramway   39
6 Mount Baldy and Te
   Rereatukahia Hut   42
7 Mount Pirongia
   Crossing   44

Raukumara Range and Urewera National Park
8 Mount Hikurangi   45
9 Lake Waikaremoana
   Circuit   47
10 Lake Waikareiti   50
11 Mount Manuoha   52
12 Whirinaki River   54
13 Whirinaki Forest   57

Tongariro National Park
14 Tongariro Crossing   59
15 Oturere Crossing   62
16 Tama Lakes   63
17 Lake Surprise   66

Mount Taranaki and Whanganui National Park
18 Mount Taranaki:
    Round the Mountain 1   68
19 Mount Taranaki:
    Round the Mountain 2   71
20 Pouakai Range
    Crossing   74
21 Matemateaonga
    Walkway   76

Kaimanawa Range and Kaweka Range
22 Umukarikari and Urchin
    Tops   79
23 Kaweka Hot Springs   82
24 Kaweka Range   84
25 Kiwi Mouth and Kiwi
    Saddle   87

Ruahine Range
26 Parks Peak and
    Makaroro River   89
27 Sunrise Hut   91
28 Sawtooth Ridge   94
29 Rangiwahia Hut   97

Tararua Range
30 Mount Holdsworth and
    Jumbo Circuit   99

31	Totara Flats (Holdsworth to Kaitoke)	102
32	Southern Crossing	105
33	Mount Kapakapanui	108

Rimutaka Range and Hauragi Range

34	Mount Matthews	109
35	Haurangi Bush Track	111

South Island

Richmond Range

36	Dun Mountain	115
37	Pelorus River	117
38	Mount Richmond	120
39	Wakamarina Crossing	121

Abel Tasman National Park

40	Abel Tasman Coastal Track	123
41	Abel Tasman Inland Track	128

Kahurangi National Park

42	Heaphy Track	130
43	Cobb Valley	134
44	Mount Arthur and the Tableland	136
45	Karamea River	140
46	Wangapeka Track	143
47	Owen Plateau	146
48	1000 Acre Plateau	148

Kaikoura

49	Saw-Cut Gorge	151
50	Kowhai River and Hapuku River	154
51	Mount Fyffe	156

Nelson Lakes

52	Travers River and Sabine River	158
53	Lake Angelus Tops	162
54	Waiau Pass	165
55	Matakitaki Valley	168

Lewis Pass and Lake Sumner

56	St James Walkway	172
57	Lake Daniells	175
58	Lake Christabel Crossing	177
59	Harper Pass	179

Victoria Range and Paparoa National Park

60	Kirwans Knob	184
61	Lake Stream	186
62	Inland Pack Track	188
63	Croesus Track	192

Arthur's Pass

64	Lake Minchin	195
65	Hallelujah Flat and Binser Saddle	197
66	Tarn Col (Edwards River to Hawdon River)	199
67	Mingha River to Deception River	202
68	Carroll Hut and Hunt Creek	204
69	Avalanche Peak	206
70	Three Pass Trip	209

West Coast

71 Arahura Valley 212
72 Cedar Flats 215
73 Frew Saddle Circuit 217
74 Whitcombe Pass 220
75 Welcome Flat Hot
   Pools 222
76 The Paringa Cattle
   Track 225
77 The Coast (Barn Bay to
   Martins Bay) 229

Canterbury

78 Jollie Brook 232
79 Wharfedale Track and
   Black Hill 234
80 Cass Saddle and
   Lagoon Saddle 236
81 Rakaia River 239
82 Mount Somers
   Walkway 242
83 Arrowsmith
   Approach 245

Mount Cook and Mackenzie Country

84 Mueller Hut 247
85 Huxley Valley and
   Brodrick Pass 250
86 Dasler Bivouac 252

Mount Aspiring National Park

87 Gillespie Pass 254
88 Wilkin Valley 258
89 The Waterfall Face and
   Rabbit Pass 260
90 Matukituki Valley 263
91 Rees Valley and Dart
   River 266
92 Routeburn Track 270
93 Greenstone Valley and
   Caples Valley 273
94 Mavora Walkway 277

Fiordland National Park

95 Hollyford Track 280
96 Milford Track 284
97 Kepler Track 287
98 Dusky Sound 291
99 Waitutu Tramway and
   Port Craig 294

Stewart Island

100 Rakiura Track 297
101 The Stewart Island
    Circuit 300

Authors' note

Guide books seem to go out of date faster than last year's computer. Since *101 Great Tramps* was first published (as *75 Great Tramps*) in 1986 there have been numerous reprints, revisions, and new editions, but despite all this the book was, in all honesty, getting steadily out of date.

The system of tramping times was not detailed enough, the introductory notes were skimpy, the gear notes designed for the Neolithic period, and as for the photographs ...

On top of these stylistic problems the tramping world has evolved considerably. The Department of Conservation (DOC) has introduced the Great Walks, encouraging a whole new type of tramper to go back-country. There have been several new National Parks, hut fees have come in, and large open-air fires (sob) have gone out of fashion. The tramper, walker or hiker is a recognised type of consumer, and all sorts of new products from transport packages to backpacker hostels have sprung up to meet the demand.

For all these reasons it was decided to produce a completely new edition of *101 Great Tramps*, not only scrutinising all existing tramps but replacing them with others where appropriate.

Since many tramping books cover the more off-the-beaten-track areas, it was felt that *101* should concentrate on the classic tramps in each region, which are usually better tracked and better marked. Some fifteen new tramps have been added, most wilderness or bush-bashing routes have been deleted, and there are more tramps in the easy to easy/medium category. Because more people are using cars for access, circuit trips have been emphasised wherever possible.

Another book, called *New Zealand's Top Tracks*, replaces the earlier *New Zealand's Top Ten Tracks*, and covers in much greater detail the showpiece tracks on the DOC estate. People only intending to do a Great Walk will probably find that book more directly useful.

Mark Pickering, Rodney Smith

Acknowledgements

I'd like to thank Sven Brabyn and Geoff Spearpoint for reviewing the text and updating my tramping information, and Steve Kennedy for assistance with the Milford Track text. I would also like to thank the staff of various field stations and conservancies of the Department of Conservation who commented on some of this text. Their comments were appreciated if not always absorbed into the text.

Especially deep thanks to my partner, Rachel Barker, who shares my enthusiasms and lets me wander off into the hills — yet again.

Mark Pickering

Introduction

This book offers 101 of the classic New Zealand tramps, the 'must-dos' of any region, from the internationally known tracks such as the Milford Track and the Routeburn, to such well-known local tramps as Totara Flats in the Tararuas, and the Round-the-Mountain trek at Taranaki.

101 Great Tramps is intended as an ideas book, to give people the information, and the inspiration, to have a go at some of the tracks in the New Zealand back-country. In the descriptions we have tried to convey a sense of what the place is like, a bit of ambience, and hopefully an enticement.

Long-fingered fiords, lakes, smoking volcanoes, natural hot pools, the great glacier fields of the south, and the rolling carpet of forest between make up the substance of the New Zealand mountain world. Over this humans have imposed a matrix of routes, tracks and walkways, and have dotted the landscape with tough little mountain huts. The result is incomparable tramping opportunities.

Nor are there any dangerous insects, leeches or bears to worry about. Too good to be true? Paradise does have its imperfections. The New Zealand sandfly is one of them (take repellent) and the weather can be the other. Carry a good weatherproof jacket and a philosophical attitude. A spare day and a book is also not a bad idea, but New Zealand's weather changes so fast that yesterday's perfect horror of a storm can give way to a promising dawn of blue skies — time to go.

TRAMPING IN NEW ZEALAND

In New Zealand back-country walking, hiking, backpacking etc. is simply called tramping. Most tramps in this book take a minimum of a weekend, require overnight camping gear, and often cross high passes — they are tramps, not walks!

You will need a basic level of fitness if your trip is not to become a tiring, blister-plagued ordeal. People not used to tramping often find a backpack rather debilitating, and the odd jog or game of squash will not necessarily provide sufficient preparation for a long tramp.

The best training is tramping itself, day walks at first, then short weekend tramps. If you are inexperienced or unfamiliar with New Zealand conditions, give yourself an extra day in case you find you are not covering the distances you expected. And since in most cases you will be travelling long distances just to reach the tracks, it's worth giving yourself plenty of time and making a thorough holiday of it.

Several difficult tramps have been included simply because they are popular among experienced trampers and are considered a classic trampers' challenge. The Southern Crossing in the Tararuas would be one example, the Waterfall Face in Mount Aspiring National Park another. People should work up their tramping experience before tackling such routes.

Alpine tramping

In general any routes or tramps that require alpine experience, or the carrying of crampons and ice-axe, have not been included, the exception being the Three Pass Trip in Arthur's Pass. The classic Copland Pass was excluded because of the steep and permanent snow slopes leading up to the pass, and the fact that lots of people die on it.

HOW TO USE THIS BOOK

The book is divided into 101 descriptions of different routes: 35 in the North Island, 66 in the South Island. The disparity reflects the greater amount of mountain land available for tramping in the South Island — eight of the country's twelve National Parks are in the South Island.

Grades

Each trip is graded. 'Easy' usually means a walk on very good tracks; 'medium' refers to longer tramps, always on tracks and often over passes. 'Fit' is hard, uncompromising tramping, with long days spent on rough tracks and open exposed tops. 'Easy/medium' and 'medium/fit' are useful halfway classifications indicating that travel and conditions will be mixed.

'Easy' is suitable for the beginner tramper, 'medium' for the more practised tramper. 'Medium/fit' and 'fit' are suited only to the experienced and well-equipped tramper — you have been warned.

No grading system is infallible. It should be used as a yardstick to your own ability, and after a couple of trips you will be able to relate the grade descriptions to your own fitness and temperament.

Linking tramps

Some of the tramp descriptions overlap, and this can work to your advantage. By joining two or more trips together you can construct longer and more ambitious tramps; for example, in the Tongariro National Park, the three trips of 'Tongariro Crossing', 'Oturere Crossing' and 'Tama Lakes' can be joined into one all-inclusive circuit. The same is true for many other areas, and the potential for extended trips is considerable.

Short tramps

Alternatively, if you prefer shorter, easier trips, many of the tramps can be cut down to suit individual needs, or even made into day trips; for example, the routes to Ketetahi Springs or Mountain House. Take a flexible approach to the trip descriptions, and design a tramp around what you want to do.

Left–right, right–left

If you are tracing a route back in the opposite direction to that referred to in the trip description you should alter the left–right directions accordingly. For example, if you are walking down the left bank of a river, then in reverse it will be the right bank. Wherever possible, trip descriptions have tended to avoid left–right terminology in favour of east–west descriptions, which are not so ambiguous.

Distances

The **total tramping distance** gives the entire tramp distance, including the return distance if the tramp is an in-and-out type. It also attempts to allow for the actual foot distance, taking into account criss-crossing rivers and track perambulations. A rough rule of thumb on a map is to add 1 km to every 6 'crow flies' kilometres, but this is only an approximate assessment.

There can be considerable variation between guide books and DOC pamphlets as each struggles to give a fair representation of the actual tramping distance.

Times

Total tramping time means the estimated entire time the tramp may take, including the return. It is notoriously hard to suggest tramping times that make sense for everyone, and the times suggested here are conservative, designed for the slower and more cautious user. Most fit and experienced trampers will reduce these times.

As a rough rule of thumb the following scale can be used for flat or well-graded track travel, such as on a Great Walk:

0.5 km = 10 minutes

1 km = 20 minutes

1.5 km = 30 minutes

2 km = 40 minutes

3 km = 1 hour

For rougher track travel, or boulder-hopping down rivers, you might want to add 10 minutes per kilometre at least, and possible 20 minutes if there is a lot of river crossing.

For hill climbs the actual distance is not as relevant as the amount climbed. Again as an approximate rule of thumb, on a good track a tramper could expect to climb 300 metres in an hour:

100 m = 20 minutes

300 m = 1 hour

600 m = 2 hours

1000 m = 3 hours

Surprisingly, many people find it harder going downhill than up, and indeed for inexperienced trampers it can take almost as long to go down a track as it was to climb it. Such is the strain on knees and joints. For a 1000-m descent allow about two-thirds of the climbing time, say 2 hours, but fit trampers may cut that down to half the climb, 1.5 hours.

Planning and safety

Entering the mountains carries some risks, and to a degree that's part and parcel of the sport. Tramping offers the challenge that you will enter an unfamiliar environment, negotiate your way around it safely, and have an enjoyable time doing it. Tramping in a party is one of the safest outdoor pursuits in New Zealand, and you are far more likely to be involved in a crash on your way to the road-end than to encounter serious problems on the tramp itself.

- **Trip planning**
  Do take special care when planning your trip, and remember that most trips run into difficulties because of poor decisions made at home. Spend some time before the trip with a map, and find out what other members of your party can cope with. Bear in mind the number of days planned and take into account the level of fitness and ability of the party members. If you are unsure, give yourself an extra day.

- **Maps and information**
  Maps are a wonderful first source of info, and there are many

guide books available these days. Compare several if route descriptions conflict. DOC pamphlets are often available as well. If you know someone who has done the tramp recently, talk to them. Knowing a lot about a route doesn't spoil it, but makes you better able to enjoy it.

Always take a map with you! The metric topographical are best, and National Park and Forest Park maps are not bad; anything less is inadequate.

They are expensive but maps not only give you an idea of where you are going, but a sense of the landscape and mountains around you. They also provide a record, and even a memento of your trip. The appropriate map(s) are listed in the introduction to each track and are available from some retail bookshops and DOC information centres.

- **Weather**
New Zealand's weather is famously unpredictable, and it is surprising how even innocent side-creeks can become impassable after torrential rain. Every year bridges are washed out and people stranded, even on such well-known tracks as the Routeburn and the Milford. Fronts barrel along with astonishing speed, and it is quite possible you will get a different sort of weather every day.

Most of New Zealand's weather comes from the west, bringing moist winds and sometimes heavy rainfall. A sharp southerly frontal change usually brings rain, and if it's cold enough, snow, although it will often clear dramatically afterwards.

The mountains of New Zealand act as a block to the westerly or north-westerly winds, and this means that the west coast gets a lot of rain, while the eastern side of the divide is much drier. If you are planning a tramping trip bear in mind that a forecast 'nor'wester' invariably means rain for the mountains, and it often takes a southerly or sou'wester to clear it. This pattern of north-west/south-west is common in the summer months.

Depressed already? The only thing to be relied upon is that long settled periods are rare, so if the day is fine, make the most of it. An early start is always a good precaution, wet or fine, and you should not be afraid to turn back if the weather is getting unpleasant.

- **Weather forecasts**
Love 'em or hate 'em, we still listen and make plans accordingly. Weather forecasts are presented in various different forms — newspaper, television, radio — and combining several at least gives you the opportunity to compare the information. There are also specific mountain forecasts, and DOC gets daily updates on the weather for the Great Walks.

When you are planning a trip and you are not sure what the weather is doing 'down there', or if you think the rivers may be 'up' with that recent rain, ring the nearest DOC office, or a local farmer. They are right on the spot, and the cost of a toll call could save you a lot of petrol money. Always plan a bad weather option in case the weather turns nasty.

- **Being flexible**
Rigid timetables, rigid ambitions can get you into trouble in the hills. The weather may not always behave as expected, or an injury may slow the party down. Relax, don't force it. You can always have another go, another day.

- **Winter tramping**
All the descriptions in this book are written for summer users only. Winter snowfalls make tracks such as the Tongariro Crossing, Milford, Routeburn and Kepler hazardous, and people should be equipped with full mountaineering gear such as

ice-axe and crampons. You should get the latest track updates from the Department of Conservation.

However, you can often make attractive use of short sections of the tracks in winter without having to cross the alpine passes. For example on the Routeburn Track, you could tramp in to Routeburn Flats or Falls Hut, or from the other end into Howden Hut or even Mackenzie Hut if the snow permits. This way you get to enjoy a winter wonderland without the risks. It will be perishingly cold of course, and the gas in the huts will probably be switched off, but you will probably have the track to yourself.

- **Solo tramping**
  Although solo tramping is not encouraged, if you do tramp alone be aware of the extra risks involved, and take special care to leave accurate intentions with someone reliable.

- **Clear intentions**
  Before you set off, it is important to leave clear intentions of where you are going with friends, family, flatmates, or the local DOC ranger.

  All huts have logbooks, but some people have got into the habit of not putting their names in the logbooks so as to avoid paying hut fees. This is an irresponsible practice that can cause considerable inconvenience in the event of a search and rescue operation being necessary.

Department of Conservation and visitor centres

The Department of Conservation (universally known by the acronym DOC) is the main public body responsible for the protection and management of wilderness areas in New Zealand. That includes both coastal and mountain areas, high-country tussock landscapes and urban swamplands. DOC manages all National and

Conservation Parks as well as Marine Reserves and many other types of land. Something like 25 percent of New Zealand's land area is in wilderness regions of one type or another, so you can see DOC has a massive job.

Nearly all the National Parks and Forests have visitor centres and these are excellent places to start from, with track advice, pamphlets and maps, weather updates, information on track closures and upgrades, and of course hut tickets. DOC publishes handbooks to most of the National Parks, which are mines of information, full of facts, figures, flora and fauna.

Because local transport operators, commercial track guides and places of accommodation change hands (and telephone numbers!) frequently, these have not been listed in this book. The town information centres and DOC visitor centres invariably have all the up-to-date guff on these private operators.

- **Huts and tickets**

  Throughout the mountains of New Zealand there are over a thousand public back-country huts and bivouacs. Few countries can boast such a system, and it is one of the glories of Kiwi tramping. Hut tickets or hut passes are required for most huts and can be bought from DOC or a licensed retail ticket seller.

  All huts are on a first-come first-served basis except some of the huts on the Great Walks, where a booking is required. It is important to realise (especially for New Zealand trampers) that the Great Walks huts and hut fees operate under a different system to the ordinary back-country huts; the standard DOC hut pass is not valid for Great Walks huts, and neither is the yearly hut pass. You will need a Great Walks Pass, which has to be pre-paid before you go.

  Huts in New Zealand are generally classified in one of the four following categories:

  Category 1: usually in excellent condition with a warden in

attendance in the summer season. Most of the huts on Great Walks are in this bracket. They have toilets, bunks with mattresses, a wood stove and gas cookers. Nightly fees are $12–28.

Category 2: in good condition, with a wood stove or open fire, and bunks with mattresses; $8–12 per night.

Category 3: usually four-bunk or six-bunk huts with an open fire; $4.

Category 4: old huts in poor condition or small two-person bivouacs, no charge.

- **Great Walks booking systems**

  The Department of Conservation has a booking system for the Routeburn Track, and this may be extended to all the other Great Walks. The booking system for Great Walks is designed to guarantee a bunk in a hut, and to avoid having trampers sleep on the floor of overcrowded huts.

  (Please note that the Milford Track was always an exception and still is, so see page 284 for details on booking that walk.)

  The booking system means that trampers have to be more organised. You have to have a clear idea of how long you will take on the track, and how many nights you plan to stay in each hut. You cannot suddenly change your mind and stay a night longer because someone else might be heading for your bunk!

  Booking forms are available from DOC, and passes must be purchased prior to departure. Phone bookings can be made (keep your credit card handy!) but you still have to pick up the passes at a DOC Great Walks Booking Desk.

  The booking system only applies at present to the Routeburn Track during the summer season. Outside of that season it is first-come first-served again, and normal hut charges apply. If the gas is switched off the hut usually drops to Category 2.

It can get expensive; for example, 1998 prices on the Routeburn were $28 per adult per night for a hut, $6 per night for a campsite. Children are half-price, and there are family discounts available. Children should be at least 10 years of age and accompanied by an adult. Since most people take three days to walk the track that means you are up for $50 per person for two nights in the huts at least.

Because the booking system is new, changes may occur after this book has been published. For details of track cancellations, alterations and refunds, contact a DOC Great Walks Booking Desk directly.

- **Wardens**

Wardens are appointed by the Department of Conservation throughout the summer to assist the public, collect hut fees, and maintain facilities. They are often volunteers who are provided with a small wage, accommodation and food. They do it more for love than for money, and they are really on your side even when they are doing their job, like collecting hut passes.

They are usually knowledgeable about the landscape and local weather conditions, and are in radio contact with DOC headquarters. Weather reports are posted daily in the huts.

- **Camping**

Basically you can camp anywhere within a National Park or Forest Park and no charge applies (Great Walks excepted). However, some courtesies to the environment should be observed:

1. Give other tramping parties space.
2. Bury all toilet wastes.
3. Keep the fire modest.
4. Destroy the fireplace afterwards, and remove or bury the ashes.
5. Leave only footprints, take only photos.

- **Camping on Great Walks**
  Camping is not allowed on the Great Walks except at the designated camping areas. A charge is made for use of the area, which usually has a water supply, toilets, and sometimes a shelter. The camping areas are often in attractive spots, and on some tracks (like the Routeburn) have to be booked. If you use the hut facilities (e.g. gas cookers) you can expect to be charged the full hut rate.

- **Which way to go?**
  It's up to you. For some reason DOC Great Walk pamphlets always seem to recommend starting with the big hill first — Heaphy, Waikaremoana, Kepler — which seems a bit perverse. However, you may want to go with the flow, as going the opposite way will see you meeting every party on the track. On the other hand, if you go against the flow you won't have to share the hut with the same party, day after day after day.

Public transport

The availability of public transport to the hills has increased dramatically in recent years, especially to the popular tramps such as the Great Walks. During the summer season timetabled shuttle buses offer very convenient pick-up and delivery services to the track ends. About 50 of the tramps in this book are served by either public bus transport or summer season transport operators. You should not have too many problems at all.

The best sources of up-to-date information are the various Department of Conservation information centres and the local town information centres. Many of the smaller transport operators change hands, names, timetables and service availability relatively frequently.

Some mountain areas such as the Tararuas, Ruahines, Kawekas and Kaimais are home tramping grounds for local clubs and are regularly visited. It is usually fairly easy to join one of these local club trips.

Car security and vandalism

Vandalism on cars happens from time to time, and all road-ends have had their share of break-ins and vandalism. To avoid becoming a victim don't leave valuables in cars, or arrange to park your car in a secure area in town and get a taxi or mini-bus to the road. It's some scrap of consolation that cars are usually burgled and not vandalised.

On many of the popular tracks (such as the Great Walks) there are transport packages that automatically include a safe holding area for your car while you are out in the hills. And in many local towns there are taxi services and car-valet services to the track-end. Alternatively you may be able to arrange to park your car with a local farmer.

Gear

When deciding what equipment to carry, you should strike a balance between usefulness and weight. The less you carry, the more comfortable the walking will be. But there are some items, such as food, warm clothes and a sleeping bag, that you cannot afford to skimp on.

- **Footwear**

  Footwear should be solid as New Zealand tracks and routes are generally rough. Although you can get away with sandshoes on some tracks, it's hard on both shoes and ankles. For better ankle support there is a good range of lightweight tramping boots that are impressively comfortable compared to the older-style tramping boot. It is well worth spending the dollars to get a comfortable pair of boots — you are practically going to be living in them.

  Take plenty of dry socks. Getting wet feet is a fact of life for New Zealand trampers, so a dry pair of socks and lightweight jandals are handy to change into at the end of the day.

- **Raincoat**

  Wet-weather gear is always essential; it rains a lot in the mountains. Heavy nylon, Gore-Tex and PVC are common materials for raincoats (Kiwis usually call them 'parkas'). A hood is important, and for people with glasses a peaked cap can keep most of the rain off.

- **Warm clothing**
  Adequate warm clothing is essential, particularly on alpine tramps, where mittens and a woollen hat are a must. Always carry a dry set of spare clothes to change into when you get to the hut.

- **Sleeping bag**
  A good, warm sleeping bag is essential. No blankets are provided in any of the huts.

- **Tent**
  A fly or tent should be carried, although it's common for tramping groups to take no outdoor protection and just rely on huts. Apart from the fact that the hut may be overcrowded, noisy and smoky, you may not get there. Who wants to spend a miserable night huddled under a groundsheet because it got dark too soon, you couldn't find the hut, or somebody sprained an ankle?

  The range of modern tents available is stunning. Domes, half-domes, tunnels — every available aerodynamic shape has been thought of. They are not cheap, but if you are an aficionado of tramping then it is well worth investing in a good tent. It gives you the freedom to stop in the places you choose, and get away from the crowds.

  A fly (a large square nylon sheet with long cords at the corners and sides) is light and offers very good protection from bad weather in bush country.

- **Cooking equipment**
  As a minimum you will need a billy (cooking pot), plus knives, spoons, plates and mugs. A portable cooker (gas cooker, primus, burner, whatever) is almost a necessity as well these days, particularly if people feel uncomfortable about lighting fires.

  Although many Great Walk huts have gas burners for cooking the gas can get used up. There have been suggestions too that the gas burners may be removed in the future, as the gas is expensive and there are safety concerns.

- **Food**
  Energy foods such as chocolate, dried fruit and biscuits are useful to munch on during the day. You'll need a substantial meal in the evening; rice or pasta are familiar and lightweight options.

- **Medical kit**
  This doesn't have to rival a small pharmacy, but insect repellent, burn cream, headache pills and bandages are all useful. Some sort of bandage for pre-binding feet to prevent blisters is also useful.

- **Camera**
  A small, lightweight camera is always nice to have with you, as well as a spare film, and a spare battery if you have one of those one-zoom-does-everything types. People shots are often more memorable than landscape views.

Fire

Fire is a special danger in some areas, particularly in late-summer beech forest and scrub country. Be sure to use the purpose-built fireplaces, or build your fireplaces out on the shingle riverbeds. Keep fires small and make absolutely sure they are put out afterwards. Observe fire bans.

Drinking the waters

A water-borne parasite protozoan called giardia has become something of an issue in New Zealand in recent years, and has been identified in some freshwater streams throughout the country. It's an intestinal bug that causes diarrhoea and vomiting and, in extreme cases, death. Fortunately it is easily cured and for most people is a nuisance rather than a threat.

Although it has been called the 'travellers' disease', giardia actually occurs mostly in cities as a result of poor hygiene where contact with faeces is possible. Places such as kindergartens are particularly vulnerable.

You should carry your own water if you are doubtful of the local stuff, or else boil creek water thoroughly, or filter it. Generally any water running through farmland should be treated with suspicion, and you should wash your hands carefully after going to the toilet.

It is a pity to have to automatically distrust all freshwater creeks in wilderness areas, and the authors have no intention of doing so. Recent scientific articles suggest that in order to absorb the 10 giardia cysts necessary to start an infection you need to drink something like 100 litres of water from a stream. Cheers!

Insects and precautions

Sandflies are the worst insect pest you will encounter, though mosquitoes are a close second. Sandflies are active only in the daytime and mosquitoes take over at night, a charming ecological conspiracy. Take insect repellent for the sandflies and an insect-proof tent (if camping) for mosquitoes. Sandflies are most active before or after rain and on greyish, dull days. They are not supposed to like hot sun, wind, frosts and campfire smoke, but take insect repellent anyway. Mosquitoes bite when the buzzing stops, which is very demoralising.

Wasps too are beginning to prove a nuisance in the beech forests. They tend to be seasonal (January–May) and have a painful sting. If you are allergic, take extra precautions. There are no snakes or leeches in New Zealand.

New Zealand has many unique insects, but most of them are shy. Our only native poisonous creature is the katipo spider, usually found on beaches, and though they exist in the millions most New Zealanders have never seen one. They are not found in the mountains.

Wetas are a type of grasshopper, large, ugly but harmless. They come out at night and live in the bush and alpine regions. You'll get a fright if you see one, but then so will they. On Great Barrier Island you can hear them grinding their back legs at night, so zip that tent up! One rare species of weta weighs up to 70 grams, making it one of the heaviest insects in the world.

Farm courtesy

Many tramps start by crossing farmland. Unless there is a marked route indicated it is sensible to ask the farmer's permission first. Usually this is freely given, and often extra information is volunteered at the same time, which helps with planning your trip. It is best to ring up before leaving town if possible.

If a homestead is located at the very end of the road, a pile of noisy trampers arriving at midnight on a Friday is seldom appreciated. Be considerate, camp lower down the valley and pay a visit in the morning.

Remember too that gates should be left just as found, whether open or shut, and if you have to climb a fence do so at the strainer post. Firearms and dogs must not be taken onto a farmer's land without permission.

Looking at the wild things

New Zealand is rich in unique plant and bird species, and if you are new to the country it really is quite worthwhile to learn a plant a day (or a bird), a good method of getting to grips with all the unfamiliar flora and fauna. Although there are many excellent books on New

Zealand plants and birds, most field guides are probably too detailed (and too heavy) for the casual tramper.

There are two main forest types in New Zealand: the beech forest with its characteristic spacious, dry, dappled interior; and the rainforest composed of the podocarps such as rimu, kahikatea, miro and matai. A rainforest is usually a densely packed assemblage of ferns, mosses and epiphytes. Beech is particularly dominant on the eastern side of the Southern Alps and in Fiordland. Rainforest, as its name suggests, prefers the wetter West Coast of the Alps and is extensive all over the North Island.

Birds are the occupants of the mountains that the tramper usually encounters first. Fantails, wood pigeons, riflemen, robins, pipits, weka and kea are the most inquisitive (in their respective habitats); tui and bellbirds are often heard, but not so easily seen; and kaka, blue ducks, rock wrens, kiwi and parakeets tend to be shy of human company. Takahe, kakapo and kokako are very rare and localised.

Of the large mammals, red deer are generally present throughout New Zealand forests. Although deer are wary, a keen tramper is bound to stumble across one of them before long. Chamois occupy high slopes in the South Island, and thar are found on the highest and remotest slopes of all, around Mt Cook/Aoraki National Park. White-tailed deer are a feature of Stewart Island and there are very scarce wapiti in Fiordland. It is unlikely you will see a deer or chamois but if you do, stay still and watch, because it is probable that they have not yet seen you.

Conservation

'Take only photos, leave only footprints' is the best motto. The hills are not replenishable resources and we cannot buy any more of them if we run out. Nor can we preserve their peaceful and uncluttered environs if we take our noisy, busy culture into them.

Many huts these days do not provide a rubbish pit, and you are expected and required to 'carry out what you carry in'. Soaps (either personal or for washing clothes) should be used carefully, never in alpine lakes, where they can have a serious ecological effect.

If staying in huts, be considerate towards other users and do not spread your gear too much over bunkrooms and tables. Hospitality is an old-fashioned virtue still very important in the hills, and the offer of a cup of tea to new arrivals is usually very welcome.

Things change

Every effort has been made to keep the information in this book up to date, but nothing stays the same. Tracks get rerouted or washed out, huts burn down or get shifted.

It is the publisher's intention to update the book on a regular basis, but since the difference between writing a book and seeing it on the shelves can be as long as 1–2 years, anyone reading the text should make allowance for altered situations and author fallibility.

If you do see any real errors please write to the authors (via the publisher) and we will make every effort to incorporate the changes in the next edition. No, you don't get your money back. Happy tramping!

NORTH
ISLAND

Cape Reinga Walkway

Total tramping time: 15–18 hours/2–3 days
Total tramping distance: 46 km
Grade: easy/medium
Highest point: 300 m; Darkies Ridge
Maps: North Cape M02, N02

This fine tramping trail at the top of New Zealand links remote beaches with magnificent headlands. Scenic coastal views, swimming bays, sand dunes, Cape Reinga lighthouse, tidal platforms and plenty of remoteness. One of the best coastal tramps in New Zealand, the tramp suits self-sufficient trampers as there are no huts, and it can get pretty dry in summer. People may prefer to take weekend bites at it. Two official camping areas, several informal campsites. Carry water.

From Kaitaia drive north almost 100 km on Highway 1 to Waitiki Landing road junction, where there are tearooms, a small store, and an information centre. It's about 12 km along Te Hapua and Spirits Bay Roads to the coastal campsite at Kapowairau at the eastern end of Spirits Bay. Regular bus day tours go to Cape Reinga, but there's no public transport to Spirits Bay or the Te Paki Stream road-end.

Kapowairau is worth exploring first. There's a tidal lagoon here, Pananeke Island and the pretty Te Karaka Bay. There are at least two old pa sites on Maungapika Hill.

From Kapowairau the route follows the huge sweep of Spirits Bay (Piwhana Bay) some 9 km/2–3 hours around to Pandora at the far western end, passing alongside the large coastal lagoon and the Paranoa Swamp, both important wetlands. Old fruit trees mark the site of an informal camping area at Pandora, and there are two more pa sites here. The track leaves the coast and climbs steadily up an old

Cliff track between Tapotupotu Bay and Cape Reinga

farm track 3 km/1–2 hours to the Darkies Ridge junction at about 300 metres.

A short side-trip can be made from this junction either to Te Paki Trig (310 m high; 1 km) or around to a rare patch of kauri forest (2 km). Tracks signposted.

Darkies Ridge continues a roistering up and down for 6 km/2–3 hours with splendid views till it drops steeply alongside the cliff edge to Tapotupotu Bay. Very good official campsite and toilets here in a real gem of a bay, many people's favourite in fact, as you will find out if you come in the height of the summer season.

From the west side of Tapotupotu Bay a modest grassy trail zig-zags up the headland, with occasional red marker posts. The views are good and in places the track leers very close to the cliff edge. A thick Kenyan grass, kikuyu, abounds on either side of the track, and it looks as if you can walk on it. But a couple of steps and you find yourself up to your knees in something that is more sponge than plant. The track climbs to the top of the headland, where it turns inland along an old vehicle track, then cuts across the top of a gully onto another headland.

You can see the Cape Reinga lighthouse now, as the track descends into a lovely bay given the rather prosaic name of 'Sandy', 3 km/1–2 hours from Tapotupotu Bay. This cove is pretty and secluded, with shady pohutukawa and more rock platforms to explore.

It's a steep climb up the open spur 1.5 km/1 hour to the lighthouse, but again the views are superb, and at the carpark the world is suddenly crawling with people. The distant sand-dunes of Cape Maria van Diemen look stunning, and there's a tempting track down the other side of the carpark to Te Werahi Beach. But first you have to look at the lighthouse, and take a photo or two.

The track leads easily to Te Werahi Beach and cuts across the wide open sands past Te Werahi Stream (preferably at low tide), some 4 km/1 hour. At low tide you can walk around to Cape Maria van Diemen (around or over Te Kohau Point), but otherwise follow the orange posts 2 km/40 minutes up and over Herangi Hill, where a side-track takes you to the Cape (2.5 km/1 hour).

The main track south fossicks among the clifftops in flax and manuka for 3 km/1 hour, and every now and then the grass and manuka have slipped away to reveal gashes of bright red earth. The track drops down to the romantically named Twilight Beach (Te Paengarehia). A side-track here climbs up to Te Werahi Gate on the Cape Reinga road, 4 km/1–2 hours. There are informal campsites at the northern and southern ends of Twilight Beach, which is 3 km/1 hour long.

The Cape Reinga walkway track dodges inland over Scotts Point and Tekepoutu Point, edging along cliffs and into scrub gullies for 4 km/1 hour via a boardwalk and steps down to the top of Ninety Mile Beach. Another attractive informal campsite here at the part of Ninety Mile called Kahokawa Beach.

A brisk 4 km/1 hour down the beach to Te Paki Stream, where the numerous tracks of the four-wheel-drive tours disappear inland. Following them you pass the famous Te Paki sand dunes and after 3 km/1 hour reach the picnic area at the road-end.

No one in their right mind would really want to walk all the way down Ninety Mile Beach (actually 84 km long), not when you can hitch a lift on the zillions of recreational vehicles that whizz by.

Whatipu Coast

Total tramping time: 4–5 hours/1–2 days
Total tramping distance: 11 km
Grade: easy
Highest point: 300 m; coastal track
Maps: Waitakere Q11, also map in *A Walking and Tramping Guide to the Waitakere Ranges*

Whatipu Beach is a wild and wonderful spot at the north heads of Manukau Harbour, at the foot of the Waitakere Ranges. Only 35 km from Auckland, there is enough wilderness and lonely spaciousness to satisfy the most claustrophobic town-worker. Coastal scenery and beach plain, headlands, islets and islands, dune ponds, historic tramway and tunnel, tidal platforms. The coast route and inland bush track make an easy weekend tramping loop, with one official campsite, which has to be prebooked at the Arataki Park Visitor Centre. A tramp suitable for most school-age children.

From downtown Auckland drive to Titirangi and follow the twisting coastal road past Huia to the north head of Manukau Harbour at Whatipu carpark, about 25 km. The last 7 km is narrow, unsealed and corrugated. Toilets and information board.

On such a short trip there is no requirement to keep to any tight schedule. From the carpark you can wander 1 km/20 minutes onto the beach, perhaps first looking around Paratutae Islet with its tiny harbour and old wharf blasted out of the rock. HMS *Orpheus* was wrecked here in 1863, with the loss of 167 lives. Then you can head across the wide sands to Ninepin Rock or Cutter Rock, and follow the coast north past sand dunes with their graceful assortment of grasses.

Eventually you will come across a four-wheel-drive track (which you could take from the carpark, past the sea-caves if you wish). There's a marvellous openness along this track between the dark coastal cliffs and the distant shining surf. All too soon you turn Pararaha Point to the Pararaha River, 5 km/1–2 hours from Whatipu carpark.

Headland on Whatipu coast

A big headland traps a coastal wetland and a huge sand dune blocks the valley entrance. It is worth wandering north, investigating the old tunnel made by the kauri loggers, and walking on to where the surf thumps against the rock cliffs. At low tide you can go on to Karekare Beach.

The inland tracks start just behind the big sand dune at Pararaha Point. After 100 m/5 minutes there's the first junction with an inland track that carries on north, eventually to Karekare Beach. On the Pararaha Valley Track it is a short 1 km/20 minutes to the junction with the Muir Track, where there are toilets and an official campsite on grass flats by the Pararaha River.

From the shelter it's a sharp climb up Muirs Track, almost 300 m to the top of the coastal plateau; 1 km/40 minutes. There's a generous gully of nikau palms on the way up. At the top track junction turn onto the Gibbons Track, which is easy, wide and mostly manuka forest with one very good lookout about halfway to Whatipu.

After 3 km/1 hour of this easy travel the track descends and you gradually get good views over Whatipu Beach. Then some sharp zigzags through the nikau to the flat coastal plain, where the track rejoins the vehicle track and follows alongside the fence back to the carpark and the hour's drive back to hot water and headaches.

Great Barrier Island

Total tramping time: 5–7 hours/1–2 days
Total tramping distance: 11 km
Grade: easy/medium
Highest point: 627 m; Mt Hirakimata (Hobson)
Maps: Barrier, Great Barrier & Little Barrier 259;
   Barrier S08, T08; Colville S09

Great Barrier, first named by Captain Cook, sounds romantic and remote, and the first glimpse of the island emerging out of a squall or burnt black against a brilliant Hauraki Gulf day fulfils expectations. The island is now well serviced with fast ferries and aircraft, but still the remoteness lingers, making the Barrier, with its low population and rust-rotten cars, a unique place. This track goes through the heart of the island, past some outstanding kauri dams and up onto the high peak Hirakimata, then down past hot pools to the eastern side of the island. Lots of track junctions, one hut, some campsites.

The Barrier is an easy place to get to. There are regular passenger services from Auckland's downtown ferry terminal to Tryphena, Whangaparapara and Port Fitzroy, as well as regular small-plane services flying to Okiwi and Claris airstrips.

From Port Fitzroy's wharf (a well-stocked store 5 minutes away) walk 3.5 km/1 hour on the road round to Kaiarara Bay. Traffic is infrequent and you can check in at the DOC office on the way through. At the road-end there is a locked gate, a ford, then a track junction.

Turn left following the hut sign and two fords later you reach Kaiarara Hut (24 bunks). Camping in the grass clearings seems more attractive than the gloomy hut, and there's a vocal and busy population of kaka overhead, and noisy night-time wetas scratching their legs.

The road-track continues upstream to a junction, where the main track leaves the road, crosses the stream and wanders up beside a pleasant side-branch of the Kaiarara, passing the south fork track junction after 500 m/15 minutes. From here on the track climbs

Historic kauri dam

steadily some 300 metres as the valley closes in, with occasional stream crossings and dense groves of nikau palms. It passes the side-track to Coopers Castle.

After 2 km/1–2 hours there's a side-track (and logbook) to a kauri dam. This is the best preserved on the island, and once you've negotiated the wire past the slippery track you can appreciate this massive piece of bush construction.

The main track continues easily at first, then crosses the stream and passes some more ruins of kauri dams (last water before Hirakimata) at 500 m/20 minutes, before climbing steeply some 200 m out of the valley up a spur to top out at yet another track junction (500 m/30 minutes) which goes to the Fitzroy–Claris road. Turn south and another short climb to the Mt Heale junction.

Here you could drop your pack and walk 300 m/15 minutes up the last climb (with extensive boardwalk and steps) to the viewing platform that surrounds the beacon on the summit of Mt Hirakimata. Virtually the whole island can be seen, and it's not a bad idea to have lunch and gaze at the nearby rock pinnacle of Mt Heale and the golden beaches of Whangapoua and Kaitoke in the distance.

Back at the Mt Heale junction the track drops 200 m smartly, sidles Mt Heale and runs down to another track junction (1 km/30 minutes). Turn east down the long and generally open manuka spur which twists in and out of some gullies before reaching the main track at Kaitoke Creek, almost 3 km/1 hour and a 400-m descent.

Almost immediately you will cross a small side-stream, and just beyond that is an unmarked trail on the right, which wriggles through bush for 5 minutes to the hot pools upstream. The pool is often too hot, and a bit scungy, but the campsite under the nikau palms is as calm as a chapel.

The main track turns sharply inland to avoid the flax-filled Kaitoke Swamp and after 1 km/20 minutes it comes to another track junction. Follow the track signposted 'Hot Pools' as it climbs for a while before dropping down into a small valley to the second set of hot pools (1 km/20 minutes). These are bigger, cleaner and the right temperature, and you'll need little persuasion to linger for a dip or two, or three ... There is one smallish campsite on the other side of the stream.

It is a short walk (1 km/20 minutes) out to the road, and about another 4 km/1 hour to Claris, where there is a store and arrangements can be made for a taxi either to Tryphena or back to Fitzroy.

The Pinnacles

Total tramping time: 7–8 hours/2 days (including
   return via Billy Goat Track)
Total tramping distance: 15 km (including return via
   Billy Goat Track)
Grade: easy/medium
Highest point: 773 m; The Pinnacles
Maps: Coromandel Forest Park 274; Thames T12

A great short tramp which follows a track through
the twisted volcanic plugs and pinnacles of the
Coromandel landscape, with native forest, nikau
palms and waterfalls. Plenty of history too, with an
historic stone staircase, pack-track, trestles and kauri
dams. A large, comfortable trampers' hut on the tops, and a side-
track to the Pinnacles, one of the best viewpoints in the Park.

From Thames drive south 2 km to the Kauaeranga Valley Road,
and follow the attractive valley 13 km to the visitor centre and
carpark. Note the gate closing times. It is another 9 km on winding
unsealed road to the road-end and the start of the Billy Goat Circuit.
The park headquarters has a nature walk, working log dam, historical artefacts, information and toilets. Many camping grounds with
fireplaces along the roadside, no free camping.

From the carpark follow the main Pinnacles track as it crosses the
Kauaeranga River on a long footbridge and follows the river for 1
km/20 minutes at an easy grade through groves of nikau palms. At
the junction, take the Webb Creek/Pinnacles track as it climbs
steeply up this attractive and narrow stream.

There are several waterfalls in this tight valley, as well as three footbridges, and the original hand-cut stone staircases that were built to
assist the packhorses up this steep grade. It's a climb of almost 300
m, and after rain these steps can get as greasy as a politician's
promise; 2 km/1–2 hours.

Bluffs lean over the track as it wriggles up to the open manuka terrace and the Billy Goat Track junction at the Hydro Camp. During
the late 1940s workers camped here when establishing the 'hydro-
line' (powerline) over to the east coast, and the lines are still there.

This area was devastated by a flash-flood in 1993.

Easier in grade now, the Pinnacles track sidles on wet, stony ground for 2 km/40 minutes with the gloomy plug of Tauranikau coming into sight, and the views become more general as the track winds through stunted scrub forest to a track junction. The side branch heads north towards Moss Creek (a half-day walk away), but instead drop down the partly boardwalked track past the Pinnacles trail to the spacious Pinnacles Hut (40 bunks, gas cookers and a warden in season).

Some camping space below the hut, halfway between the hut and the dam. This kauri log dam is impressive, but sadly the bare stripped hillsides around testify to the awesome effectiveness of the loggers' simple methods.

The side-trail to the Pinnacles begins gently enough, then gets steeper as it approaches the Pinnacles (1.5 km/40 minutes). It has to twist up and around severe rock and scrub gullies with the assistance of a couple of ladders before it reaches the final top, a total climb of 200 m from hut to the first and highest pinnacle at 773 m.

Much of the Coromandel is visible, especially in the immediate foreground of contorted rock outcrops and white-stumped hillsides. Sea on both sides and the Hauraki Plains fade into haze. It's not a bad idea to bring some sustenance and slowly digest lunch and the view.

For an easy variation on the homeward plod to the Kauaeranga carpark you can take the Billy Goat Track; allow an extra hour.

From the Hydro Camp junction this track passes through manuka forest on a bulldozed track which is lethally slippery. You get some excellent views over the Kauaeranga Valley. The track winds for 2 km/1 hour through thick manuka, young rimu and the occasional juvenile kauri down to the headwaters of the Atuatumoe Stream, where you have to boulder-hop if you want to avoid wet feet.

Shortly on from here is a side-track to the remains of the long trestle, originally 160 metres long, and 11 metres above ground at the highest point. Blown up by the army for sheer joie de vivre and apparently for safety reasons. The track passes a junction with the Tarawaere Dam track and you get good views of the Billy Goat Waterfall, as the Atuatumoe Stream plunges down a series of cascades.

View from the top of The Pinnacles

After 1 km/20 minutes from Atuatumoe Stream (and some tramway cuttings and the remains of the short trestle) the lovely graded track becomes extremely steep and slippery as it descends 200 m down the historic Billygoat incline (500 m/20 minutes). This steep tramway used steam-haulers to lower the kauri logs down to the valley.

Eventually the track sees sense, leaves the incline, and becomes well-graded again for 1 km/20 minutes as it winds down to the Kauaeranga River by the old swingbridge. Usually you can boulder-hop directly across the tea-stained river, and the bridge is only for emergency use. It's about 500 m back along the road to the main carpark.

Waitawheta Tramway

Total tramping time: 8–10 hours/2 days
Total tramping distance: 17 km
Grade: easy/medium
Highest point: 600 m; near Cashmore's Clearing
Maps: Kaimai Mamaku Forest Park 274-8;
   Paeroa T13

This tramway travels through the heart of the largest bush area in the Kaimai mountains, and gives easy, relaxed tramping along one of the many noteworthy remains of the kauri loggers. There are also pack-tracks, kauri dams and old mill sites, and the lower Waitawheta gorge is a charmer. Several river crossings, one hut, one shelter, and some good campsites.

Travel 7 km west from Waihi on Highway 2 to the Waitawheta Road, then 4 km to Spence Road and immediately Franklin Road. It's 2 km down Franklin Road to a carpark at the road-end. You need to arrange a pick-up at the Lindemann Road end.

A marked route crosses farmland and close-by the Waitawheta River meets the old tramway (1 km/20 minutes). A signposted side-track fords the river for a visit to two massive kauri, but the tramway potters alongside the river for 1.5 km/30 minutes to Daly's Hut junction. This hut is actually 1 hour up a side-track.

A further 500 m/15 minutes on, another side-track goes off to visit the same two kauri and also connects with the long inland route to Waitengaue Hut.

A gorge squashes the river above the junction and obliges the tramway to criss-cross about four times through graceful loggers' cuttings and past concrete bridge placements. Deep pools and segmented volcanic rock formations compensate for the exertion of boulder-hopping the river.

After 1 km/1 hour the gorge eases and the tramway keeps steadily to one bank for a while, crossing after 3 km/2 hours to Waitawheta Hut. The regrowth of hardwoods and podocarps along the track is abundant, though the kauri are mostly gone.

Waitawheta Hut (16 bunks) sits on a big grassy flat. Many campsites around the clearing, which is populated by busy Welcome swallows in season. Wood is scarce. A side-track goes up to Mt Te Aroha, but the main Waitawheta track

Footbridge across Waitawheta Stream

continues up the tramway and after 1.5 km/40 minutes reaches a track crossroads, the first side-track leading to the Old Mill Site, the second to Waitengaue Hut.

A fixed bridge spans a waterfall and leads to the discarded bogie wheels and general metal debris of the log site. A sheltered campsite, side-tracks to the river, and distinctive rock forms make the mill locality a delight to explore.

Back on the main tramway it is 1.5 km/40 minutes to another clearing with the remains of a kauri log dam signposted up a side-track. The tramway stops here, and a tramping track resumes for 2 km/1 hour, crossing two footbridges and climbing 200 m up a zig-zag track onto the track junction on the scrubby ridge.

There are side-tracks to Cashmore's Clearing and the Wharawhara

Stream, but the main trail turns uphill slightly then begins to sidle, giving better views over Cashmore's Clearing and to the coast. The track gently twists down and emerges at an open area with a tumble-down log dam and a ponga shelter; 1.5 km/30 minutes.

From here a pack-track continues through the bush, graded nicely past a clearing with a stream and the remains of another log dam, shortly reaching the Lindemann Ridge Track by a decrepit slab hut (1 km/30 minutes). Follow the main pack-track as it sidles around bush spurs (with incongruous pine trees poking through) to the junction with the Wairoa Stream track; 500 m/15 minutes.

Good views here. Stay on the Lindemann's pack trail for the last gently descending 2 km/1 hour to the picnic site and carpark at the end of Lindemann's Road.

Mount Baldy and Te Rereatukahia Hut

Total tramping time: 6–8 hours/2 days
Total tramping distance: 11 km
Grade: easy/medium
Highest point: 735 m; Mt Baldy
Maps: Kaimai Mamaku Forest 274-8;
  Morrinsville T14

Baldy is an unassuming tussock knob that commands tremendous views of both sides of the Kaimai Range, the Hauraki Plains, Mayor Island, Tauranga and Mt Maunganui. A circuit track varies the return route and includes the old Maori Tuahu trail, and there is the bonus of occasional pockets of kauri forest. One ridge-top hut; portable cooker essential.

Travel 33 km west from Tauranga on Highway 2 to the Hot Springs Road, 4 km before Katikati. Follow this 5 km past the Sapphire Springs motor camp to the road end and carpark. The motor camp has a large tepid swimming pool, cold pools, and basic food store.

The track to Te Rereatukahia Hut and the main range is 50 m before the carpark. It drops steeply to the river, crosses it (the last water), then saunters on a benched track to a kauri stand (1 km/20 minutes).

From here the track starts climbing steeply, brushing its way past thick bush and a grove of pole kauri up a long spur. After 250 m the track softens and dips over two or three small 'saddles' with occasional glimpses of the coastal plains. A final rise of 150 m to the ridge top and hut, a total distance of about 3.5 km/2–3 hours.

Te Rereatukahia Hut sits in the midst of a semi-cleared area, with many old stumps protruding above thick regrowth. The hut has sleeping benches for about 16–20 people, with a smidgin of camping around the hut.

To reach Baldy follow the trail northwards a short way to the junction with the main north–south track. Continue uphill, gradually leaving the bush for a climb of 100 m to the windswept tussock and dracophyllum knob of Baldy; 500 m/30 minutes. A panorama of the

Bay of Plenty and back over the Kaimai and Mamaku forest, all the more surprising from such an unassuming knob.

To complete a loop trip back to the Hot Springs Road carpark (rather than return by the steep spur) follow the main north–south track as it descends 2 km/1 hour to meet the Tuahu Track.

This old Maori trail across the range was later turned into a bridleway, and still later a walkway, so the downhill travel is excellent. Signposts are generous and this is a very pleas-

Studying the map at Te Rereatukahia Hut

ant 3.5-km/2-hour descent past several track junctions and across a number of gully streams. At the road-end, the hot springs are a very tempting way to round off the weekend.

Mount Pirongia Crossing

Total tramping time: 10–12 hours/2–3 days
Total tramping distance: 23 km
Grade: medium/fit
Highest point: 959 m; Mt Pirongia
Map: Te Awamutu S15

Mt Pirongia is a near 1000-m bush-clad mountain with dominant views of the Waikato. Several tracks cross the mountain and this crossing takes in most of the good scenery, including the crater hut at the top. This is a fairly strenuous weekend tramp. A portable cooker is essential.

Take Highway 23 from Hamilton for 13 km, then turn onto Highway 31 for some 20 km to Te Rore Road (5 km before Pirongia village), then 5 km up Te Rore, Hodgson and Grey Roads to the carpark near the Forest Park Lodge.

The Mahaukura Track climbs steadily some 4.5 km/2–3 hours to the track junction with the Wharauroa route and the Wharauroa lookout. Another 500 m/20 minutes to Mahaukura volcanic rock lookout at 899 m. Both rock outcrops have good views.

With the bulk of the climbing done the track turns for 2 km/1 hour along the bushy ridge to a junction with the Tirohanga Track, and shortly afterwards the very summit of Pirongia (959 m) is reached. Pahautea Hut (6–8 people) is 750 m/20 minutes along the track.

It's almost 1.5 km/30 minutes along the crater crest to the second dominant peak of The Cone (945 m) and then the Bell Track starts its long descent, 6 km/2–3 hours down to an old hut site. Camping here and a small stream nearby.

More easily now the track passes through Taylors Clearing and drops down to the Blue Bull Stream, and a side-track to New Zealand's tallest recorded kahikatea — 66.5 m (4 km/1–2 hours). Only 1 km/30 minutes to the Nikau Loop Walk (worth a short diversion) and another 500 m/15 minutes to the junction with the Tahuanui Track. A short way up this track there is a campsite.

The main Nikau trail takes 2 km/40 minutes to reach the Kaniwhaniwha carpark beside the Karamu Limeworks Road.

Mount Hikurangi

Total tramping time: 7–10 hours/2 days
Total tramping distance: 20 km
Grade: medium
Highest point: 1752 m; Mt Hikurangi
Map: Hikurangi Y15

Hikurangi is claimed to be the first point in New Zealand to see the morning sun. A fine, craggy peak, with relatively easy if steep access. One hut, and camp sites around the hut. Carry water and a portable cooker.

From Gisborne take Highway 35 for some 120 km and turn off down Tapuaeroa Road for about 18 km to the bridge leading to Pakihiroa Station. Carpark on the other side. You should ring Pakihiroa Station first to gain access permission. At the time of writing an access charge is being imposed, however, this situation may change.

A farm vehicle track loops past the station buildings and climbs remorselessly up the spur, the views getting better and better as you climb. It's almost 8 km/3–4 hours up over 1000 m to reach the Gisborne Canoe and Tramping Club Hut, which has a magnificent north situation. The hut is open to the public but contact the club beforehand.

Dead tree stumps surround these top slopes like obscure sculptures. Cloud often settles up here and can make the last part of navigation to the hut confusing. The hut holds 12 people; portable cooker essential.

The view from the hut is pretty stunning but most people will want to have a crack at Hikurangi. Whether it's worth trying to beat the sunrise is a moot point; you'll need a good torch.

An old tree stump and the view from the Gisborne Canoe and Tramping Club hut

A well-marked track climbs steeply up through the bush for 200 m then sidles around the mountain through a number of alpine scrub basins; 1.5 km/1 hour. Directly under the summit the track scrambles up steep rocky slopes for 200 m to the craggy double top with the beacon on the high point (500 m/30 minutes).

Tremendous views of Hikurangi's lower peak and the gnarly looking Mt Aorangi, and beyond that to the coastline of East Cape. If you've lucked out with a calm, clear morning you can do nothing worse than lie back and enjoy the view.

Lake Waikaremoana Circuit

Total tramping time: 4–5 days
Total tramping distance: 46 km
Grade: medium
Highest point: 1180 m; Panekiri Hut
**Maps: Urewera National Park 273-08; Lake
    Waikaremoana 239; Waikaremoana W18**

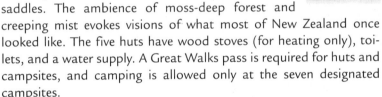

A lakeside track between the sparkling waters of Waikaremoana and the dense Urewera bush. A justly famous tramping trip but not a doddle; there's a big climb up onto Panekiri Bluff, and many smaller bush saddles. The ambience of moss-deep forest and creeping mist evokes visions of what most of New Zealand once looked like. The five huts have wood stoves (for heating only), toilets, and a water supply. A Great Walks pass is required for huts and campsites, and camping is allowed only at the seven designated campsites.

Waikaremoana is remote! There is a regular bus service along State Highway 38, which passes alongside Lake Waikaremoana and the Park Visitor Centre. Check latest timetable details from the DOC visitor centre at Waikaremoana. The two track ends at Onepoto and Hopuruahine Landing are widely separated, but there are boat ferry services and a van shuttle during the summer season. These services may operate on demand during the quieter winter months; check with DOC first. The motor camp has basic tramping supplies and a small foodstore.

The track begins at Onepoto Bay 6 km south of the park headquarters. Extensive and attractive rest and picnic areas beside the lake. Toilets, shelter, boat landing and track information signs. A side-trail leads to Lake Kiriopukae.

The main track zig-zags past the commodious shelter and onto the historic redoubt's parade ground before entering the bush proper. It's a good track, sometimes gouged out in places, and it climbs steadily through the red beech forest. Crown fern dominates the understorey, and Maori travellers used to bend their leaves as track markers; the pale undersides are distinctly visible, even at night.

Although you get good glimpses of the lake through the trees it's not till the lookout at Te Rahui (964 m) that you see a first-class panorama, and sandstone rocks provide a good seating 'possie' to enjoy the splendid views. The beacon has been well inscribed by passers-by. It's a 500-m climb from Onepoto to Te Rahui over a distance of 2.5 km/2 hours, then another 2.5 km/1–2 hours to Pukenui and a superb vista. For most of the next 3 km/1 hour to the hut the track winds up and down through mixed forest, and a wire and timber stairway that has to be scaled up a rock outcrop just before Panekiri Hut. An alternative track around the stairway is marked though seldom used.

Panekiri Hut is perched astride a ridge dropping hundreds of metres on both sides, with a bird's-eye view of Lake Waikaremoana. In the evening you can see the twinkling lights of the East Coast town of Wairoa. The hut has 36 bunks, and no camping is allowed here unless the hut is completely full.

The track follows the main Panekiri Range for 3 km/1–2 hours until it veers off the range and sneaks over and under a line of bluffs, then breaks out into rock gullies that face into the Wairaumoana, a side-arm of the main lake.

The track then descends 300 m over 3 km/1–2 hours through dense forest to the 24-bunk hut at Waiopaoa. A 5-minute side-track through manuka glades leads to a sandy lakeside bay and campsite. If the lake level is low you can wander around the shoreline on the exposed lake beach towards the secluded Wairoa Bay.

The main lake track turns inland to cross Waitehetehe Stream and Waiopaoa Stream over two footbridges, then follows the shoreline through terraces of sinewy manuka. Inlets and deep sluggish creeks often force the track inland. It's 2.5 km/1 hour to a junction where a side-path leads to Korokoro Falls, a shining band of water under the bush canopy, well worth the 30-minute or so diversion.

Back on the main trail which climbs a little past a lakeside shelter (and campsite) until it is about 30 m above the waterline, then sidles past a sequence of sheltered rock bays. A short bash down through the bush gives you a private bay for lunch and perhaps a sunbathe. There is plenty of birdlife all around the lakeside, even if more heard than seen, especially tui, bellbirds and shining cuckoos.

After 3 km/1 hour the track reaches Te Kotoreotaunoa Point and slips down into the rock-lined Maraunui Bay. There's a ranger base hut at Maraunui, but this is not for public use. A further 2.5 km/1 hour and the track meets the Te Wharau Stream inlet. The track skirts around another small bay where there is a shelter and designated campsite, and dips over a low saddle for 1 km/30 minutes to reach the hut at pretty Marauiti Bay.

A short side-track leads to the 18-bunk hut, which is snuggled on a grass flat beside the sheltered lake shores. The 'plop' of trout, the buzz of evening insects and the morepork's distinctive call drift across this still bay at night.

Across the footbridge the foreshore track wanders around rocks which intrude into the bay, forcing the track to clamber over and around them until it turns the corner into Te Kopua Bay (1.5 km/40 minutes). This intimate inlet has smooth protected waters and is popular with anglers.

The track heads inland across a wide peninsula for 1 km/30 minutes to Te Totara Bay, then skirts around the bay and dips over another peninsula (almost an island) to where sandy beaches broken by boulder outcrops continue for 2 km/1 hour to a shelter and campsite at Upokorora Bay. A circuitous track goes around to Te Puna Hut, which has 18 bunks. Panekiri Bluff can be spotted through the inlet channel.

From Te Puna the track goes inland over a 100-metre-high bush saddle to Tapuaenui Bay where there is a shelter and campsite. The track negotiates a series of small bays and promontories to the hut at the very end of Whanganui Inlet (3 km/1 hour from Te Puna). Sited by the Whanganui Stream flats, the hut has the standard 18 bunks. There is a good beach on the lakeside, and to get to it you pass two curious stumps of bush-clad rock.

Whanganui Hut is only 4 km/1 hour from the western road-end. The track winds above the lake to Huiarau Stream Bay, then out past a spur before turning into the wide grassy Hopuruahine Valley. A short way further along a bridge crosses the river to the public road, carpark, toilets and picnic area.

Lake Waikareiti

Total tramping time: 6–8 hours/2 days (allow longer
  for Ruapani circuit)
Total tramping distance: 16 km
Grade: easy
Highest point: 853 m; bush saddle
Maps: Urewera National Park 273-08; Waikaremoana
  W18

An intimate forest landscape of lakes, lagoons and
rare wild flowers surrounds the Ureweras' second
largest lake. Apart from the usual foot-track the hut
can be reached by hiring a rowboat across the lake.
Potter among the peaceful islands and bays which no
power boats are allowed to disturb.

Take Highway 38 to the park headquarters. There are regular bus
services along the highway. Dinghies can be hired at the park headquarters, where keys and rowlocks are given in exchange for the
hireage price, plus deposit. The boats are chained up by the lakeside,
and the oars are available from a locker beside the shelter.

The track to Lake Waikareiti begins just over the Aniwaniwa
Bridge. A large sign displays the routes and the location of the huts.
Almost immediately the track passes the side-track to Lake Ruapani,
which can be taken as an alternative on the return journey.

Continue strolling on the 1-metre-wide benched trail as it eases
through a stately forest, with salubrious seats provided at regular
intervals. It's a 300-m climb over 2 km/1 hour to the lake edge. Here
the dinghies, lockers, toilets and a comfortable shelter are sited. The
shelter is enclosed and contains a wall map and window seats which
look out to Lake Waikareiti. A good brew stop.

Turn left from the shelter (unless you have taken the option of a
rowboat) and walk for 2 km/1 hour to reach the other end of the
Lake Ruapani loop trail. From this junction travel 4 km/2 hours
along the lake's northern edge to Sandy Bay Hut.

The lake is rarely visible from the track, and only at one point does
the track come down to the shore. The bush has a rich canopy and
subcanopy of plants, as you would expect in a wet mountain

Waikareiti Track

climate. Rata, rimu, tawa and matai are typical trees, overtopping an abundance of ferns, epiphytes (hanging plants) and flowers. Birds are equally prolific, but unless you have patience you are likely only to hear their songs.

Ten minutes before you reach the hut a sign marks the junction of the Kaipo Lagoon track. The track turns downhill to the 18-bunk hut, which is equipped with a wood stove and a verandah that looks back over the lake.

The side-track to the Kaipo Lagoon is well formed and worth a day trip as it wanders amid bush lakelets and tussock openings for 4 km/2 hours to a large silted clearing at the head of the Kaipo Stream. Here there are more rare plants for the keen-eyed naturalist. A comfortable and much-used campsite is situated where the main track ends.

The Lake Ruapani diversion adds another 8 km/3–4 hours to your return time, and includes many peculiar inland ponds and wetlands. The forest on the Ruapani circuit is consistently beautiful while the ponds have an eerie tranquillity and provide a welcome respite from the all-enclosing bush. Orchids are often found on the wetland margins and black-backed gulls and spur-winged plovers can be seen at Lake Ruapani. Some of the smaller ponds dry up and such is the remoteness of the scene that you fully expect to see a moa strolling across the meadow.

Mount Manuoha

Total tramping time: 7–8 hours/2 days
Total tramping distance: 15 km
Grade: medium
Highest point: 1403 m; Manuoha
Maps: Urewera National Park 273-08;
  Waikaremoana W18

Mt Manuoha is the highest peak in the Ureweras, just protruding above a circle of bush hills that stretches as far as the eye can see. Only Lakes Waikareiti and Waikaremoana and the Panekiri Bluffs interrupt this vast forested tract. There is one hut.

Turn off Highway 38 by Waiotukapuna Stream, 1 km north of Hopuruahine Road, 6 km from the park headquarters.

The Manuoha track begins on the left of the stream by the gravel turn-off area and proceeds inland 50 m to a pretty side-creek. Cross over and turn up along this little valley for 500 m/20 minutes until the track begins to sidle out of the creek. Winding slowly upwards, the track lazily switches back across an open gully (the last water), then goes up a steep bush face to the main ridge. It's a 400-m climb over 1.5 km/1 hour.

The next 6 km/2–3 hours to Manuoha is along an undulating bush ridge with few views. The scarcity of trampers up to this peak encourages the wary deer to browse along the slopes, and there is always a chance of seeing one. It is 4.5 km/2 hours and 300 m before you reach the only major clearing before the summit.

There are a series of gouged rockbeds at the head of Taparawera Stream before the track turns back into the tangled mountain bush for 1.5 km/1 hour to the scrub-crowned peak of Manuoha (1403 m). A large trig occupies the high point, which offers an unbroken vista of rolling bush tops. A cut track through scrub leads down 30 m to an open bush terrace and a 6-person hut. Return the same way unless doing route below.

Mt Manuoha to Lake Waikareiti

Total tramping time: 6-7 hours one way
Total tramping distance: 9.5 km one way
For experienced parties only

Mt Manuoha can be combined with Lake Waikareiti, for a route is marked from Manuoha Peak over Pukepuke Peak to Lake Waikareiti, but take care. The Pukepuke route is not a formed track and only markers in the bush indicate the way, making this track strictly for experienced trampers only.

The Pukepuke route is completely waterless. You should allow 5-6 hours in descent or 7-8 hours if climbing.

For the Pukepuke route to Lake Waikareiti, go east from the trig down a badly overgrown track. Waist-high scrub hides many of the markers (white plastic rectangles) until the bush edge, where the route becomes clearer.

At first there is the vestige of a worn trail as the markers follow the ridge crest for 2 km/1 hour, dropping 100 m, and passing an open earth gully. Then the route veers right for 2 km/1 hour off the ridge and down a spur for 180 m to a bush saddle.

The track then climbs and turns east up 100 m over 2.5 km/1-2 hours in dry undulating forest to reach Pukepuke (1220 m). From here you can glimpse Kaipo Lagoon. The markers continue along the ridge for 2 km/1 hour, then they swing south and sidle downhill to the head of the lakebed for 1 km/30 minutes. A spacious campsite on a grass clearing marks the beginning of a good track to Lake Waikareiti.

For access and route information to the main highway see Lake Waikareiti (page 50).

Whirinaki River

Total tramping time: 9–12 hours/2 days
 (Central Whirinaki Hut return)
Total tramping distance: 28 km
Grade: easy
Highest point: 600 m; Central Whirinaki Hut
Maps: Urewera National Park 273-08;
 Whirinaki V18

This ancient forest is one of the finest to be found anywhere in New Zealand — a dense assemblage of marvellously tall rimu, kahikatea and other podocarps in the lower valley and beech forest higher up. Whirinaki was at the centre of a famous conservation battle in the eighties, with all these great podocarps being eyed up for logging. High-grade tracks and huts have made this a very approachable tramp for family groups and the less active.

From Murupara on Highway 38 it's about 16 km to the Minginui turnoff. It's a 7-km sealed road to Minginui but you do not have to go into the township itself, instead turn right over the Whirinaki River bridge to meet River Road. There's a DOC camping area at this road junction. Follow River Road upvalley about 5 km to the Whirinaki carpark and signboard. Some of the signposting is unclear and it is useful to have the overall Urewera National Park map.

The first part of the track passes through a scientific reserve 500 m/15 minutes to the deep slot of the Te Whaiti Nui a Toi canyon and footbridge. The track stays on the far bank for the rest of its journey up to Central Whirinaki Hut. It is superbly graded, with boardwalks over streams and smooth cuttings through spurs.

After 500 m/15 minutes the Moerangi side-track heads away uphill, then another 2 km/40 minutes on the river track leads to the footbridge over the Mangamate Stream. A track goes up the Mangamate River, which is part of the back-valley route described under Whirinaki Forest (page 57).

With easy curves the benched track wanders alongside the Whirinaki River, sometimes closer, sometimes cutting inland over spurs. The forest dominates, with alternating stands of rimu, tawa,

Riverside track

matai and kahikatea. There is a profound, nearly churchy silence, and it's almost a relief when a robin lets loose with a volley of territorial calls or a wood pigeon whooshes by. Both the shining and long-tailed cuckoos live in Whirinaki, as well as parakeets, kaka, song thrushes, blackbirds, tui and bellbirds.

A further 1 km/20 minutes to a side-track leads to a signposted waterfall, with steps and a viewing platform overlooking the plunge of water into a deep rock bowl.

It's 5 km/1–2 hours to the Kakanui Stream, suspension bridge and an open clearing giving rare relief from the forest canopy. There is camping here. Neatly sidling some river bluffs the track ambles another 4.5 km/1–2 hours (including a tunnel!) to the Central Whirinaki Hut. The hut has 17 bunks and a verandah, and sits in a wide clearing with tall podocarps as dignified companions, and ample good camping on the flats around. A signposted track to Pukeroa (a minute before the hut) fords the Whirinaki River and climbs 250 m to a lookout over the Whirinaki Valley and as far as Mt Edgecumbe, Tarawera and the Tongariro massif. A good day trip.

The hut is a handy base for trips upvalley, either to the cave or to

Upper Whirinaki Hut. It's 2 km/1 hour upstream to the Taumutu Stream bridge and junction. Stay on the valley track and note how the forest is predominantly silver and red beech.

Another 2 km/40 minutes to the caves junction. One track goes to Upper Whirinaki Hut. Take the alternative over the footbridge towards the Plateau carpark, but immediately past the bridge a short unmarked track nips upstream to the cave entrance. There's an excellent campsite here, and a deep swimming hole. The cave is about 60 m deep and also provides shelter.

The track to Upper Whirinaki Hut starts from the caves junction and winds through lovely beech forest, crossing the river as it suits and passing several fine campsites. After 2 km/40 minutes it reaches a signposted three-forked junction. One track goes up the ridge to the Plateau road-end, another continues to Upper Te Hoe Hoe Hut, and the third goes 700 m/10 minutes up a side-stream track to the expansive grass clearing of Upper Whirinaki. The hut has 9 bunks and a broad verandah.

For the back-valley route to the Mangamate see Whirinaki Forest. This route is suitable for more experienced groups.

Whirinaki Forest

Total tramping time: 6–7 hours/1 day
  (one way to Upper Whirinaki Hut)
Total tramping distance: 15 km
  (one way to Upper Whirinaki Hut)
Grade: medium
Highest point: 800 m; unnamed saddle
Maps: Urewera National Park 238-08;
  Whirinaki V18

This is a harder alternative to the main Whirinaki Track, and goes through back-valleys to the Upper Whirinaki Hut. Tracks are rougher over a number of low bush saddles, and there are oodles of river crossings. Two huts. This trip can be linked with the main Whirinaki River track to make a varied 3- to 4-day tramp.

See Whirinaki River (page 54) for access and route description to the start of the Mangamate track, 3 km/1 hour from the road-end.

The first part of the Mangamate Track is possibly the roughest. It stumbles back and forth over the stream 12–14 times as it heads upvalley. After 1 km/1 hour it unexpectedly meets a four-wheel-drive track. Travel is much more pleasant, but wetter still, for this vehicle track fords the Mangamate something like 50 times, in complete disregard of trampers' feelings on the matter.

Still the bush is nice and after a sloshy 3.5 km/1–2 hours you arrive at Mangamate Hut in its ponga-fringed clearing. Nine bunks, wood stove and verandah.

The route upstream persists with its river-crossing for about 3 km/1 hour, sometimes skirting thick patches of native stinging nettle. Then the track climbs 100 m to a low bush saddle, entering the headwaters of the Kakanui Stream after 1 km/30 minutes. A longish sidle around streams and grass clearings for 2 km/1 hour leads to another subtle saddle, then drops into a branch of the Kakaiti Stream, criss-crossing for 1.5 km/1 hour to the forks with Taumutu Stream. There is a campsite here.

Turn up the Taumutu track (which changes banks fairly frequently) in this pretty valley for 2.5 km/1 hour as it starts to clamber

Top Whirinaki Hut

up onto bush river terraces to a low, disguised saddle. After a modest 50-m climb the route descends into a grass gully with tall beech forest for 1 km/20 minutes to the Upper Whirinaki Hut. The hut looks small in the large grass clearing, but it has 9 bunks and a sunny verandah, and is altogether a pleasant place to linger.

If you want to rejoin the main Whirinaki River track rather than return by the back-valley route, follow the track across the flats beside the side-stream. It's about 700 m/10 minutes to the main Whirinaki River and the major track junction.

For access and a route description down the Whirinaki River see Whirinaki River (page 54); 14 km/6 hours to Whirinaki carpark.

Tongariro Crossing

Total tramping time: 12–14 hours/2–3 days
Total tramping distance: 23 km
Grade: medium
Highest point: 1886 m; hill overlooking Red Crater,
   Tongariro plateau
Maps: Tongariro National Park 273-4;
   Tongariro T19 (optional Ruapehu T20)
(See *New Zealand's Top Tracks* by Mark Pickering
for a more detailed description of this track.)

There is no other track in New Zealand quite like the
Tongariro Crossing. A lunar landscape of young
steaming mountains surrounded by the intricate
debris of old craters, brilliantly coloured lakes and
bubbling hot pools. Allow extra time for bad weather and side-trips.

The two huts have gas cookers, gas heating, toilets, water supply
and a warden through November to April. A Great Walks pass is
required for both huts and campsites. Camping is allowed only at
the two designated campsites, Ketetahi and Mangatepopo.

Ketetahi Springs are on the northern edge of Tongariro National
Park. From Turangi take Highway 1 to the Rangipo turnoff then take
Highway 48 to the Ketetahi Springs side-road, about 25 km. From
the Chateau take Highways 47 and 48 some 35 km. Carparking,
shelter, information boards and toilets at road-end.

For the latest information on the various transport operators in
the district ring the DOC visitor centre at Whakapapa. Whakapapa
is on the western side of the park, off Highway 4 from National Park,
then some 9 km to the turnoff onto Highway 48, 7 km to the
Chateau. Mangatepopo access is off Highway 47 and down a 6-km
gravel road.

At Ketetahi carpark the track starts gently through the totara forest of Okahukura Bush, and crosses a stream which is sparkling, but undrinkable, for it's been liberally dosed with chemicals from the hot springs. There's a side-track to a waterfall-cascade before the main track gets suddenly serious, climbing up a series of steps to the bush margin. About 2 km/1–2 hours from the carpark.

There are fine views of Lake Rotoaira and the graceful bush-clad cone of Mt Pihanga (1325 m). The well-formed track steadily climbs a long spur over 2 km/1 hour aiming for the brown flanks of North Crater, then drops off the spur into the steam-veiled valley of Ketetahi Springs.

The hot springs are in an enclave of Maori land and the Ketetahi Trust has given permission for walkers to cross the area. The springs have long been used as a recuperative spa, and escaping fumes and steam cover the small valley, creating a strange primeval landscape.

It's a short final heave up to the hut (200 m/10 minutes), which has splendid panoramic views. Camping permitted here. The hut has 24 bunks and gas burners for cooking. A cup of tea on the verandah goes nicely with the stunning view.

The stretch of track between Ketetahi and Mangatepopo Saddle is open and exposed, and since in bad weather you are not going to see a thing (and will probably have a miserable time doing it), if you have a spare day, sit it out.

From the hut the track zigzags steeply for 2 km/1–2 hours up the slopes for a climb of 200 m, before easing along the gully that leads to the saddle between Blue Lake and North Crater. The sudden emergence out of the saddle onto Central Crater is marvellous — you feel on top of the world.

The main track heads confidently across the Central Crater for 1 km/30 minutes, following marker poles and rock cairns, and skirts the brilliantly coloured Blue Lake (past the track junction to Oturere Hut — see Oturere Crossing, page 62) to the ridiculously turquoise-coloured Emerald Lakes.

After a steep 200-m climb, 700 m/1 hour past the steamy Red Crater the track reaches the spur crest, the highest point of the track at about 1886 metres. There's a poled side-trail marked to Mount Tongariro (1968 m), a rocky scramble somewhat overshadowed by the symmetrical beauty of Mount Ngauruhoe.

The main track descends 200 m down a sharp spur to South

Crater and wanders across this vast bowl to the low saddle on the far side (2 km/1 hour). If you have allowed the time Ngauruhoe is a tempting side-trip.

It is 600 m up to the summit of Ngauruhoe, and poles mark the start of the route but peter out after a while, though on a fine day the route is not difficult to follow. Without a pack it is 1 km/1–2 hours to the top, and about 15 minutes down, moon-walking down the soft gravel.

From the saddle the main track tips into the head of the Mangatepopo Stream and the smell of

Lunch by Emerald Lake, Mt Tongariro

the Soda Springs. It is a fast 1 km/20 minutes descent through interesting rock formations to the side-track to the Soda Springs (which are not hot), then 2 km/40 minutes downstream to the 24-bunk Mangatepopo Hut and campsite.

The track to Whakapaka cuts across-country and numerous side-streams, and in places the tussock tracks have been deeply eroded by use, but the sweeping views make up for some of the mud. After 8 km/2–3 hours you reach the junction to the Taranaki Falls. The falls are impressive and are well worth a diversion, but the Chateau is only 1 km/30 minutes further through a brief margin of mountain beech forest then back onto the open plain, and a few more tussock gullies to cross and you are at the carpark, still at an altitude of 1140 m. No wonder the air is bracing.

For access and route description to Tama Lakes and Waihohonu Hut see page 63.

Oturere Crossing

Total tramping time: 4–5 hours/2 days
  (Emerald Lakes to Waihohonu Hut one way)
Total tramping distance: 10 km
  (Emerald Lakes to Waihohonu Hut one way)
Grade: medium
Highest point: 1650 m; Emerald Lakes
Maps: Tongariro National Park 273-4;
  Ohakune S20; Ruapehu T20

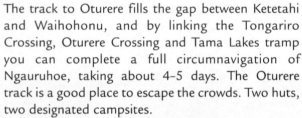

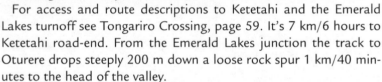

The track to Oturere fills the gap between Ketetahi and Waihohonu, and by linking the Tongariro Crossing, Oturere Crossing and Tama Lakes tramp you can complete a full circumnavigation of Ngauruhoe, taking about 4–5 days. The Oturere track is a good place to escape the crowds. Two huts, two designated campsites.

For access and route descriptions to Ketetahi and the Emerald Lakes turnoff see Tongariro Crossing, page 59. It's 7 km/6 hours to Ketetahi road-end. From the Emerald Lakes junction the track to Oturere drops steeply 200 m down a loose rock spur 1 km/40 minutes to the head of the valley.

Here you have left the crowds behind, and the track snakes pleasantly down the Oturere Stream for 3 km/1 hour, until it climbs up through some dramatic and weird rock formations for 1 km/20 minutes to the discreetly placed Oturere Hut — 24 bunks, gas cookers, wood stove and warden in the summer. Campsite by hut.

The track continues to Waihohonu, dipping up and down over a series of pumice gullies for 4 km/2 hours. In fine weather the views are tremendous.

The last 1 km/1 hour is a long drop into the broad Waihohonu Valley and a gradual climb through beech forest, then a final quick descent to the sunny hut — 24 bunks, gas, wood stove, and warden in the summer. Sheltered beech campsite 150 m below the hut.

For access and route descriptions to the Desert Road and Waihohonu Hut see Tama Lakes, page 63. It's 6 km/3 hours to the Desert Road, 13 km/7 hours to the Chateau.

Tama Lakes

Total tramping time: 8–10 hours/2 days
Total tramping distance: 19 km
Grade: medium
Highest point: 1300 m;
   saddle near Lower Tama Lake
Maps: Tongariro National Park 273-4;
   Ruapehu T20 (optional Ohakune S20)

Between the volcanoes of Mts Ngauruhoe and Ruapehu are the twin jewels of the Tama Lakes, occupying two former vent holes. A good well-marked track crosses this volcanic panorama, and includes an historic hut, tussock plains, alpine plants and a freshwater spring. One hut, several campsites.

Along the Desert Road (Highway 1) the turnoff and carpark for Waihohonu is not conspicuous, a small sign and carpark about 25 km north of Waiouru. You are already at an altitude of 1000 m when you get out of the car, and the winds can howl across the Rangipo Desert, and even bring snow in the middle of summer.

From the carpark you follow an old vehicle track and dry sand streambeds for 1.5 km/30 minutes to Te Mako bush, an attractive copse of trees beside the Ohinepango Stream. Established campsites are found here in sheltered beech clearings.

The track bridges the Ohinepango Stream, then climbs through a little bush to emerge back onto the tussock plain. Marker poles lead across the plain for 4.5 km/1–2 hours to Waihohonu Bush. On the way across the plain it is worth studying the ground level panorama as well, where multi-coloured scoria mingles with prostrate creeping plants, bunches of hebes and shy alpine flowers.

At the four-way track junction, the right-hand choice goes 100 m/5 minutes past a sheltered camping area and across a footbridge up to Waihohonu Hut. Good views from the 20-bunk hut, which has gas cookers and a warden in summer. The left branch track travels about 1 km/10 minutes in and out of a large scoria gully and across the Ohinepango Stream to the natural springs, which are nestled in a bush grotto, usually loudly occupied by a pair of paradise ducks.

Crossing a stream, with Mt Ruapehu behind, Tama Lakes Track

The track straight ahead leads to the old Waihohonu Hut (1 km/20 minutes), painted bright red and well sheltered in a glade of beech forest and manuka scrub. This is listed by the Historic Places Trust as Category 1, the highest protection able to be given to any building. Built in 1901, it has an unusual construction, for pumice was used as a filler between the double-wooden walls. The walls are covered in graffiti, some of it going back to the 1920s.

The main Tama Lakes track goes past the old Waihohonu Hut and follows a branch of the Waihohonu River, crossing a complex of side-streams as they cut through the thin covering of tussock. At 1200 m this rolling plain is a barren but beautiful region, miserable on a stormy day but magnificent if fine. On one side there is snow-crusted Ruapehu, and on the other the stark symmetry of Ngauruhoe.

After 7 km/2–3 hours from Waihohonu Hut, and a barely noticeable climb, the open basin which holds Lower Tama Lake should become obvious to the right. Rocky bluffs ring the lake and the only easy descent is from the north side. Continue along the track for 1.5 km/1 hour to the junction of a side-trail which follows along the top of Lower Tama, where you can descend 100 m down into the lake basin.

On the main track more open tussock travel follows, muddling in and out of streambeds for 3 km/1–2 hours to the tip of Taranaki Falls. To appreciate the sudden burst of water over the rock edge, another track can be taken to the foot of this waterfall. This track continues downstream, offering an alternative route to the Chateau, but the main graded track takes about 2.5 km/1 hour to reach Whakapapa village with the Chateau sternly guarding its golfcourse.

Lake Surprise

Total tramping time: 10–12 hours/2–3 days
Total tramping distance: 24 km
Grade: medium
Highest point: 1450 m; on the track
Maps: Tongariro National Park 273-4; Ohakune S20

A short trip to an alpine lake on the more remote western flanks of Mt Ruapehu. A wide belt of upland forest gives way to scoria gullies above the bushline. There are impressive views and the trails are easy to follow, although muddy in places. Two huts.

Travel 6 km east from the National Park township along Highway 47, and turn right down a short road to the secluded and comfortable Mangahuia campsite.

The track wanders inland for 5 km/2 hours, a gentle gradient of 200 m in forest to the bushline. After 1 km/20 minutes crossing tussock slopes the track does a sharp east turn, and it's a further 1.5 km/30 minutes to a track junction.

Turn north towards Ruapehu as the track winds for 2 km/1 hour beside Whakapapaiti Stream to the hut (20 bunks). An elegant stream, but in high rainfall it can flood dangerously.

Above the hut the track goes 1 km/20 minutes to a track junction and a circ of cliffs at the head of Whakapapaiti Stream. Curious rockforms in the creekbed and waterfalls breaking over the line of bluffs make for interesting travel. The poled trail swings south some, climbing out of the Whakapapaiti Valley to a height of 1450 m. Staying very roughly at this level the track crosses deep scoria gullies and alpine fields. On a clear day Taranaki's distinctive cone stands out over Tongariro's western bush.

After 8 km/3–4 hours of up-and-down travel the cross-country track comes out on a spur above the Mangaturuturu River. Turn south-west down this spur for 1 km/20 minutes (a 150-m descent) to Lake Surprise, which sits in an unexpected place on the spur's broad crest. It is a quiet, undramatic spot with a shortage of dry campsites. Mixed alpine shrubs and grasses ring a swampy shoreline.

The track enters the bush, which is only a little beyond the lake,

The daily diary

and descends 150 m in a swinging curve to the valley floor, crossing one branch of the Mangaturuturu to come out beside the hut after 1.5 km/1 hour.

This hut belongs to the Wanganui Tramping Club and has space for 10 people, a wood stove and a fine outlook up the snowy sides of Ruapehu. Outside the hut stands a memorial to four members of the club who were killed when the Three Johns Hut at Mt Cook was blown over the ridge in a violent storm.

The track diverges at the hut. One branch heads down-country some 9 km to the Horopito road-end, but the main Round-the-Mountain trail continues climbing 250 m around the base of Ruapehu to the Turoa Skifield road (2.5 km/1 hour).

Mount Taranaki:
Round the Mountain 1

Total tramping time: 13–16 hours/2–3 days
  (North Egmont to Ihaia Track)
Total tramping distance: 26 km
  (North Egmont to Ihaia Road end)
Grade: medium
Highest point: 1300 m;
  track under Dieffenbach Cliffs
Maps: Egmont National Park 273-09; Egmont P20

Mt Taranaki (also called Mt Egmont) is the elegant cone that dominates the province and coastline of the western bulge of the North Island. At 2518 m the old volcano can be seen from as far south as the Heaphy Track in the South Island, although many people drive right past the mountain without even seeing it. Westerly cloud and storms batter the peak and have given it a nasty reputation as one of New Zealand's most dangerous mountains. Ease of access and sudden changes of weather are a bad combination. Those wishing to climb the mountain itself need to consult a proper climbing guide and DOC.

The following route descriptions concentrate on the round-the-mountain tracks (RTM) which encapsulate the diverse forest types and alpine scenery of this unique mountain. For ease of use the description has been divided in two, and if you want to circumnavigate the entire mountain you will need to walk both tracks, allowing perhaps 5–6 days. RTM 1 has some well-graded tracks and three huts, but camping opportunities are limited. A portable cooker would be useful.

From New Plymouth drive 29 km to North Egmont, via Egmont

Early morning, Mt Taranaki

Village, where there is a visitor centre and teashop. The camphouse offers basic bunk accommodation.

From the camphouse take the Razorback or Holly Hut track past the monument and climb a remorseless staircase for 250 m (past the Veronica track); 1 km/1 hour to Tahurangi Trig (1181 m). Shortly after the Razorback track junction follow the clean-cut main trail as it winds around gullies towards and under the Dieffenbach Cliffs (1 km/40 minutes). This is the track's highest point, with a marvellous outlook back to New Plymouth and the Taranaki plain.

The track wriggles and descends slightly for about 1 km/40 minutes to Boomerang Slip (where signs warn against stopping on this still-shifting rock slope) and the track curves around the head of Kokowai Stream to Kokowai track junction; 1 km/20 minutes. Keep to the higher RTM track as it threads through the dense belt of leatherwood and drops 200 m over 2.5 km/1–2 hours to the Ahukawakawa track junction.

Bear left, and a couple of gullies and 5 minutes later is Holly Hut, named after the mountain holly growing around it. This hut has 38 bunks and a verandah outlook to the Pouakai Range.

There are two good side-trips here. One follows a well-signposted track to Bells Falls (1.5 km/30 minutes one way), a spectacular 30-m waterfall at the head of the Stony River. The second trip goes to the Ahukawakawa Swamp (1 km/30 minutes one way), which is the feeder for the Stony River Bells Falls, and is reached via the Ahukawakawa Track. A boardwalk is provided across the vast spongy wetland.

The RTM track continues from the hut across the tall alpine scrub of Holly Flat (past Bells Falls junction) and drops sharply in and out of Peters Stream, a wide bluffed channel (1 km/40 minutes). Then it's a steady climb, sidling for 2 km/1–2 hours around Hook and Skinner Hills past the etched gullies of Upson Stream and Hidden Valley.

An energetic 150-m climb alongside the gash of Pyramid Stream takes the track on to tussock grassland, and just when you are beginning to enjoy the views the track descends sharply 200 m down open slopes into the tall scrub again (2 km/1 hour). After another 1 km/1 hour through several bitsy gullies Puniho junction is passed, and after another 1 km/30 minutes Kahui Hut is reached. This hut has 6 bunks and is one of the older huts on the mountain. There's a small grass flat below it for campers.

From here it's an easy 300-m descent over 2.5 km/1 hour down through kamahi and totara forest to the Kahui cross-junction. Turn south onto the Oaonui Track. In 3 km/1–2 hours this track crosses three prominent side-streams and several smaller creeks, many of which have now been bridged.

Across the Oaonui Stream is the site of the old Oaonui Hut (good camping here) and the Ihaia Track junction. Continue for 500 m/10 minutes until you reach a footbridge which spans a curious dry flood-channel of the Oaonui. On the other side is the Waiaua Gorge Hut beside the broad, deep-cut Waiaua, with an unobstructed view of the western slopes of Egmont. The hut sleeps 16 and has a wide verandah.

If you are exiting here return to the Ihaia Track and continue out to the road-end 5.5 km/2 hours away. Alternatively resume the RTM walk by referring to Round the Mountain 2, which follows.

Mount Taranaki: Round the Mountain 2

Total tramping time: 11–14 hours/2–3 days
  (Ihaia Track to North Egmont)
Total tramping distance: 25 km
  (Ihaia Track to North Egmont)
Grade: medium
Highest point: 1500 m; Tahurangi Lodge
Maps: Egmont National Park 273-09; Egmont P20

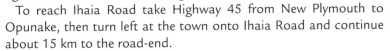

The second half of the Round the Mountain track is slightly longer, and has more choice and complexity. In places almost separate alpine and bush routes can be taken, or a mixture of the two. Initially this description stays on the lower slopes where the tracks are well maintained, but from Dawson Falls to North Egmont it takes the excellent higher track.

To reach Ihaia Road take Highway 45 from New Plymouth to Opunake, then turn left at the town onto Ihaia Road and continue about 15 km to the road-end.

From the Waiaua Gorge Hut the track drops dramatically via a ladder and steep trail to the Waiaua bed, then clambers 30 m up the other side. The track follows the cliff edge upstream for 500 m/30 minutes to a track junction.

(The Brames Falls track continues as an alpine route, bypassing Lake Dive hut and dropping down to Dawson Falls via Hooker Shelter; 11 km/4–6 hours.)

The Taungatara Track sidles slowly for 6 km/2–3 hours through thick supplejack forest and crosses several prominent open streams to a junction with the Lake Dive Track. This track steadily climbs 400 m inland for 4 km/2–3 hours alongside the impressive Punehu Canyon to the quiet lapping lakeside. A 16-bunk hut overlooks the far end of the lake, a secluded place.

(The Upper Lake Dive track goes to Dawson Falls via Hooker Shelter; 7 km/3–4 hours.)

From the hut follow the bush RTM track as it winds in and out of gullies for something like 6 km/2–3 hours to Dawson Falls. On the way there's a side-track to Hasties Hill (996 m), and a fine lookout just afterwards. Signposted track junctions lead to Dawson Falls carpark and information centre. There is also a public shelter here, and a tearooms in the motel; you might even care to visit Dawson Falls themselves.

To take the high route from the carpark or visitor centre study the map boards carefully, for there are numerous tracks in this area and there is plenty of opportunity for confusion. The Wilkies Pools track immediately plunges into a forest thickly crusted with lichens and mosses, giving the trees a shaggy, fairytale look. Many visitors find this 'goblin' or 'cloud forest' eerie.

The spur is easy for 500 m/20 minutes, and at the track junction you drop down and cross the bubbling Kapuni Stream (which after heavy rain may be impassable) then pass another junction to meet the Ridge Track (300 m/15 minutes). Follow this up to the junction with the Waingongoro Track (250 m/10 minutes).

(The low route to North Egmont starts from here and follows the Waingongoro Track to Mountain House Lodge, then along the Curtis Falls track to Maketawa Hut (16 bunks), and around to North Egmont; 12 km/3–4 hours.)

Back into the leatherwood line the upper track traverses a delicate waterfall at the head of the Waingongoro around to the Stratford Plateau (1 km/1 hour). The Plateau carpark is at an altitude of 1100 metres, the highest carpark in Taranaki National Park, with out-standing views across the well-ordered plains to the squat volcanoes of Ruapehu and Ngauruhoe on the horizon. Toilets here.

The first part of the high track to North Egmont is also a service link to the skifield, and the angle is well graded and easy. You pass through a thick shrub belt of alpine leatherwood and koromiko and past the flying fox arrangement, where the skifield sends its supplies across the Manganui Gorge, then the track angles into the narrow valley.

Signs warn against lingering in the gorge, mostly as a winter pre-caution against snow avalanches but you can also often get rock-fall. Even late in the season the gorge bed is full of old avalanche debris, and it can get quite exciting negotiating your way across the hard-packed snow. A short sidling climb out of the gorge and you are at the skifield, and practically the first building is a large public shelter with toilets (1.5 km/1 hour).

The track crosses in front of the skifield buildings and across a mountain stream, sidling around small alpine gullies filled with buttercups and daisies in spring. The track climbs steadily all the way to Tahurangi Lodge (some 2 km/1 hour), crossing several creeks. The gradient is gentle, and the track well poled as it sidles under the volcanic outcrop of Warwick Castle.

Waterfall, Mt Taranaki

It is not long before the TV pylon and Tahurangi Lodge come round into view, and there is a small unlocked emergency public shelter underneath the lodge. For the North Egmont carpark go down 'The Puffer' vehicle track (which services the TV tower) some 3 km/1 hour.

For access and route description from North Egmont to Ihaia Track via Holly Hut see Round the Mountain 1, page 68.

Pouakai Range Crossing

Total tramping time: 9–11 hours/2–3 days
Total tramping distance: 22 km
Grade: medium
Highest point: 1400 m; Pouakai Trig
Maps: Egmont National Park 273-09;
  New Plymouth P19; Egmont P20

The rolling tops of the Pouakai Range lie on the northern flanks of Mt Taranaki. A good track traverses the range and gives tremendous views. Two huts; a portable cooker is definitely useful on this trip.

It is a 30-km drive from New Plymouth to the Kaiauai carpark on the North Egmont road. There is a visitor centre, tearooms and toilets 2 km up the road at North Egmont.

From the carpark walk briefly to a track junction with the Waiwhakaiho Track, then turn north along this for 500 m/20 minutes to the footbridge across the Waiwhakaiho River. Immediately there is another track junction with the Kokowai Track. Keep north as the track passes through a dense matrix of ponga, ferns, vines, pepper trees and canopy podocarps.

For 1.5 km/1 hour the track sidles in and out of slippery gullies, finally reaching the 4-bunk Kaiauai Hut, which sits on a shelf beside the deeply incised Kaiauai Stream.

The track continues by descending into this gorge then climbs out, following beside it uphill for a while; it's a solid rise of 500 m to Henry Peak (2.5 km/2–3 hours). The track, particularly above the bushline, is often gouged out and slippery with mud. Snow poles lead the last 150 m to the top of Henry Peak (1222 m) with its dominating views along the hillocks and plateaus of the Pouakai Range.

Following poles and a wide track, slide down 150 m to a low saddle, then sidle past Maude Peak and the Maude Track junction onto the Pouakai Plateau (1 km/40 minutes).

With Mt Taranaki sharply symmetrical on your shoulder, it's a steady 100-m climb over 1 km/1 hour past twin tarns which sparkle on a lush wet flatland to the Mangorei junction. The Pouakai Hut is 5 minutes beyond this junction.

Pouakai tops

This 16-bunk, three-roomed hut is spectacularly sited. A spacious verandah gazes out towards New Plymouth and the arc of coast, and at night the lights from the Taranaki plains seem dreamlike.

You can exit via the Mangorei road-end, an almost 750-m descent over 6.5 km/2–3 hours. Another good exit option is to return to the ridge and follow the broad track past the Hump (1292 m) to a high scrub saddle and track junction (1 km/40 minutes). (The Ahu-kawakawa Track south can be linked with Holly Hut; see RTM 1.)

Take the Pouakai Track west as it sidles up past Tatangi (1366 m) for 50 m onto a small plateau then sidles a further 100 m up and around to Pouakai Trig (1400 m), where the entire upland of the Pouakais lies spreadeagled before you (2 km/1 hour).

The Dover Track is a long, even descent of 900 m over 5.5 km/2 hours to the Carrington Road. The top 300 m of tussock and alpine shrubs have a couple of rock outcrops that have to be negotiated. Then it's duck and dodge through the twisted upper bush canopy until you emerge into the taller lowland trees where the occasional rimu or rata grows. From there it's a stroll to the end of the track to the carpark.

Matemateaonga Walkway

Total tramping time: 11–14 hours/3–4 days
  (Kohi Saddle to Whanganui River one way)
Total tramping distance: 35 km
  (Kohi Saddle to Whanganui River one way)
Grade: easy/medium
Highest point: 732 m;
  Mt Humphries (Whakaihiwaka)
Maps: Matemateaonga R20

This is the longest track in Whanganui National Park and the longest walkway in the North Island. It follows the tops of bush ridges all the way and is well suited to less experienced trampers and lovers of bush and birdlife. However, on dull wet days the walkway can turn into a monotonous exercise in simply covering ground. The birdlife is excellent though usually unseen, and you will hear a variety of shrieks, coughs and chortles that could be blamed on anything from pigs to kiwis, or the goats that infest the range. Six huts and shelters, limited camping. Carry water; it gets pretty dry between huts.

For those who don't fancy going the whole hog across the range to the Whanganui River, a good weekend option is to Omaru Hut, with a side-trip up Mt Humphries which offers impressive views.

Access to the Matemateaonga Walkway is not easy and because most people only want to do the walk one way, you have to book transport for the entrance and exit. This can be expensive so a party of four is an efficient cost-spreader. The Kohi Saddle end of the track is a long way from anywhere (60 km from Stratford), though transport operators in Stratford do run a trampers' service. At the Whanganui River if you have booked a jetboat you can exit via the river, a most satisfying way to end the walk. Ring DOC Wanganui (the headquarters for the Whanganui National Park) for a list of current transport operators and prices.

From the Kohi Saddle carpark follow the track as it crosses a fence and sidles through manuka before entering the bush proper. Here the old dray road is broad and comfortable to amble along, glimps-

Puketotara Hut

ing views of endless bush-covered hills. After 1 km/30 minutes the walkway brushes disconcertingly close to a disused logging road.

It's 3.5 km/1 hour to Omaru Hut, which accommodates 12 people and is surrounded by tall podocarps. There's a short side-trail down to the head of Omaru Stream. From Omaru Hut the walkway continues along the ridge for 6 km/2 hours and sidles under Mt Humphries (Whakaihiwaka) crossing a few small side-streams to the side-track to Mt Humphries.

This side-trip is a must on a fine day. The track is steep at first, then sidles under a rock overhang. After another short steep scramble it takes it easier in the summit area, winding up to the first peak and in and out of a small gully to the beaconed high peak (1 km/1 hour); a 200-m climb. The view is a mass of mountain ridges blueing into the distance, along with Mt Taranaki's clean cone.

Back on the main track it is 1 km/20 minutes to Humphries Hut, a quite useable 6-bunk hut with a fireplace. You could camp around the hut.

The walkway continues (past a side-track and Puteore Hut) for 3 km/1 hour to the 18-bunk Pouri Hut, set in a small clearing. The dray road ends just beyond Pouri, becoming a narrower, muddier bridle track, and the next stage is a long one, 7 km/2–3 hours to Otaraheke Hut (2 bunks and a fireplace). Two good bush campsites just along the Maungarau side-track.

(On the Pouri–Otaraheke section the track passes near the peak Te Mapua, which at 746 m seems to be the highest point in the Matemateaonga Range. No side-track to it unfortunately.)

From Otaraheke hut it's 3 km/1 hour to Ngapurua Shelter, with three sides, benches and picnic tables. A reasonable number of campsites here, with tap water and fireplaces.

From Ngapurua there are occasional glimpses of islands of farm-land in swathes of bush. After 9 km/2–3 hours the track starts to slide noticeably downhill to Puketotara Hut, which sleeps 12, has a wood stove and verandah. Sometimes there's a voluntary warden over the summer.

This is the best-placed hut on the whole walkway, with vistas of the bush hills and the mists that characteristically fill the valleys in the mornings and evenings. The Mt Ruapehu lookout seat is just 30 m from the hut, and there is one good campsite just above the hut.

Oddly, the kilometre posts reach 0 km at Puketotara Hut, but there's still 2 km/30 minutes to go. From the hut the track drops abruptly and steeply 300 m, initially through bush, then grass glades and manuka forest down a narrow spur to the banks of the great Whanganui River, where a muddy back-eddy swirls logs around like reptiles.

Here you either wait for your booked jetboat, try to hitch a ride on an unbooked one (a long shot), or turn back and retrace your steps across the Matemateaonga Range.

Umukarikari and Urchin Tops

Total tramping time: 12–15 hours/2–4 days
Total tramping distance: 31 km
Grade: medium/fit
Highest point: 1591 m; Umukarikari
Maps: Kaimanawa State Forest Park 274-11;
** Tongariro T19; Ruapehu T20**

A varied circuit trip in the Kaimanawa Range, smooth, apparently endless tussock tops on the Umukarikari Range, and then a pleasant meander down the Waipakihi Valley, with a return over Mt Urchin. One hut, good tracks, many river crossings, but plenty of camping down the Waipakihi. Alpine conditions can be expected all year round on the tops and this trip is suitable for experienced trampers only.

Entrance and exit are off the Desert Road (Highway 1). Drive 15 km south of Turangi and turn left on to Kaimanawa Road. Travel 2.5 km along this short sealed road past the Poutu Inlet Scenic Lookout to the Waikato Falls across the Tongariro River, then after 500 m veer left at the next junction, and after another 500 m sharp left again across the Waihaha Bridge. 500 m along a river terrace turn right at the last junction to reach the signposted Umukarikari Track, 1 km.

From the road-end carpark the tramper faces a 650-m haul up to the tops, in mostly beech forest interspersed with an occasional rimu. A total of 4 km/2–3 hours of hard work to the gentle gradients of the tops. As the forest falls away the views dramatically increase with the striking volcanic trio of Tongariro, Ngauruhoe and Ruapehu rising to the west, and the lovely bush cone to the north is Pihanga.

Kaimanawa tops

About 2 km/1 hour around to Sharp Cone, and then the poles lead a further 1 km/30 minutes on to the low flat mound of Umukarikari.

This time the views to the east are what attract the eye. Looking out past the Waipakihi Valley you can see the plains of tussock and forest so characteristic of the Kaimanawas.

The marker poles lead slowly downhill at first, a gradual descent of 400 m over 6 km/2 hours, as the trail runs along the wide and easy Umukarikari Range. The trail then drops more sharply through the bush to end at the headwaters of the Waipakihi River. Cross the river and the hut (12 bunks) is prominent on a grass terrace above the river.

The Waipakihi River is some 20 km long. There is no specific track along its length (except those that tramping parties etch out) and no real need for one. It's delightfully easy to travel down the grass river flats and beech terraces, and the river can be forded at most sites. There are abundant campsites, and only in one place is there anything like a gorge, and that's easily negotiable.

About 6 km/1–2 hours down to the first major fork, then 2 km/30 minutes to the next major side-stream and 1 km/20 minutes to where a track on the east side climbs and disappears into the Kaimanawa hinterland. A further 2 km/40 minutes down the Waipakihi is a track that offers a good return trip back to the Poutu Intake road-end, without the transport hassles of coming out at the Waipakihi. The short sharp track leads abruptly some 300 m back onto the Umukarikari Range (1 km/1–2 hours).

From here on the poled track leads for 2 km/40 minutes around to Mt Urchin (1392 m) at the end of the Umukarikari Range. Enjoy the last great views before the 3 km/2 hour descent of 600 m to a carpark near the turbine station, and you have quite a long road walk (perhaps you have left a mountain bike?) of 5 km back to the Umukarikari carpark.

For the Waipakihi River exit it is still a good 12 km/3–4 hours to wend your way down the river, through a short gorge, on to where the Waipakihi Road comes down from the tussock plateau just before a big U-bend in the river. It's 6 km to the Desert Road, and the Waipakihi Road exit is 38 km south of Turangi, 24 km north of Waiouru.

Kaweka Hot Springs

Total tramping time: 9–12 hours/2–3 days
Total tramping distance: 26 km
Grade: easy/medium
Highest point: 1100 m; Makino ridge
Maps: Kaweka Forest Park 274-12; Kaweka U20

Tucked up in the northern Kawekas are two natural hot springs beside the mighty Mohaka River. This is an area well known to Hawke's Bay trampers, but the drive to the start is almost as arduous as the tramp itself. This short circuit includes both hot springs, plenty of kanuka and beech forest, some river travel and two huts, one of them on the tops. The river track to Te Puia Lodge is suitable for most ex-trampers who want to get back into it.

From Napier take the winding back-country road 60 km through Rissington, Patoka and Puketitiri to the Makahu Stream Ford. The public road continues for 1.5 km beyond the ford, and four-wheel-drive vehicle access exists right to the Mangatutu Hot Springs road-end 6 km further on, but people in humble cars may have to walk this stretch.

From the Maungatuku hot springs and picnic area on a high terrace, a well-graded track follows the south bank of the Mohaka River to Te Puia Lodge. This track is 7 km/2–3 hours long and hugs the sinuous river, passing mostly through kanuka forest. The large lodge sits on a grassy clearing at the junction of the Makino and Mohaka Rivers, and holds 20 people. Plenty of camping on the flats.

A few minutes past the hut clearing is a track junction and a footbridge across the Makino River. It is worth continuing along the Mohaka River track for 2 km/40 minutes to the Mangatainoka hot spring, where a spa tub arrangement catches the hot water as it trickles off the hillside. Nice campsite nearby, and a generally salubrious spot for doing not much at all.

There is a direct inland track to Makino Hut, starting from Te Puia Lodge and climbing a steep 500 m straight out of the Mohaka River (2 km/2 hours), but a more pleasant route is straight up the Makino River. Lots of river crossings, but on a summer day the next 5 km/2 hours slip easily by. Bright shallows and small pools, with manuka on the sides at first, quickly giving way to beech forest. Some attractive camp-sites along the route.

The track to Makino Hut starts on the east bank some 1.5 km above Wai-matai Stream; it should be well marked. You'll guess if you've gone past it, because you will shortly meet the top forks with a prominent track lead-ing to Mangaturuturu Hut on the west bank.

The spur track to Makino Hut climbs steeply some 500 m and tops out on a

Criss-crossing the river

flat-topped bush spur 1.5 km/2 hours. It's an easy 2.5 km/1 hour through bush and manuka ridge down to Makino Hut, a 4-bunk old Forest Service type.

From Makino out it's a brief 500 m/15 minutes to the top of the spur where the short-cut track goes down direct to Te Puia Lodge. The main ridge track rambles along for 5 km/2 hours, at first through bush (past Middle Hill track junction), then open scrub, gradually descending to the Makahu or Hot Springs Road.

Kaweka Range

Total tramping time: 17–19 hours/3–4 days
  (Makino Hut to Kuripapango)
Total tramping distance: 27 km
  (Makino Hut to Kuripapango)
Grade: fit
Highest point: 1724 m; Mt Kaweka
Maps: Kaweka Forest Park 274-12; Kaweka U20

The Kaweka Range lies on the sunny side of the main ranges, shielded from the prevailing westerlies by the bulk of Ruapehu and the Kaimanawa Range. This tops-traverse from one end to the other is only suitable in fine weather, but it's a good leg stretcher, and the rewards are tremendous views. It would be hard yakker in cloudy conditions, and it can blow forty bastards when it wants to. Good navigation skills are needed as the range has only sporadic markers and cairns, and this trip is suitable for experienced trampers only. Four huts; carry water.

Obviously you need to arrange transport pick-ups as the road-ends are widely separated. If you fancy a shorter version of this range trip then the entrance via Kaweka Road and Makahu Saddle has a good track leading up just short of Mt Kaweka, about halfway along the range.

For access and route descriptions to Makino Hut/Kaweka Hot Springs and Kuripapango see Kaweka Hot Springs (page 82) and Kiwi Mouth and Kiwi Saddle (page 87). Hot Springs road-end to Makino Hut is 5.5 km/2–3 hours.

From Makino Hut a good bush track climbs steadily up the spur past the Makino River turnoff some 5.5 km/2–3 hours to the bush line, about a 300-m climb. It's about a 2 km/1 hour climb over 300 m over the tussock tops to Whetu peak, which occupies the northern end of the Kaweka Range. Ballard Hut is about 30 minutes away, west from Whetu about 1 km, then down the poled spur some 200 m to the tidy 6-bunk hut.

From Whetu the Kaweka Range lies before you and the travel is good but with plenty of ups and downs. Poles and cairns sporadi-

The dry tops of the Kawekas

cally mark the route. It's 150 m and 1 km/20 minutes down to the top of a prominent spur leading to Middle Hill track and hut, then 2.5 km/1–2 hours along the rolling tops around and up to North Kaweka (1707 m), which is only 20 m lower than the high peak.

A further 1.5 km/30 minutes past a natural spring (somewhat off the western side of the range and not always easy to find), past the Makahu track (a good escape route down to Makahu Saddle), a memorial cairn and finally Mt Kaweka itself (1724 m). With Ruapehu and Ngauruhoe on one side and Hawke's Bay on the other you feel on top of the world, with 2 km/40 minutes of easy travel down to Mad Dog Hill and a steep 1-km/30-minute drop of 250 m to Studholme Saddle.

Both Studholme bivouac and Studholme Saddle hut can be reached easily from here. Drop down to the west side-stream from the saddle and follow this around barely 1 km/30 minutes to the dog-kennel bivvy. Studholme Hut is 500 m/15 minutes up the side-stream beside the bivvy, 4 cosy bunks.

It's a bit of a haul from Studholme Saddle up to Kaiarahi peak (1.5 km/1 hour) and a quick 1 km/20 minutes along the sharper ridge to the aptly named The Tits. Cook's Horn rock outcrop is off to the east. The main ridge and route turns west a bit and after about 500 m/15 minutes some markers should indicate a trail down a subtle spur to the bush edge. Navigation here requires particular care; it's easy to miss the various turn-offs in the mist. It's a steep 250 m down to the bush edge, and markers continue with a good track down a further 150 m to the old Kaweka Hut (1 km/40 minutes).

This hut has 6 bunks and is owned by the Heretaunga Tramping Club (Hawke's Bay). A good track leads down 100 m into a side-stream, and wriggles around and down to the Tutaekuri River (1.5 km/1 hour). Across the river the track picks up a vehicle track, climbing briefly, and links up with an old bridle track that jogs past The Lakes for about 5 km/2 hours to the Napier–Taihape road, about 3 km east of Kuripapango.

Kiwi Mouth and Kiwi Saddle

Total tramping time: 13–16 hours/2–3 days
Total tramping distance: 28 km
Grade: medium
Highest point: 1394 m; Kuripapango ridge
Maps: Kaweka Forest Park 274-12; Kaweka U20

A circuit trip from Kuripapango encompassing dense kanuka forest, tussock hills and the lovely windings of the Ngaruroro River. The Kaweka Range is usually hot and dry in summer, an ideal place for a river trip. Three huts, several good campsites.

From Fernhill (Highway 50) follow the metalled Napier–Taihape road some 44 km, just 1 km short of Kuripapango. A short vehicle track leads down to the river, a cableway and a small shelter by the water gauge.

A track leads down to the Ngaruroro River, then it's predominantly river travel to Cameron's Hut (7–8 km/2–3 hours). In normal river flow the travel is straightforward, and on a hot day enjoyable. There are lovely deep pools on the way with some striking rock formations, and short, often overgrown trails along the banks.

Cameron's Hut is a 6-bunk hut on a grass clearing beside the river. A track leads around to the footbridge upstream from the hut, and past an old side-track going up to Kiwi Saddle. From the bridge the 7–8 km/2–3 hours of river travel to Kiwi Mouth continues as pleasantly as before.

There's a footbridge 500 m/20 minutes short of the hut, and a short track leads to the sheltered and sunny grass clearing at Kiwi Mouth. It's a warm 4-bunk hut, and because of its central location provides at least 6 different routes into various parts of the southern Kawekas.

There are two possible routes to Kiwi Saddle hut, but both depend somewhat on the state of the tracks (which can get overgrown), so a good check of the Kiwi Mouth logbook first might sort out the best option.

The easiest way to Kiwi Saddle is to criss-cross up Kiwi Creek, an attractive small stream, for about 3 km/1 hour to just above a

Ngaruroro River

prominent fork in the stream. On the south bank a track should be marked leading up a steep manuka spur for 200 m before meeting the ridge track junction. Here the climb is a more gradual 200 m up the main ridge then the track sidles into beech forest for the final 100-m climb up to the low-lying saddle and the old-world hut (6 bunks). All told a climb of 1.5 km/1–2 hours.

The alternative is the ridge-line track from Kiwi Mouth to Kiwi Saddle. This starts behind the hut and climbs a severe 750 m or so onto a flat-top peak and then discouragingly drops 300 m again into a side-creek, meets up with the track from the river and climbs on up the ridge to the hut (4 km/3–4 hours).

The Smith-Russell track back to Kuripapango has some splendid views, but is rather up and down. In misty weather you should watch out carefully for the cairns and other markers. It's 300 m up to the first knob (1 km/1 hour), down and up 150 m to the second (1 km/40 minutes), then a long, easier drop some 200 m around to Kuripapango Peak (2 km/1 hour).

The bleached eroded hillsides are not everyone's cup of tea, but you get sweeping views over to the Kaimanawas and look down on the twin jewels of The Lakes. The long 3 km/2 hour descent down the Kuripapango spur is a bit hard on the knees, over 700 m down to the carpark.

Parks Peak and Makaroro River

Total tramping time: 12–14 hours/2–3 days
Total tramping distance: 25 km
Grade: medium
Highest point: 1300 m; Parks Peak Hut
Maps: Ruahine Forest Park Map 274-5; Kereru U21;
 Ongaonga U22

An interesting circuit in the eastern Ruahines with
beech forest on the ridge and easy travel down a
shingle-filled Makaroro River. This is a solid weekend tramp, with plenty of river crossing, so it makes
a good summer tramp. Four DOC huts and some
good campsites along the river.

From State Highway 50 turn west onto the Wakarara Road, and
drive past the locality of Wakarara to the road-end beside the
Makaroro River.

The road bridge across the Makaroro River has long since fallen
away and you will have to ford the river. From here follow the road
for 1.5 km/20 minutes (past the Wakarara Road leading to
Makaroro Base) to the second road junction. Makaroro Hut (9
bunks) is 300 m to the west, however continue straight ahead on the
north road branch to a bush track (500 m/10 minutes). A signpost
indicates the route and after 5 minutes you reach the junction with
the Yeoman Track (which continues to Ellis Road and Whitnell
Lodge).

With these preliminaries over, the main hill track has a steady haul
of 750 m up a side-spur on to the main ridge (3 km/2–3 hours).
There's a track junction down to Barlow Hut in the Makaroro River,
but the main trail ambles along the ridge which, because it lies just
below the bushline, has the characteristic vegetation of stunted trees
covered in wet moss and hanging lichen.

Makaroro River

The track is well marked for 4.5 km/2–3 hours to Parks Peak Hut, which is sited in a tussock clearing at 1300 m (or 'in a swamp' as one logbook entry comments). The hut has 4 bunks and a cosy wee wood stove.

At a junction before the hut a track descends to the Upper Makaroro Hut, down a long 650 m to the Makaroro River (3 km/2 hours). This hut has 4 bunks and sits on a narrow grass terrace on the west bank of the river.

Like many rivers in the eastern Ruahines, the Makaroro has been filled with gravel eroded from the tops, which makes it a veritable trampers' highway. From Upper Makaroro Hut the river winds for 5 km/2–3 hours downstream and swings easily through thick bush-clad banks to Barlow Hut (6 bunks). There are several suitable camping spots between the two huts.

After Barlow Hut the river continues its meandering progress for 2 km/40 minutes to a commemorative cairn, then another 2 km/40 minutes to farmland. From here the river widens considerably and it's 3.5 km/1 hour of shingle flats back to the old bridge and its junk-yard of history.

Sunrise Hut

Total tramping time: 6–8 hours (Armstrong Saddle return)
Total tramping distance: 12 km (Armstrong Saddle return)
Grade: easy
Highest point: 1300 m; Sunrise Hut
Maps: Ruahine Forest Park Map 274-5;
   Ongaonga U22

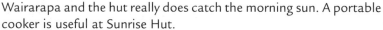

The track to Sunrise Hut is one of the most accessible trips to the tops on the western side of the Ruahine Range. A well-maintained 'garden path' zigzags up through some splendid mature forest to a sunny hut beside a small tarn. The rocky lookout nearby provides a panorama of Hawke's Bay and the Wairarapa and the hut really does catch the morning sun. A portable cooker is useful at Sunrise Hut.

(Note: for fitter trampers there is an interesting circuit option over Mt Te Atuaoparapara, down to Waipawa Saddle and Waipawa River to Waipawa Forks Hut and back onto the Sunrise Track. See track details at the end of this entry.)

From Hastings follow the Tikokino back-road some 50 km to the Wakarara Road, and follow this 18 km to the junction with the North Block Road. From here it's another 7 km to the signposted Triplex carpark, with several farm gates to open and close. If you continue along the road you reach the Waipawa River, and access upriver to Waipawa Hut.

For Sunrise Hut follow a four-wheel-drive track for 1.5 km/30 minutes around the hillside (some 10 minutes past the Swamp Track junction) to the start of the Sunrise track. A few minutes further on the vehicle track reaches Triplex Hut, a 12–16 person hut, still in reasonable condition. Heaps of camping space in the grassy glade.

From the hut the signposted track dips across a stream past the Swamp Track junction, and many lazy zig-zags later (and after climbing almost 300 m) the track flattens and sidles round to a discreet saddle and a track junction to Waipawa Forks Hut (2 km/2 hours). The forest is a lovely mixture of beech and native conifers.

The Sunrise Track climbs slowly up 2 km/2 hours to the hut, the

Serving up

first 250 m through impressive red beech forest with occasional podocarps like rimu and kahikatea poking through. Bellbirds and tomtits are active vocally, and parakeets can often be heard chattering in the canopy, though you rarely see them.

After passing the old Shuteye Shack hut site there's another 250-m climb through mountain beech and Sunrise Hut comes as a surprise as you pop out of the bush into 'buttercup hollow' (the buttercups have gone unfortunately) where the hut stands beside a small tarn. Sleeping platforms for 8–10, a wood stove, ample portable cooker benches and tables make this a roomy, relaxed hut. Gas heater and gas cookers. The windows face the sun and a fine view over Triplex Hut to the plains and sea.

There are lots of little hummocks and viewing points around the hut for sunning on. It is also an easy walk up the cairned trail to Armstrong Saddle and tarn, and a prominent knob to the north of the saddle (1499 m) gives wide-ranging views over the Ruahine Range with not too much effort (a 200-m climb from the hut; 500 m/30 minutes).

The saddle was named after Hamish Armstrong who crashed a

light airplane here in 1935 and whose body was never found, only a shirt with the trademark 'Triplex' (or in another version of the story a shirt marked with three 'X's).

Te Atuaoparapara and Waipawa Saddle Circuit
Total tramping time: 6–7 hours
  (Armstrong Saddle to Waipawa River carpark)
Total tramping distance: 9 km
  (Armstrong Saddle to Waipawa River carpark)
Grade: medium/fit
Highest point: 1687 m; Te Atuaoparapara

For trampers wanting more of a challenge it is about 4 km/2–3 hours from Armstrong Saddle over the tortured scree ridges of Te Atuaoparapara and round to Waipawa Saddle. The travel is not as rugged as it looks, mostly tops travel with some scrub in the dips, but you still need a fine day, and some experience.

From Waipawa Saddle a well-marked trail cuts down through a steep scrub and bush spur some 600 m to the top forks (1.5 km/1 hour). From here on the travel is in the gravel river and much easier, some 2 km/1–2 hours down to Waipawa Forks Hut (12 bunks). Just before the hut on the north bank a good track leads back up to the Sunrise Track junction (500 m/20 minutes), or you can continue past the hut for 2 km/1 hour to the road-end and carpark.

Sawtooth Ridge

Total tramping time: 15–18 hours/2–3 days
Total tramping distance: 24 km
Grade: fit
Highest point: 1686 m; Ohuinga
Maps: Ruahine Forest Park Map 274-5;
   Ongaonga U22

The Sawtooth Ridge is a famous stretch of tops-travel in the Ruahine Range, a series of knobs strung together for 2 km. Its reputation is arguably greater than its difficulty because there is a pretty passable worn trail most of the way, and none of the bumps are unduly steep. Even so, it's a trip for experienced trampers in good weather. There's scarcely any point in going in a storm, unless you are particularly weird. This trip description is almost a circuit, with river crossings, bush ridges, open tops and four huts.

Access to the start of the Daphne Track is off Highway 50 some 8 km south of Ongaonga, turning into Makaretu Road for 4 km to Mill Road, through Ashley Clinton for 10 km to Kashmir Road, then 3 km to the former Forest Service base at Moorcocks and the park boundary. About 1 km past the cattlestop the road turns right for 500 m to a parking area near Moorcock Stream, and the Daphne Hut track is poled from here.

For access to the Tukituki River continue to the end of Mill Road, then turn right by some buildings and follow a farm road for 1 km. Legal access follows a track down to the Tukituki River and upstream to the park boundary.

(Note: it is possible to travel directly to Daphne Hut up the Tukituki in the streambed through the gorge, however there are some deep wades and it should not be attempted after rain; 7 km/3–4 hours. This option does make an attractive way of completing a circuit, and avoids the longish road walk between Tukituki and Kashmir carparks.)

From the Kashmir Road carpark cross Moorcock Stream and the farmland to a steep scrubby spur, eventually meeting the main ridge in red beech forest after 2.5 km/2 hours; a climb of 500 m. Take the

Looking across to the Sawtooth Ridge

north (right) junction and follow an open ridge (past a good look-out after 20 minutes) then the track descends, steadily at first, then steeply into the Tukituki River (2.5 km/1 hour). Criss-cross up the incised river gorge for 500 m/20 minutes to Daphne Hut (4 bunks).

The track to Howletts Hut (10 bunks) starts just before Daphne on the north bank of an obvious side-stream (there are two tracks, choose the upstream one) and doesn't muck about. It's a 750-m climb over 2 km/2–3 hours straight to the tops where Howletts sits in an attractive spot, straddling the ridge with views in all directions.

From here to the Sawtooth it's all tops travel — 2 km/1–2 hours up and around to the corner peak of Tiraha, a climb of almost 300 m, then there's a great tarn on a small saddle about 150 m before the peak. It would make a superb evening campsite. From Tiraha the Sawtooth Ridge lurches away north, and a 200-m descent sets the ball rolling as the worn trail worms its way past, over and around various lumps on the ridge. About 3.5 km/2–3 hours up to the deceptive double peak of Ohuinga (1686 m), a grunt of 200 m.

In misty weather it might be confusing getting off Ohuinga and negotiating the big saddle (200 m down and 200 m up), onto the ridge (1 km/1 hour) and then a sharp east turn down the Hinerua Ridge. This ridge-spur is rather scrambly up and down travel for 3 km/1 hour to the bush edge, then a good track for 1 km/30 minutes down to Hinerua Hut (6 bunks) which sits on a bush flat. Total descent of 600 m.

The main track dips across a small bush saddle (500 m/10 minutes), and at the track junction turns sharply south down a prominent spur for some 4 km/2–3 hours, with a final 300-m descent over farmland down to the Tukituki River. This track is no longer being maintained.

A final 1 km/20 minutes downriver then pick up the steady farm track on the south bank that climbs up to the Tukituki carpark.

Rangiwahia Hut

Total tramping time: 3–4 hours/1–2 days
Total tramping distance: 5 km
Grade: easy
Highest point: 1327 m; Rangiwahia Hut
Maps: Ruahine Forest Park Map 274-5;
  Mangaweka T22 (optional Ongaonga U22)

At Rangiwahia you can see the great triptych of North Island volcanoes, Taranaki, Ruapehu and Ngauruhoe, and that's just from the carpark. 'Rangi' Hut is one of the most accessible alpine huts in the North Island, and few tracks can offer such a comfortable trip to the tops — two easy hours to the hut, with waterfalls, gorges and mountain cedar forest on the way. Take a portable cooker.

A road map would be useful as there's a lot of potential for getting lost. The easiest route is probably via Highway 1 to Mangaweka township, then turn off to Rangiwahia. It's about 15 km to the turnoff onto Te Para Para Road, a further 4 km to Renfrew Road, and 4 km to the carpark. There are at least two gates to open and the road is steep towards the end.

From the carpark the track wanders up 2 km/1 hour through some attractive rimu forest with pepper tree (horopito), rangiora and wineberry underneath. A grove of red beech then an area of felled and ring-barked pine trees gives the impression that some ardent conservationists have been very busy.

The bridge is balanced elegantly over the gorge, and on the other side you enter mountain cedar forest, which is now becoming rare. Kaikawaka was known to the early settlers as 'bucket of water tree' because it was notoriously difficult to burn.

The track maintains its easy grade for the last 1.5 km/1 hour, and zig-zags up through the subalpine leatherwood forest, which the Maori knew as 'tupare'. Beyond the winsome waterfall you are on the tussock grasslands and there's the 12-bunk hut, with a colour scheme that makes it appear oddly like a marae.

There's a verandah on which you can eat lunch and gawp at the

Rangiwahia Hut

views, and an even better lookout on the small hilltop beside the hut. Gas rings and heater in the hut.

It's certainly worth following the well-worn tussock track a wee way above the hut just to sample the expansive views of snowgrass, but the distance to the main ridge itself is deceptive. Mt Mangahuia is 1580 m high, and it's more than 3 km/1 hour one way to the summit from the hut.

You can find old pumice deposits throughout the Ruahine Range, and even on the tops as the old volcanic layers get exposed by the winds. You can't help but look back at Ruapehu, and wonder whether the recent abdominal rumblings are just a case of indigestion or whether she really will blow. Tell you one thing, the view from Rangi will be superb.

Mount Holdsworth and Jumbo Circuit

Total tramping time: 12–15 hours/2–3 days
Total tramping distance: 21 km
Grade: medium
Highest point: 1470 m; Mt Holdsworth
Maps: Tararua Forest Park 274-2; Carterton S26

A popular circuit track over one of the dominant peaks of the Tararuas, with extensive views of the range and the Wairarapa Plains. Well-formed and signposted tracks, but the long tops section requires good weather. A hard weekend trip, but cruisier over three days. Five huts.

If travelling from Wellington on Highway 2, turn left 4 km before Masterton into Norfolk Road and Mt Holdsworth road (well sign-posted), 15 km to the road-end and carpark. At the road-end there is a picnic area, toilets, camping ground, caretaker and Holdsworth Lodge, a roomy hut available for the use of trampers, school parties and others (sleeps 20).

From the carpark the track begins by crossing the footbridge over the Atiwhakatu Stream, then passes the turnoff to Holdsworth Lookout and Gentle Annie and carries on through to the wide grassy clearing of Donnellys Flat (1 km/20 minutes). Good camping here.

From the flat the well-graded Atiwhakatu Stream track climbs gently above the short crisp gorge, with good river and forest views. In average flow you can easily wade through the gorge though it is probably not much quicker than the track these days. The track passes an old side-track up to Mt House hut and reaches the unbridged Holdsworth Creek after 2 km/40 minutes. The East Holdsworth side-track is marked just on the other side.

An easy 3 km/1 hour up a trampers' highway to the knocked-around

Jumbo Hut junction

Atiwhakatu Hut, which sleeps 10 and has an open fire. This may be replaced soon, or just removed.

About 1 km/30 minutes up the Atiwhakatu to the signposted junction, where the grunt begins, a climb of 750 m up 'Raingauge Spur'. The track is steep at first, and rougher, then climbs steadily, before it reaches the bush edge and sidles the last 15 minutes or so to Jumbo Hut (2 km/2–3 hours). The hut has room for 30–40 people, gas cookers, and sits right on the bushline but below the ridge, so you need to go above the hut to get the really good views.

The next stage onto Mt Holdsworth is all open tops. The poled track climbs above the hut into the tussock and scrambles along the spur to the main ridge and signposts (1 km/1 hour). The views are excellent all along this broad poled and cairned ridge as it dips up and down a few times before the final climb to the peak (3 km/2–3 hours). A tremendous panorama, encompassing the main Tararua Range, Waiohine Valley, Mt Hector and the town of Masterton. A large beacon, scraped with many years of initials, stands on top of Mt Holdsworth.

It's about a 1200-m knee-popping descent down to the

Holdsworth carpark, though the first part down the rolling snow-grass spur to Powell is a relatively gentle 1.5 km/1 hour.

Powell Hut was built in 1981 by the New Zealand Forest Service and Hutt Valley Tramping Club co-operatively. It sits exactly on the bushline, with 30 beds and gas cookers. The verandah, a great sun-bathing spot, looks out over the Wairarapa Plains and at night the glow of Masterton and car lights on Highway 2 can be seen.

The track from Powell to Mt House is unrelentingly steep, and rutted out with the passage of a zillion boots. In rain the stream also likes to go down the track. It's quite a scramble at times, and it takes longer than you think to get the 1 km/1 hour down to the old Mountain House, which is signposted down a side-track. It's about a 20-person hut, but may be removed in the future.

The 'Gentle Annie' track is a doddle, a lovely gradient with good views from a rocky knob on the way down to the carpark (5 km/2–3 hours).

Totara Flats (Holdsworth to Kaitoke)

Total tramping time: 15–18 hours/2–3 days
Total tramping distance: 36 km
Grade: easy/medium
Highest point: 780 m; Pig Flat junction
Maps: Tararua Forest Park 274-2; Carterton S26

A nicely varied trip down the Waiohine and Tauherenikau valleys, with spacious river flats and three short climbs over bush saddles. Nowhere does the track go on to the tops. Although the tramp is often done as a fit weekend trip, a leisured 3-day crossing may suit many people. Six huts and two shelters.

If travelling from Wellington on Highway 2, turn left 4 km before Masterton into Norfolk Road and Mt Holdsworth road (well signposted), 15 km to the road-end and carpark. At the road-end there is a picnic area, toilets, camping ground, caretaker and Holdsworth Lodge, a roomy hut available to trampers, school parties and others (sleeps 20).

Follow the easily graded 'Gentle Annie' for 4 km/2–3 hours up to the clearly signposted Totara Flats junction at Pig Flat, about a 450-m climb. From here the track sidles and nips down 1.5 km/20 minutes into the pretty Totara Creek; the old cattle track is scoured out in many places. A track travels for 3.5 km/2 hours along the creek on the west bank, although it can be quicker tramping down the creek itself. There is a nice campsite where the creek meets the Waiohine River.

A long footbridge spans the Waiohine River, and it's 1 km/20 minutes to Totara Flats themselves. This is the largest clearing in the Tararuas, nearly 2 km long and 500 m wide. There are plenty of campsites around the perimeter and by the river.

The Totara Flats Hut sleeps 24 people and commands a grand view of the flats, and gets well used. Much less so is Sayers Hut (6 bunks) on the east bank of the Waiohine, approximately halfway along the flat. A curiosity in its snug clearing, this hut is decorated with antlers and road signs, and was originally built in the late 1940s for a grazing lease on the flats held by Sayer. Worth a visit.

From Totara Flats Hut follow the main trail across the flats and up onto a river terrace, down the Waiohine River (or alternatively hop along river boulders) to Makaka Creek (3.5 km/1–1.5 hours). The river route is slightly quicker. At the Makaka track junction there is a solid 300-m climb up to a false saddle and sidle into Clem Creek, then it muddles across various branches of Clem Creek with a final zigzag up to Cone Saddle at 540 m, a meeting place of tracks from Mt Cone, Tauherenikau and Mt Reeves (3.5 km/2 hours).

Old Cone Hut

The descent to Tauherenikau is 200 m over 1.5 km/30 minutes to Cone Hut. This is an historic hut, built from totara slabs, and sited on a small promontory overlooking the Tauherenikau River. The hut was restored in 1988, though its rustic qualities remain.

The track from Cone Hut continues gently on the east bank over bush and grass flats for 3.5 km/1 hour to Tutuwai Hut (sleeps 20). Good camping spots by the river.

From here it's easier to criss-cross the Tauherenikau River downstream rather than follow the track, which occasionally sidles high to avoid slips and bluffs. A footbridge 1 km/30 minutes below Tutuwai Hut allows those who prefer the track to keep dry feet. From Tutuwai it's 7 km/2–3 hours of easy flats travel down to Smith's Creek Flats, with some swimming holes on the way. The river track on the west bank is a bit longer and slower.

At Smith's, the Tauherenikau River swings sharply away through its lower gorge, and there is a shelter in the forks between Smith's Creek and the Tauherenikau River. There are many campsites on these flats.

The main well-graded track up Smith's Creek is a painless 4-km/1–2-hour climb of 300 m to the gorse saddle at the top of the 'Puffer'. From the saddle the track drops 200 m over 1.5 km/30 minutes to the Kaitoke Shelter and carpark.

Southern Crossing

Total tramping time: 14–16 hours/2–3 days
Total tramping distance: 34 km
Grade: fit
Highest point: 1529 m; Mt Hector
Maps: Tararua Forest Park 274-2; Carterton S26

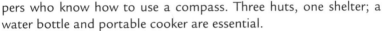

A classic tops traverse of the Tararua Ranges with outstanding views as far north as Taranaki and south to Wellington and the Kaikoura mountains. This is a popular but exposed alpine route which should be taken very seriously. Excellent navigation skills are needed, and it is suitable only for experienced trampers who know how to use a compass. Three huts, one shelter; a water bottle and portable cooker are essential.

From Highway 1 just before Otaki township and Otaki River, turn onto the Otaki Gorge Road and follow it some 19 km to the Forks. The last 5 km are narrow and winding, with one ford.

The tramp starts from Boielles Flat carpark and picnic area at the end of the Otaki Gorge Road. Cross the footbridge (Parawai Lodge is one minute off to the left; 30 people) and follow the signposts up a track to the farm plateau, where poles lead across and climb beyond several farm terraces up an open bracken spur to the bush edge, a vigorous 300-m climb (1 km/1 hour).

Follow the Judd Ridge Track as it winds up 500 m over 4 km/2 hours to Field Hut. Older trampers will remember the notorious mud on this track, but it is now gravelled in many places and almost mud-free and well graded as it follows a fine forested spur up to the historic Field Hut (20 bunks). The place reeks of nostalgia, starlight and storms. There's a small campsite on an unnamed knob 5 minutes before Field Hut.

Above the hut it's a short climb of 30 m through leatherwood to the flat tussock of Table Top (1035 m); 1 km/30 minutes. There's talk DOC may put a hut here; now it's open, exposed tops, with splendid views in fine weather. Boardwalks and muddy tracks lead up past Dennan Peak and on to Bridge Peak, a climb of 350 m (3 km/1.5–2 hours).

Southern Crossing near Mt Hector

The main track ambles over Hut Mound (1440 m), following snowpoles for 1 km/20 minutes to the door of Kime Hut. The flat terrain can be confusing in misty weather, and the hut sits in a shallow dip. It holds about 30 people on bench bunks.

The next stage of the Southern is the crunch, a long open ridge with quite a few bumps and sudden changes of direction. You must have a map and compass with you, and a low expectation of fine weather. Many people do the Southern without seeing a thing.

From Kime Hut it's a quick climb up on to Field Peak (1483 m) then a cruel descent of the same hard-earned 100 m, and up 150 m to the War Memorial Cross on Mt Hector (1.5 km/1 hour). It's a marvellous vantage point over the crumpled tops and deep-set valleys of the range, and on a good day both Mt Taranaki and Mt Tapuaenuku (in the Kaikouras) can be seen.

The route slips south around two lumps called the Beehives then into a feature nicknamed the Dress Circle, a half-arc of small peaks on a curving ridge. They start with Atkinson (1472 m) and Aston (1376 m) and end with Alpha (1361 m), with many dips and rises on the way round. Almost 5 km/2–3 hours. In misty conditions this can be a particularly tricky feature to navigate along.

It's a fast 250-m descent over 1 km/1 hour off Mt Alpha and the alpine slopes to Alpha Hut (12 people).

From Alpha Hut there's a 100-m climb over a knob then a sharp 150-m drop down into a saddle meaningfully called Hells Gate. Then it's another 100-m hike back up and out on to Omega (1118 m) in semi-open scrub country (2.5 km/1–1.5 hours).

Here the track swings south (away from the Bull Mound and Omega Track junctions) and sidles along the Marchant Ridge with its many bumps and dips. Some people vary it by dropping down into the Tauherenikau River, but this hardly makes the day shorter.

It's 6 km/2 hours past the Block XVI track to the old burn-off and dead stumps at Mt Marchant, and then a descent of 300 m over 3 km/1–1.5 hours to the old Dobsons Hut site. The track now slowly descends 100 m over 5 km/1.5–2 hours through bush, then scrub and gorse country to the junction with the well-graded Puffer track. Then 500 m/15 minutes down to Kaitoke Shelter and carpark.

Mount Kapakapanui

Total tramping time: 5–6 hours/1–2 days
Total tramping distance: 10 km
Grade: medium
Highest point: 1102 m; Kapakapanui
Maps: Tararua Forest Park 274-2; Carterton S26

It seems to be a good rule of thumb that mountains offset from the main range often have the best views, and this is certainly true of Mt Kapakapanui. You can see Mt Taranaki, Ruapehu, the Kaikouras, the Tararuas, Kapiti Island and the Marlborough Sounds. So you want a fine forecast for this simple weekend circuit tramp (often done as a day tramp), and if camping on top take a portable cooker and plenty of water. One hut. Access is from Highway 1 at Waikanae; turn down the Akatarawa Road for 4 km then take the Ngatiawa Road some 4 km to the carpark.

A poled route leads across the farmland and fords the river; 1 km/20 minutes to the track junction up to Ngatiawa and Kapakapanui Hut. It's easy to walk right pass this junction.

It's a steep 1.5 km/1 hour up 450 m to the bush knob called Ngatiawa, but the track eases and gradually turns a long corner climbing slowly to Kapakapanui Hut (2 km/1 hour). The hut has 6 bunks and a wood stove. There are some campsites round the hut, but they're nothing startling. If you are prepared to carry lots of water there is plenty of good camping on the flat summit of Kapakapanui, and on a fine evening this is an unbeatable option.

The track winds up through forest for another 1 km/1 hour, climbing some 300 m to the bush edge and the huge summit clearing. The actual summit is still a kilometre away but the views are well worth the effort.

To complete the tramp circuit carry on past the beacon and follow the reasonably well-marked track through a scrub belt and quite quickly into the bush edge (200 m/10 minutes). It's 3.5 km/2 hours down the long bush spur to the Ngatiawa River, and the track emerges right on the forks. Another 1 km/20 minutes back down to the carpark, and hopefully a camera full of good views.

Mount Matthews

Total tramping time: 13–16 hours/2 days
Total tramping distance: 30 km
Grade: medium
Highest point: 941 m; Mt Matthews
Maps: Rimutaka and Haurangi State Forest Parks
  274-4; Wellington R27

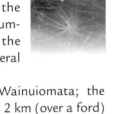

A tramp to the highest peak of the Rimutaka Forest Park. The tracks vary from high grade in the Catchpool to a rougher tramping track to the summit. No huts, but plentiful camping in the Orongorongo Valley, where DOC also has several bush cabins for hire.

From Wellington or Lower Hutt travel to Wainuiomata; the Catchpool is 10 km south on the Coast Road. It's 2 km (over a ford) to the main carpark, with extensive parking and picnic areas along the Catchpool Stream.

The Orongorongo Track climbs easily through pine trees before dropping down into native bush. The side-creeks are well bridged and after 30 minutes or so there is a side-track called the 'Catchpool Loop' which takes you back to the carpark.

Gradually the well-graded path reaches the head of the valley (passing the Cattle Ridge track) and crosses a low almost indistinguishable saddle. It slopes past the McKerrow Track junction and descends sharply to the graceful arched bridge over the Turere Stream. There's a dark brown swimming hole here, with toilets and a picnic area a minute or so further, out on the wide Orongorongo riverbed (5 km/2 hours).

Across Turere Stream a sign indicates the Big Bend Track. This is a side-track that connects upstream some 3 km/1 hour to the

Whakanui Track, a perma-
nent wet weather route. It's
an interesting track in good
bush, with glimpses of the
many private baches that
are secreted along the
Orongorongo River. This
track can be used for travelling upstream, but it is usually easier and quicker to
follow the bleached open
riverbed to Matthews
Stream.

There are good camping
sites at Big Bend and
Manuka Flat and many
open sites on the river, with
a few more discreet bush
sites on the banks. Any-
where in the bush you are
likely to stumble on a private bach. It's 3 km/1 hour
from Turere Stream to
Matthews Stream on the
south-east bank.

*Footbridge across a side-stream near
Orongorongo River*

A signpost indicates the Mount Matthews Track. This slips past
the private Baines Hut (Hutt Valley Tramping Club) and crosses
Matthews Stream a few times (two campsites here), then slogs up a
spur dominated by kidney ferns. A 400-m climb to the South Saddle
junction, which is worth visiting as this blowy tussock area has better views than the summit of Matthews (2 km/2 hours).

The summit track continues steeply, passing a grassy knoll that has
some good views back over the Orongorongo and South Saddle. The
track grinds up and flattens onto a long plateau of gnarled, moss-
crusted trees. This plateau takes a long time to travel along, but
eventually you get to the top where you can see trees everywhere (1.5
km/1–2 hours).

Haurangi Bush Track

Total tramping time: 14–17 hours/2–4 days
Total tramping distance: 26 km
Grade: medium
Highest point: 700 m; bush ridges
Maps: Rimutaka and Haurangi State Forest Parks
   274-4; Palliser S28

This attractive bush traverse sidles the Haurangi Forest Park on good tracks via four huts. Lots of up and down tramping, but the teeming birdlife, healthy forest, occasional views over the coast and nifty campsites more than compensate the visitor on this private and rather personal mountain track. Stinging nettle (ongaonga) can be a problem at times, so take some overtrousers. You need to arrange a car-switch, or leave a concealed push-bike at the Mangatoetoe track exit.

From Featherston on Highway 2 it's a longish drive on mostly good roads, past the turnoff to Lake Ferry, to the Ranger Station at Te Kopi and the short side-road to the Putangirua Pinnacles, where you can start the track. About 60 km.

From the picnic area follow the track and riverbed to the Pinnacle Stream (1.5 km/30 minutes), where you can drop your packs and explore these strange gravel columns. Back on course the main track zig-zags steeply to the splendid lookout over the Pinnacles (and incidentally the Kaikoura mountains of the South Island) and continues to another track junction. Turn up the inland track as it climbs through manuka to the beech forest and a vehicle track on the main ridge crest (1 km/1 hour).

Follow this farm road as it does a wandering climb through beech forest, then changes down into a mere track, which continues to climb to a 700-m ridge crest and a grassy knoll where there are good coastal views (4.5 km/2–3 hours). The track is close to the oddly named peak called Surf, but turns away and drops down a side-spur to Washpool Hut (6 bunks and an open fireplace), which sits on a terrace 30 m above the river (2 km/1 hour).

Follow the main track down to the river and head upstream a few

Mangatoetoe Hut

minutes to the Pararaki Track. One minute upstream there is an excellent campsite by the forks. The Pararaki Track doesn't mess about and climbs a lively spur for some 2 km/2 hours, with some fine totara and matai among the beech. Occasional clearings give views before the track pops over the 700-m crest and slips down quickly to Pararaki Hut (2 km/1 hour), another 6-bunker, with plenty of camping on flats around the hut.

The track into the Otakaha starts across the river from Pararaki Hut and slightly downstream. It climbs steeply at first, then eases casually across a side-stream and onto a subtle saddle with a smidgin of a view (1 km/1 hour). The track then drops into the head of the next valley and begins a stinging sidle, with plenty of heart-shaped kawakawa lining the tracks. This sidle makes some sense when it reaches an open beech spur and the track romps down it to a fork (1 km/1 hour). There's a sheltered campsite half a minute upstream. An easy amble downriver 1.5 km/30 minutes in shady kanuka forest (past many possible campsites) to the sunny Kawakawa Hut (6 bunks).

From the hut take the old vehicle track up the south branch past a sign and along the track that dodges back and forth up this pretty and intimate stream. Watch for a prominent side-creek which the track turns up (1 km/30 minutes). Occasional markers lead the way up the riverbed to where the creek narrows at a small fork. The track goes straight up a spur between these forks, then settles down into a sidle that slips almost unnoticed over the saddle, dropping furtively under fern trees down the other side, and then down a steep slidy spur to the main stream (2 km/2 hours).

From here on it's easier, with a prospective lunch spot at every bend as the river broadens and the track experiments with both sides of the stream, making an idle path through the kawakawa and kanuka terraces to Mangatoetoe Hut (2.5 km/1-2 hours). The predictable 6 bunks, but lots of floor space and spacious camping under the tall kanuka trees.

For the final exit keep to the east side of the Mangatoetoe (the only legal access out) for 4 km/1 hour down scrubby terraces and farmland to where the route leads round to the carpark and the sea.

SOUTH ISLAND

Dun Mountain

Total tramping time: 10–13 hours/2 days
Total tramping distance: 32 km, including Dun Mountain
Grade: easy/medium
Highest point: 1129 m; Dun Mountain
Maps: Richmond State Forest Park 274-6;
  Nelson O27

From Nelson city a tramp up New Zealand's first railway to the distinctive bare tops of Dun Mountain.
Built in 1861–2 to extract copper, the historic railway
line offers plenty of history and views on this very
accessible tramp. The uncompromising bleakness of
Dun Mountain is contrasted by swathes of beech forest, giving the
geography of this area an unusual character. Shelter, bivouac, hut.

From the Nelson city centre walk/taxi/bus up Brook Street 4 km
past the start of the Dun Mountain Walkway to another entrance 1
km further on, near the motor camp. This must be the closest tramping start to any city in New Zealand.

Follow the walkway for 1.5 km/1 hour up a dusty logging road
through pine plantations to a junction with the old railway line. Turn
uphill and follow the old line as it gradually climbs through native
forest some 5 km/2 hours to Third House. This large shelter sits in
an open clearing with views back over Nelson.

Keep to the main track as it meanders past the Wells Ridge turnoff
(1 km/20 minutes) and after another 3 km/1 hour breaks out into
the alpine shrubs and bare rocky screes of the mineral belt.

The track turns a corner at Windy Point and meets a four-way
junction. One side-track goes back to Wells Ridge and up onto
Wooded Peak (1111 m), a possible alternative route on the way out,
and the second side-track drops into the head of the Roding River
and climbs directly up to Rocks Hut.

Dun Mountain

Keep to the main trail as it sidles 1 km/20 minutes to Coppermine Saddle, sometimes over a track built up on hand-stacked rocks and passing mounds of tailings that are one of the few visible remnants of the miners' activities.

From the bleak Coppermine Saddle walk up rocky slopes almost 1 km/30 minutes (past a bush side-trail to Rocks Hut) up to Dun Saddle. Here you can leave your pack and follow an open, cairned route through tussock for 1.5 km/1 hour onto the flat mound of Dun Mountain itself. A seedy-looking bivouac (2-person) stands 300 m before the inconspicuous peak.

Returning to Dun Saddle, pick up the good track that follows the ridgeline through bush and open tops for 2 km/1 hour to Rocks Hut. This has 20 bunks, a wood stove and a verandah in a superb site, standing slightly above a bush hollow with an outlook as far as Mt Richmond.

Your return could be via the short-cut track into the head of the Roding River and briskly up to Windy Point again (almost 300 m up and down, however; 2 km/1–2 hours), possibly carrying on via the Wells Ridge Track. Or you may prefer the comfort and convenience of the graded track back to Nelson, constructed by miners and railway workers who probably sweated a good deal more than you will.

Pelorus River

Total tramping time: 11–14 hours/2–3 days
Total tramping distance: 36 km
Grade: easy/medium
Highest point: 680 m; Totara Saddle
Maps: Mt Richmond State Forest Park 274-6;
  Wairau O28; Nelson O27

A famous green-blue river, known for its deep rock pools, big trout and native beech forest on the banks. A well-formed track follows the river all the way, with several DOC huts, and good campsites. Only one real climb over a lowish saddle then it's a cruise downriver.

Drive from Nelson and Richmond and turn off 1.5 km south of Hope onto the Roding River Road. It is 11 km up the twisting metalled road to Hackett Creek forks. Parking space is provided in a picturesque scenic reserve. The other road-end is 14 km up the Pelorus River from Pelorus Bridge off Highway 6. Obviously you will have to arrange transport back to your vehicle, as it's too far to walk between the road-ends.

Cross the footbridge over a deep swimming hole in the Roding River and follow a vehicle track through pine plantations up the Hackett Creek. After 1.5 km/30 minutes the road ends at a crossing of the creek. You can either ford the creek or use the footbridge to cross to the other bank where a benched track sidles above Hackett Creek for 2.5 km/1 hour. It is pleasant travel to the track junction.

The route to the Pelorus River turns left and crosses Hackett Creek then follows a graded track beside Browning Stream. Alternatively, you can reach the Browning valley by deviating via Hackett Hut. This means continuing up the Hackett Creek track for less than 1 km/20 minutes to a second junction, then turning left down to the hut and following a side-trail which leads over a low saddle back to the main Pelorus River and Browning Stream track, another 1 km/20 minutes.

Hackett Hut has 6 bunks and an open fire, and gets knocked around from time to time. There is camping space on the grass beside the hut, and if you have enough daylight this is a good place

Long footbridge over Pelorus River

to aim for on a Friday evening.

The trail up the Browning Stream is easy going. It winds through bush, bracken slopes and clearings for 3 km/1–2 hours to Browning Hut (6 bunks), about a 250-m climb. This is the last major clearing on the trip, and bush, grass and a bubbling stream make this a fine lunch spot.

The track plunges immediately into the bush and climbs a steady 150 m over 1 km/1 hour to Totara Saddle at 680 m. A side-track goes to the Rocks Hut and Dun Mountain, but the main Pelorus trail sidles from the saddle into the Roebuck Creek Valley. You tramp 8 km/2 hours in bush, barely losing 200 m in height in what is at times a monotonous descent. The last 150 m is a livelier drop to the twin footbridges.

One bridge crosses the Roebuck, the other the turquoise Pelorus River to the hut on the far side. Situated on a sunny open shelf, the 6-bunk hut is a welcome break from the bush canopy.

Cross back over the two bridges and follow the Pelorus River downstream along its north bank. It's 6 km/1–2 hours of winding and weaving to a major track junction where the inland track climbs 750 m up to the Dun Mountain Range. A side-trail crosses a footbridge to Midday Hut (6 bunks), and there is a good campsite near the junction.

Some people like to float along the Pelorus River in tubes or lilos. It's good fun although bloody cold, and is best enjoyed with a large group who can help pull you out of the back eddies. Long sluggish pools with plunging rock faces, interrupted by short rapids, typify the Pelorus, but the cold often forces a retreat to the track. Most of the length of the Pelorus can be travelled this way.

From Midday it's 6 km/2 hours along a pleasant track past a foot-bridge back over the Pelorus to the next and last hut at Captain Creek (6 bunks).

The river stays confined in its narrow valley, and the track stays on the north bank, occasionally having to climb to avoid a tight loop-ing bend. It's 7 km/2 hours to the first break in the bush, then there are farm and scrub terraces for 2 km/40 minutes around the final bend to the picnic areas and carpark.

Mount Richmond

Total tramping time: 7–10 hours/2 days
Total tramping distance: 17 km
Grade: medium
Highest point: 1756 m; Mount Richmond
Maps: Mt Richmond State Forest Park 274-6;
  Wairau O28

At 1756 m Mt Richmond is not quite the high peak of the range (it's pipped by Red Hill at 1790 m) but that's being picky, for it's a good climb up to a fine peak, with excellent views over the Richmond Range, the Wairau Valley and as far as Blenheim. One hut.

Access is off Highway 2 on the north bank of the Wairau River (4 km north of Renwick). Follow the long North Bank Road some 25 km then turn off up the signposted Top Valley Stream road and continue 6 km to a junction.

People blessed with four-wheel-drives can ford the stream and drive up a good gravel road (occasionally signposted) 2.5 km to the carpark on top of the spur, thus saving themselves at least a 40-minute tramp. Ordinary mortals in ordinary cars have to walk from the junction.

From the carpark a good track wanders resolutely up the beech spur, with occasional good views and rock outcrops to provide interest (5 km/2–3 hours). Towards the top the track suddenly starts to sidle a messy 2 km/1 hour to Armchair or Richmond Saddle and to a clearing where there is a well-situated hut; 6 bunks, wood stove and it catches the sun. All in all a 750-m climb from the carpark, and 1000 m from the valley road.

To reach Mt Richmond continue on the well-cairned trail as it scrambles through bush and up steepish rock-slides for 1 km/1 hour to the flat main ridge, and 500 m/20 minutes to the battered trig on top. A total climb of 500 m from the hut.

Apart from the distant views the immediate foreground of Johnson peak is quite eye-catching, as well as the long ridge to Mount Fell and occasional tarns dotted in the hanging basins. Mount Fishtail is also prominent.

Wakamarina Crossing

Total tramping time: 8–10 hours/2 days
Total tramping distance: 19 km
Grade: medium
Highest point: 1150 m; Fosters Ridge
Maps: Mt Richmond State Forest Park 274-6;
  Nelson O27; Wairau O28

Very little stopped a gold-digger in search of 'the colours' and all over New Zealand goldminers' pack-tracks wriggle through some improbable and lovely landscapes. The Wakamarina track was built in 1861 for the shortlived gold rush, and now provides the basis for an excellent crossing track, with the option of a harder circuit return. Three huts, some campsites.

The Wakamarina valley is off Highway 6 about 8 km west of Havelock, and 15 km down to the Dead Horse Creek carpark. The last bit down to the picnic area is quite steep. Access to the other end of this trip is down the North Bank Road alongside the Wairau River, via Bartletts Creek Road or the Onamalutu Road 20–25 km from Highway 6. Take a good road map for this access.

Four-wheel-drivers can go a little further, but for most trampers the track starts at Dead Horse Creek (great name!) and goes 2 km/30 minutes to the footbridge and hut at Doom Hut (another great name!). Six bunks and an open fireplace.

Head along the pleasant miners' track 4 km/1–2 hours to Devils Creek Hut (6 bunks). There's a side-track across the footbridge up to Mt Royal, and a short track to some old stone huts (30 minutes return).

From the hut the main miners' track zig-zags up a long bush spur for 3 km/2 hours, climbing almost 900 m to a bush knob, and it's a relief when the geography flattens and the track sidles for 3.5 km/1–2 hours to a high saddle on the ridge. There's a clearing here, a four-way track junction, some views and a rain barrel.

The side-track east goes 500 m/15 minutes to Fosters Ridge Hut — 6 bunks and a wood stove, and a great situation. On the other side of the pass a route follows the ridge for 2.5 km/1 hour to the clear rock outcrop of Baldy, and fine views.

The pack-track maintains an excellent grade down the other side for 4 km/1–2 hours, to a small side-route (not very well signposted) direct to Bartletts Creek. Otherwise it is another 1.5 km/30 minutes to the Bartletts Ridge carpark.

Mt Royal Circuit
Total tramping time: 17–20 hours/2–3 days
Total tramping distance: 42 km
Grade: medium/fit
Highest point: 1365 m; Mt Royal

Those who want to get back to the Wakamarina road-end via Mt Royal should take the roughly marked side-route from Bartletts Ridge about 3 km/1 hour direct to Bartletts Creek Road. Then follow the road for 1 km/20 minutes to the Quartz Creek road junction, and criss-cross up the Quartz Creek vehicle track some 3.5 km/1 hour to a good campsite at the foot of the Royal spur.

It's another 4 km/2–3 hours up the long 900-m spur on to the top of a high bush knob, then the good track wanders along the ridge 1 km/30 minutes to the bare top of Mt Royal. A further 5 km/2 hours back down another bush spur brings you to Devils Creek Hut.

Abel Tasman Coastal Track

Total tramping time: 3–5 days
Total tramping distance: 38 km Marahau–Whariwharangi Bay
Grade: easy
Highest point: 150 m; on the coastal track at several places
Maps: Abel Tasman National Park 273-07;
   Tarakohe N25; Takaka N26
(See *New Zealand's Top Tracks* by Mark Pickering
for a more detailed description of this track.)

Coastal tramping at its best along the bays and tidal inlets of Abel Tasman National Park. This is certainly the easiest major tramp in New Zealand. Sea-sculpted rocks, brilliant sands, easy graded tracks, large huts and native bush edging tempting sandy bays round every corner. Unique low-tide routes across the bays, where you carry your boots and wade barefoot. There's even a cafe halfway! You'll love it. Beware of fires, giardia, and sunburn.

You need to prepay your Great Walks pass for both huts and campsites during the summer season (October–April) at $12 per person per night for huts, $6 per person per night for campsites.

From Motueka drive 7 km past Riwaka on Highway 60, turn right down the Sandy Bay road and continue for 10 km to Marahau, where there is a carpark, cafe and information kiosk. With 30,000 trampers a year (mostly in the summer) public transport access to Abel Tasman is excellent. The main access point is from Motueka, and regular bus services connect to Marahau road-end. There are also good bus services from Nelson, which connect to Motueka, directly with the launch pick-up point at Kaiteriteri, or the track-end at Marahau.

Most trampers walk one way and catch a launch back, and there are several launch operators who run daily (in summer) along the coast, starting at Kaiteriteri and stopping off at various places before Totaranui. These water taxis provide a unique dimension for trampers; take plenty of cash, though some will take credit cards.

From the carpark the track first crosses the mudflats of the Marahau estuary on the boardwalked causeway and winds through bracken and gorse as it hugs the coastline for 2.5 km/1 hour to the Tinline campsite, a sheltered open clearing with picnic tables and toilet. A nice little spot.

A short way beyond is the junction with the inland track (which tackles the huge inland climb up to Castle Rock Hut) and a good lookout beyond that on Guilbert Point (1 km/20 minutes).

The coastal track ambles along the sea edge 20–30 metres above the shore, past two pretty bays, Appletree and Stilwell. Side-tracks lead down to each bay, and there are campsites at both. It is 3 km/1 hour to Yellow Point (note the Akersten campsite), then the track climbs gradually for about 1 km/30 minutes to a signposted track junction. Although there's a muddle of track junctions here, tracks to Anchorage Hut are well signposted. There's a side-track to Watering Cove, which has good camping at the bay where Dumont d'Urville filled up his watering casks in 1827. The main track gives splendid views over Anchorage Bay and drops down to this brilliant sweep of sand after 1 km/20 minutes.

Turn right along the beach to the 26-bunk hut which sits on a grassy terrace. Campsite nearby. Anchorage Bay is popular with yachties and in summer becomes a convivial and disorganised marina. If this is not your scene, at the north end of Anchorage Bay a short side-track nips over the Pitt Peninsula to cosy camping in the charming Te Pukatea Bay (700 m/20 minutes).

For Torrent Bay, go west along the beach and up an easy bush trail that dips over the headland to the bay (700 m/20 minutes). At low tide you can head north across the sand and mudflats, with the shells crackling under your feet (1 km/20 minutes). On the western side of the bay the old Torrent Bay Hut has been removed, but the void makes a peaceful campsite.

(If the tides catch you out, there's a permanent bush track that follows the edge of Torrent Bay (3 km/1 hour). Cleopatra's Pool is a deepish well of clear water, edged by smooth, sunbathable rocks. A good side-trip on a really hot day.)

Wet feet across Awaroa estuary

The main coastal track passes the dense cluster of private holiday homes at Torrent Bay, turns the corner and picks up a steep bush track that climbs inland 100 m and sidles around Kilby Stream to a subtle saddle (2 km/40 minutes). A side-track leads to a lookout over a splendid seascape of rock bays, islets and reefs. The main track drops down to Falls River, crosses the footbridge and wanders up and over another bush headland and down to the coast again at Medlands campsite (2 km/40 minutes).

Just round the corner is Bark Bay, a beaut, snug bay. Keep left for the 30-person Bark Bay Hut, which is on the all-tide track. There are campsites in the bush close to the hut, but the best spots are on the sandy spit, which juts out attractively between the estuary and the sea.

The low-tide route is straight along the spit and over the mudflats, where the coast track climbs steeply for 100 m to a low bush saddle, then slips 2.5 km/1 hour to the disused quarry by the Tonga Roadstead. There's a shady campsite here, and at low tide you can scramble around the rocks south from the old quarry to the striking sea-sculpted rocks of Arch Point (700 m/15 minutes one way).

The main track climbs briefly out of the quarry down to the gracious swing of Onetahuti Beach. Well-sheltered campsites here, and a lovely freshwater pool behind it. It's about a 1 km/20 minute plough along the beach as the track turns inland again, past the Richardson Stream swamp and up over the 150-m Tonga Saddle (2 km/1 hour).

Although the main track misses the Awaroa Cafe and Lodge, most people tend to turn off at the signposted junction and drop in for a cuppa, or something a little stronger. The track then cuts through mixed scrub and pastureland, and over the airstrip to Venture Creek (1 km/30 minutes).

Orange lollipops lead round the creek, and round Sawpit Point to the 26-bunk Awaroa Hut (1.5 km/30 minutes). Campsite here. After the intimacy of most of the bays the huge Awaroa Inlet is quite a contrast, and you have to wait for low tide to cross it. DOC recommends that you cross the estuary two hours either side of low tide. Aim directly over the wide mudflats to Pound Creek (1 km/20 minutes); large orange markers help. From here the track follows up the creek, crosses a low bush saddle, and pops down to Waiharakeke Bay (1.5 km/30 minutes), yet another perfect Abel Tassie beach, where there is good camping.

The narrow track follows an old bush tramway and climbs up from the north end of the bay, sidles and drops down into Goat Bay (sigh, more beauty), then hops over Skinner Point and through the typical coastal manuka forest to the strangely orange beach of Totaranui (3 km/1 hour).

There's a ranger station here, and a visitor centre by the boat drop-off point. Expansive areas for camping, public phone, motor camp (but no cabins), and pukeko are always scouting hopefully around.

Many trampers return from Totaranui to Marahau or Kaiteriteri by launch, but the option of going on to Separation Point and Whariwharangi Bay is becoming more popular, and is actually part of the entire Great Walk.

Follow the tree-lined avenue in Totaranui to a road junction and turn right past the Education Centre where the Anapai Bay Track begins at the end of the road (1 km/20 minutes). After a short distance the main track climbs 100 m before descending along a bush stream to the beach (1.5 km/40 minutes).

Go along Anapai Beach, then up over a headland to the campsites at the double-bayed Mutton Cove (2 km/1 hour). Weary old macrocarpas shelter the camping area, and the track to Whariwharangi starts here.

If you want to go direct to Separation Point continue on the beach route as it negotiates the headland that divides Mutton Cove and picks up a trail at the far north of the bay. This climbs up to a track junction, and soon after you reach the grass headland of Separation Point (1 km/30 minutes). You can scramble down the steep track to the lighthouse, count the loitering seals and watch the gannets plunge magnificently. People sometimes see penguins on the rocks, dolphins offshore, and even orcas.

The return route can be made along the crest of the headland and joins the Whariwharangi Bay track at the saddle (1 km/30 minutes).

For Whariwharangi Bay follow the farm road from the saddle as it drops easily through the regenerating scrubland to a fine beach backed by a stand of old macrocarpa trees (1 km/1 hour). The gorse is rapidly being overcome by kanuka and native shrubs, and turning this once dusty bay into a green haven.

The hut is the old homestead, 500 m/15 minutes inland, two-storeyed and with a unique period atmosphere. It was built in 1897 by John Handcock, who lived here for 15 years, and has been restored by DOC. There's also a campsite here.

It's 2 km/1 hour of easy tramping up the old vehicle track to the saddle overlooking the soft Wainui Inlet, then a sharp 1.5 km/30 minutes zig-zag down to the carpark.

There is a daily bus service to the carpark in summer. If you miss it you can cross the Wainui Inlet at low tide (follow the marked route) to the Totaranui Road (2 km/40 minutes), then hitch out to Takaka that way.

Abel Tasman Inland Track

Total tramping time: 3–5 days (depending on side-trips)
Total tramping distance: 37 km (Wainui Inlet–Marahau)
Grade: medium/fit
Highest point: 1015 m; Sub A
Maps: Abel Tasman National Park 273-07;
  Tarakohe N25; Takaka N26

Most people will not visit the inland mountains of Abel Tasman National Park, which are surprisingly rugged and untracked. The few tracks there are not suited to the bikini and jandals brigade, and a complete tramp around the National Park demands more planning and equipment. While this is harder tramping than the coastal route there are some remarkable places, like Harwoods Hole, Moa Park and Castle Rocks. Five huts; carry big water bottles.

Take Highway 60 from Takaka and turn right down the Clifton–Pohara road to Wainui Inlet. Pass the Totaranui turnoff and continue to the road-end at Takapou Bay (from Takaka 24 km).

At the Wainui road-end a vehicle track climbs 200 m up a scrubby spur to the crest of a ridge (1.5 km/1–2 hours). Turn south at the well-signposted junction and follow vehicle track and firebreak roads up scrub-covered spurs onto Gibbs Hill (405 m), a climb of 200 m over 2.5 km/1–2 hours. A rare view from the hilltop shows the entire length of Farewell Spit, circling around Golden Bay.

From Gibbs Hill the track drops down to a saddle and junction (1 km/20 minutes), and by turning left you descend a long spur back to Totaranui. The main route runs for 2.5 km/1 hour south along the ridge top through patches of scrub, bush and open land, mostly following farm tracks (past Lookout Rock) to Pigeon Saddle (305 m). A bone-dry route.

Cross the Totaranui road and scramble up a track through deep bush; 2 km/2 hours to Centre Peak (534 m). After all that up and down it's good to enjoy a breather, and reach some open country with a fine panorama.

Prominent orange discs show the way south along the ridge for 1 km/30 minutes to the bush edge. The track drops a little before climbing 250 m up to the main ridge (2 km/1–2 hours), where Awapoto Hut stands (12 bunks and a much appreciated watertank).

From here it is a steady rolling uphill climb for 5.5 km/2 hours until you reach the highest point, Sub A (1015 m), a trig station. The track divides a short distance from the trig. One branch turns right into the Wainui valley, while the other continues for 3.5 km/1–2 hours along the thick bush ridge to the Canaan Track junction. Turn east here and descend 100 m among dracophyllum forest to the wide open clearing of Moa Park (1 km/15 minutes).

The comfortable 4-bunk hut is a good base from which to do side-trips to Harwoods Hole, Porter Rock and Mt Evans.

The Hole is the furthest away, but the most impressive. Return to the Canaan Track junction and descend 200 m to Wainui Saddle (2 km/1 hour). Past the Wainui turnoff a vehicle track skirts the private farm basin of Canaan for 1.5 km/40 minutes to the Rameka junction. The track then continues for a further 1 km/20 minutes to a picnic and camping area at the end of the Canaan road. The track to Harwoods is 2.5 km/1 hour alongside a stream which disappears as you get close to the Hole. You cannot see right into Harwoods Hole but the quiet 'pull' of the 176-m deep vent is scary enough.

Porters Rock is a somewhat disappointing lookout 1 km/20 minutes from Moa Park Hut. Mt Evans is 2 km/1 hour away from the hut; again the view from the 1156-m peak isn't up to much but at least you have the satisfaction of standing on the highest point in Abel Tasman National Park.

From Moa Park the main track enters the bush, passes the Porter Rock turnoff, and does not leave the bush until Castle Rocks hut and clearing, a good 350-m descent over 3.5 km/1–2 hours. A 10-bunk hut here, and the rock outcrops are an interesting scramble, with a good view overlooking the Marahau Estuary.

It is a slow and at times tedious descent from Castle Rocks to Tinline Bay, a total drop of almost 800 m back to sea level. It's 5 km/2 hours to the bracken-clad Holyoake Clearing and the small 2-person shelter, then 4 km/1 hour more to the main coastal track. You pass a track junction to Torrent Bay a little after Holyoake Clearing.

A short walk from Tinline over the Marahau Causeway takes you to the road-end (2.5 km/1 hour).

Heaphy Track

Total tramping time: 4–6 days
Total tramping distance: 70 km
Grade: medium
Highest point: 915 m; Flanagans Corner
Maps: Heaphy Track 245; Kahurangi National Park
  274-13; Cobb M26; Heaphy L26
(See *New Zealand's Top Tracks* by Mark Pickering
for a more detailed description of this track.)

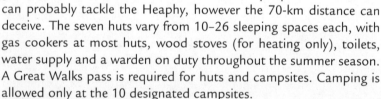

The Heaphy is an historic and scenic highway, a classic tramping traverse, travelling from the beech
forests of Golden Bay over to the moist nikau-fringed
beaches on the West Coast. There is a rich diversity of
plants and forest types, and the sweeping red and
gold tussocks of the Gouland Downs. Most people
can probably tackle the Heaphy, however the 70-km distance can
deceive. The seven huts vary from 10–26 sleeping spaces each, with
gas cookers at most huts, wood stoves (for heating only), toilets,
water supply and a warden on duty throughout the summer season.
A Great Walks pass is required for huts and campsites. Camping is
allowed only at the 10 designated campsites.

Go south from Collingwood up the Aorere Valley 35 km to the
road head. Three fords before the carpark can be impassable after
rain. A taxi service is available from Collingwood, and a local bus service connects Collingwood and Nelson. Often trampers walk the
track one way and fly back the other to avoid transport hassles.
There are airstrips at Takaka and Karamea, and at least one operator runs this service. Four packs and four people is quite economi-
cal, but prior bookings should be made. At the Kohaihai end of the
Heaphy a taxi service is available to Karamea, and Cunningham's
Coaches run a regular bus service to Westport.

Brown Hut is almost at the road-end, 5 minutes stroll, or stagger, depending on the weight of your pack. There is spacious bunk accommodation for 20 people, with an open fire and a taxi telephone. No gas cookers.

Cross the bridge upstream from the hut and follow marker poles up through scrub and pasture to the bush margin. An old packhorse track sidles evenly uphill through the rich greenery of rimu, miro and beech. It is a gradual climb of 800 m over 8 km/3–4 hours (past the Shakespeare Flat junction) to Aorere Shelter, set in a clearing. The shelter has water, and good views of Golden Bay.

Another 2.5 km/1 hour from here is Flanagans Corner, the highest point on the entire Heaphy, where a short side-track leads to a rocky lookout and more great views. On a fine day you can see Mount Taranaki. It is 2 km/40 minutes further to Perry Saddle Hut (26 beds).

With most of the climbing done, it's pleasant to amble up over the snowgrassed saddle and down past subalpine vegetation as the track slowly turns into the Gouland Downs. The Downs are a high exposed moorland basin at 600–700 m. The track winds through red tussock, herbfields and thickets of stunted beech (past the famous 'boot-pole') to Cave Brook, where a bridge crosses the limestone-gorged creek to Downs Hut (7 km/2–3 hours).

Built in 1936, this venerable hut has 10 bunks, a big fireplace and a lot of character. There are potholes and caves to explore in the bush behind the hut.

The track continues through this beech pocket and out onto the Downs again, then travels 1.5 km/30 minutes over the Shiner Brook footbridge to the long suspension bridge over Big River. After another 3 km/1 hour you cross a footbridge at Weka Creek to the 20-person Saxon Hut.

The Downs are just about behind you now as the track crosses Blue Duck Stream (1 km/20 minutes) and turns up into low bush with small grass clearings, rock outcrops and intimate back-alleys, a changing, interesting landscape. You climb 100 m or so for the rest of the 8 km/2–3 hours to Mackay Hut, as the track edges around the MacKay Downs through large clearings and scrub bands. From the 26-person Mackay Hut there is a fine outlook and beautiful sunsets, and sometimes you can hear kiwis calling at night.

From Mackay the track enters mature podocarp forest, and for

Weka

12 km/3–4 hours the track painstakingly sidles down-valley, a gentle if rather humdrum descent. It is 650 m down to Lewis Hut (20 people), which is barely 15 m above sea level.

From the hut the track leads briefly up the Lewis River, crosses a footbridge, then stays on the north bank of the Heaphy for a short while before crossing another footbridge to the south bank, which it follows among large northern rata in a gentle grade to the 26-person Heaphy Hut, 8 km/2–3 hours from Lewis.

The Heaphy is a sluggish brown river and strongly tidal towards its outlet. Swimming in the surf is obviously dangerous, but the sunsets are beautiful and harmless.

From here to Kohaihai River the Heaphy stays right by the shore and this is still an unspoilt coastline. A dark mosaic of hills runs down to the seashore, where abrupt headlands interrupt sweeps of yellow sands. The dangerous routes around rock headlands have been eliminated from the track, which stays in the salt-heavy coastline bush of kiekie, karaka, kawakawa, ngaio and nikau palms. There are several places where trampers may choose to forget the track for a while and just stroll the sands or boulder-hop on the beaches.

From Heaphy Hut the track swings around a corner past a pond and flax swamp to Heaphy Beach and shelter (1.5 km/20 minutes). A second shelter, Katipo, lies just beyond Mid Point, 6.5 km/2 hours away. The shelters are basic and gloomy.

The Wekakura Creek, Katipo Creek and Swan Burn are all bridged. From Katipo it's a walk of 6 km/2 hours to Scotts Beach, where there are several private baches. The track climbs 100 m over a low saddle (past a lookout) and dives through the last of the nikau to the long footbridge over the languid tea-stained Kohaihai River (2.5 km/1 hour).

The Kohaihai River is 16 km from Karamea, with attractive campsites and picnic places beside the river. There's a taxi phone in the shelter, toilets and a short lookout track.

Cobb Valley

Total tramping time: 8–11 hours/2–3 days
Total tramping distance: 27 km
Grade: easy
Highest point: 1000 m; Fenella Hut
Maps: Kahurangi National Park 274-13;
   Mt Arthur M27

History, geology and scenery have been squeezed into this little valley with delightful results. A fine upland valley walk, well signposted, with good tracks and a variety of huts. Excellent camping.

Turn off Highway 60 at Upper Takaka, 35 km from Motueka over the 'Marble Mountain' or Takaka hill, and 22 km before the township of Takaka. The Cobb Reservoir Road runs steeply through bush to a saddle at 1060 m. It's a rough, dusty and magnificent road, some 30 km to the carpark, camping ground and picnic area at Trilobite Hut (14 people), named after the fossils that have been found in the rocks here. There is also a short loop walk to Myttons Hut.

From Trilobite Hut follow the main track up the valley through beech forest and grass meadows for 6 km/2 hours to Chaffey Hut. There is some good camping on the way. This curious and historic 2-person slab hut is worth a close inspection. It must be the narrowest hut ever built, but sadly it's getting run down.

After this the track divides. The old track stays on the same side of the river and is quicker but a lot muddier. It remains generally in the open through large grass flats and gives excellent views of the knobbled tops of the Peel Range.

The new track crosses the river at Chaffey's and ambles most of the time in the bush, only occasionally poking out for the odd view. After 5 km/2 hours the two tracks combine, then it's another 1.5 km/30 minutes to the old but cosy 4-bunk Cobb Hut.

From Cobb Hut the main track climbs 100 m over 1 km/40 minutes through scrub and rock terraces past some pretty waterfalls to Fenella Hut. This is a civilised 12-person hut built as a memorial to Fenella Druce, one of four people killed when the Three Johns Hut in

Fenella Hut

Mt Cook National Park was blown off its site. Fenella boasts an open fireplace, drying/gear room, and a toilet with a stained glass door. The verandah soaks up the sun for an idle afternoon.

There is a short, secretive track 10 minutes further up the valley which leads to a natural swimming pool, easily 15 m long, hemmed in by rock outcrops and alpine vegetation. The saddle which sits between Burgoo and Cobb Valleys is sprinkled with hidden tarns, and there's plenty of scope for exploration. There are also side-tracks to Round Lake (via the Cobb Lake track which starts beside Cobb Hut), Gibbs Hill and Waingaro Peak on the Lockett Range.

Mount Arthur and the Tableland

Total tramping time: 8–10 hours/2 days
Total tramping distance: 25 km
Grade: easy/medium
Highest point: 1500 m; Peel Range ridge
Maps: Kahurangi National Park 274-13;
  Mt Arthur M27

There is a network of tracks and huts on this upland
plateau, with tussock downs, limestone karst formations and beech forest. Easy grades, novel rock shelters and fine views add up to a small patch of hea-
ven for trampers. The carpark is at 900 m which gives
you a very good heave up into these mountains. History is on every
step of this track, for it is the old 1850s goldminers' trail from
Nelson to Takaka.

Two trips are described here; the first crosses from the Flora over
the Tableland and down into the Cobb Valley, the second goes up
Mt Arthur. But a glance at the map reveals many other options and
side-trips, and it would take a week to thoroughly explore this area.

The Flora Road is the worst part of the access. From Highway 61
between Motueka and Kohatu drive to Ngatimoti (19 km from
Motueka) and follow the signs to Graham Valley and Mount Arthur.
Just as the road starts to climb it becomes particularly steep and
front-wheel-drive cars may have difficulty with traction here. After
this point, although still steep, the road is stable but it is a long climb
to the carpark at 900 m where there is a rewarding view looking back
to Nelson. Information boards, intentions book and toilet.

From the carpark ignore the side-tracks up to Mt Lodestone and
Mt Arthur and tramp 2 km/30 minutes to Flora Hut. Flora is actually two huts joined together by a wooden porch, with large fireplaces and bunks for 12. Two more side-trails go up to Mt Arthur
and Lodestone from here.

The vehicle track follows the Flora Stream for 3 km/1 hour to
Horseshoe Creek where a side-trail goes up to Gordon's Pyramid,
then it's another 1 km/20 minutes to the spectacular rock overhangs
at Grid Iron Gulch.

Heading up to Mt Arthur

The main rocks have various domestic features built in, such as a fireplace, swing chair and bunks. There's also a pocket 4-bunk hut squeezed under another huge rock biv, with a glass mural of kea.

The road-track continues for 1.5 km/30 minutes to where Balloon Creek enters at Upper Junction. Keep left and follow the main track up the side of Balloon Creek for 1 km/20 minutes to a small 2-bunk rock shelter by the Growler Creek.

The track climbs 250 m to open country over 1.5 km/30 minutes, and a sign indicates another rock shelter along a 10-minute side-track. This one has a sleeping platform for 10, an open fireplace and a fine view towards the Arthur Range.

The main track winds easily over tussock and alpine scrub for 1 km/20 minutes to the Gordon's Pyramid turn-off, then continues to Salisbury Hut (1 km/20 minutes), which has 20 bunks, gas heaters and cookers. It offers extensive views over the Arthur peaks, especially of the sharp-sided Twins (1798 m).

From the hut the track climbs up 100 m through open country and scrub onto Starvation Ridge, then out onto the flat tussock expanse of the Tableland. There's a large sign at the track junction (2 km/40 minutes). Turn north and go through a patch of bush where sink-holes and caves create interesting terrain, then out onto open snow-grass to Balloon Hill (2 km/1 hour).

Balloon Hut (8 bunks) is a little further around, off the main track in a bush clearing. Poles and a worn trail lead 250 m up a wide spur to an unnamed knob (2.5 km/1–2 hours).

Lake Peel nestles in an upland basin at the head of Deep Creek, a refreshing spot for lunch. The poled route leads down 150 m to the lakeside then skirts right along the side of a spur for 1.5 km/30 minutes. After a brief climb onto the spur's crest you will suddenly see Cobb Reservoir.

A track junction here, and for those who do not want to descend into the Cobb a circuit back to the Flora track at Upper Junction can be made via tracks to Asbestos Cottage (4 bunks) and Flora Stream. Reasonably well signposted but a good map is essential. It's a distance of 10 km/6–7 hours back to the Upper Junction.

The descent into the Cobb Valley is the only real downhill of the trip, some 2 km/2 hours and 450 m to Myttons Hut (6 bunks) which is perched above the reservoir in the bush. Either descend 100 m direct to the road from Myttons Hut or sidle along the scenic walk past grass clearings for 1 km/30 minutes to Trilobite Hut (14 bunks). A sculpture decorates one of these clearings.

For access and route description up the Cobb see Cobb Valley, page 134. For access and route description down to the Leslie-Karamea see Karamea River, page 140.

Mt Arthur
Total tramping time: 6–8 hours/2 days
Total tramping distance: 14 km
Grade: easy/medium
Highest point: 1795 m; Mt Arthur

From the Flora carpark a good track climbs some 300 m up to Mt Arthur Hut (6 bunks; 3 km/2 hours). There's a short side-track down to Flora Hut, which could be a nice variation on the way back.

Shortly after Mt Arthur Hut the well-marked main track leaves the bush edge behind and rambles up a wide open spur with impressive limestone formations on every side (note the side-track to Ellis

Basin), almost 4 km/1–2 hours to the first peak (the Winter Peak), and another 500 m onto the high peak itself at 1795 m.

On the return you can choose to go over Gordon's Pyramid (1489 m), a prominent rocky knoll off the leading spur from the high peak. In good visibility the travel is quite straightforward but misty conditions can make route-finding hard. If in doubt don't attempt it.

This is a devil of a place for choices — some 4 km/1 hour off Mt Arthur toward Gordon's Pyramid, one branch of the track goes east for 4 km/1 hour past an old mine on a pack-track to Grid Iron Gulch (a drop of 750 m), and another plunges west through a distinctly strange karst landscape and heads 2.5 km/1 hour towards Salisbury Hut. A descent of 450 m.

Karamea River

Total tramping time: 3–4 days
  (Tableland Junction to Helicopter Flat Hut)
Total tramping distance: 45 km
  (Tableland Junction to Helicopter Flat Hut)
Grade: medium
Highest point: 1260 m; Tableland
Maps: Kahurangi National Park 274-13;
  Mt Arthur M27; Wangapeka M28

A traverse through central Kahurangi National Park via the Leslie and Karamea Rivers. This tramp connects up the tussock plateaus of the Tablelands with the popular Wangapeka Track, and in between is a massive river with trout pools, good tracks, and seven huts. With most major side-creeks bridged, this tramp is long rather than difficult but from road-end to road-end you will need near enough to a week to accomplish it.

For access and route information to Tableland Junction see Mt Arthur and the Tableland (page 136). Allow at least one day's tramp (14 km/5 hours) from Flora carpark to Tableland Junction.

From Tableland Junction follow the track 1 km/20 minutes to the tussock edge, where it drops 50 m down a gully then winds down the grand old miners' pack-trail for 3 km/1 hour to Spurgeons Rock (a 350-m descent). A permanent fly camp has been turned into a virtual hut with fireplace and water. It holds 8-plus, and there's good camping on the helipad above the hut.

The pack-track sidles a further 300 m down to the Leslie–Peel confluence, then crosses a footbridge to the south bank of the Leslie River (2 km/30 minutes). Campsite and swimming hole here. There's mature lowland beech forest along the Leslie Track for the 5 km/1–2 hours to Leslie Clearing Hut (10 bunks). A side-track to Baton Saddle turns off 1 km short of the hut.

Leslie Hut is separated by 4 km/1 hour of easy track from Karamea Bend, so-called because the Karamea River does a wide turn here towards the West Coast. This is a popular trout anglers' spot, and Karamea Bend Hut has 20 bunks. The sandflies are murder. A few

Footbridge over the Leslie River

minutes on there is a locked staff hut, with good camping beside it.

From now on the track follows the Karamea River upstream, crossing flats and bush terraces for 10 km/3 hours until it reaches the 6-bunk Crow Hut. From the track you can catch glimpses of the sequence of deep clear pools that characterise the river. Eels and trout are plentiful.

From Crow Hut follow the track for 2.5 km/1 hour to a long dangling footbridge. After crossing to the other bank it's another 2.5 km/1 hour to Venus Hut (12 bunks). Most of the names along here show the hand of an unknown poet; they all have mythical or planetary connotations.

It's a further 1.5 km/30 minutes to Mercury Creek footbridge and a fine campsite just before it (one of the few campsites between Crow Hut and Luna Slips). Thor Hut (6 bunks) is 3.5 km/1 hour further, on a small promontory overlooking the Karamea River.

The track from here to Moonstone Lake (3 km/1 hour) is tangled with tree roots, but after Moonstone it smooths out a little for the 3.5 km/1 hour to Kendall Creek. This creek is not bridged, and could be a significant obstacle after rain. It's a short 1.5 km/30 minutes around the scrub end of a spur to Trevor Carter Hut (6 bunks) and the wide open flats of Luna Slips.

Bluffs and ribbon waterfalls surround these stony flats, where the Karamea idles through several deep rock pools. There's alternative accommodation across the river at the rather charming Luna Hut (4 bunks), 1 km/20 minutes downstream of Trevor Carter Hut.

To reach Lost Valley from Trevor Carter ford the Karamea River. At first the route up this secretive valley is indicated by only a few sporadic cairns and markers, but things improve as you climb through the scrubline. Mt Kendall (1810 m) is imposingly framed by the valley sides.

It is a climb of 400 m over 2.5 km/2 hours to the bush-shrouded saddle with its large, silent tarn. From here you sidle down 100 m to Helicopter Flat and hut (6 bunks), which connects with the main Wangapeka Track (1 km/20 minutes).

Biggs Tops is an alternative exit out to the Wangapeka Track, and on a fine day it can't be beaten. From Luna Hut pick up the reasonably marked track as it climbs steeply some 800 m out of the valley and onto Biggs Tops (2 km/2–3 hours). The views are superb as the route trails around a small half-arc of open tussock tops for 2 km/1 hour, before descending to the bush edge where a good track plops you right down 300 m onto the Wangapeka Saddle (1.5 km/1 hour).

For access and route information along the Wangapeka Track see page 143. Allow at least a day's tramp to get to the road-end at Rolling River, and 3 days to the Little Wanganui.

Wangapeka Track

Total tramping time: 4–5 days
Total tramping distance: 55 km
Grade: medium
Highest point: 1400 m; Little Wanganui Saddle
Maps: Kahurangi National Park 274-13;
  Karamea L27; Wangapeka M28

The Wangapeka Track has been overshadowed by the Heaphy, and is less well known and consequently less well used. A pity perhaps. It crosses the bottom of the Kahurangi National Park (the Heaphy crosses the top) and provides some splendid scenery on a trail that for a lot of the time follows an old 1890s pack-track across the range. Two saddles, a plethora of huts (ten in all), and some reasonable campsites.

Transport is a bit of a hassle, since the road-ends are widely separated. However, there are taxi services at Tapawera and Karamea, and bus services between the two. Some people resort to the well-known trick of sending a party to each end and have a car-and-key swap halfway across. Some keen backpackers have done the Heaphy then walked back over the Wangapeka.

For the eastern side from Tapawera follow the signs to Tadmor, 10 km along Tapawera Road, then travel 5 km on the Bush End road and finally 6 km on the Wangapeka River road. There's a large carpark here, but a concrete ford across the Dart means that at most times cars can continue 9 km to the Rolling River junction where there's an old 4-bunk hut. The western exit can be reached from Little Wanganui (18 km south of Karamea) down the road on the north bank of the Wanganui River, 8 km to the carpark. There have been access problems at times down this road as at one point it crosses private land.

A footbridge crosses the Rolling River and the good track wanders up beside the Wangapeka River for 9 km/2–3 hours to the site of an old hut known as the Kiwi Log Cabin/Shelter at the junction with Kiwi Stream. Scrubby farm flats at first then into beech forest. A side-track goes up to Kiwi Saddle Hut but the main trail continues

Old Cecil King's hut and gold claim

for 2 km/40 minutes then down a short side-track to New Kings Hut (30 bunks and a wood stove).

A more romantic hut is Old Kings, 300 m/10 minutes further on, built in 1935 by Cecil King, a part-time prospector who used to intrigue trampers by showing off his collection of gold. Despite this risky activity he died peacefully in his bed (in town). Good camping around the hut.

The pack-track follows the Wangapeka River around a corner and past a gorge for some 8 km/2 hours to the simple 6-bunk Stone Hut. Well into the head of the valley it is only 2 km/1 hour up to the subtle Wangapeka Saddle at 1100 m.

There's a four-way junction here. The main Wangapeka Track drops 8 km/2–3 hours down the headwaters of the Karamea River and slowly around to the somewhat shady Helicopter Flat Hut (6 bunks) and there's a junction with the Lost Valley track to Luna Slips. This main trail actually avoids Luna Slips by sidling some 4 km/1–2 hours around to a footbridge on the Taipo River where it meets a track that goes back to the Luna Slips.

Now you don't really want to miss out on seeing Luna Slips so you have two choices. If the weather is poor follow the Wangapeka to Helicopter Flat and take the Lost Valley track 3.5 km/2 hours over a low saddle (with tarn) and down a bush and scrub valley to the slips.

But if the weather is fine, take the track from Wangapeka Saddle as it climbs 450 m onto the tussocky Biggs Tops. It's then 1.5 km/1 hour up through the bush, and 2 km/1 hour round to the bush edge on the other side. Brilliant views, and well worth the effort. Mt Kendall dominates Luna Slips, which were caused by the huge 1929 earthquake. From here it's 2 km/1–2 hours down a steepish spur 800 m to the old-style Luna Hut (4 bunks).

At Luna Slips, a wide open and sunny flat (with several good campsites), the Karamea takes a deep breath before its long rush down to the West Coast. The river is easily crossed here in normal flows.

To get back onto the main Wangapeka Track head upstream 200 m or so (past the junction with the other end of the Lost Valley track) and there's a good ford direct to Trevor Carter Hut (6 bunks); 500 m/15 minutes. From TC Hut there's a junction with the lower Karamea track, but it's 2 km/40 minutes up to the footbridge and the main Wangapeka Track.

Another 4.5 km/1–2 hours up to the big Taipo Hut (20 bunks) then 2 km/1 hour on to Stag Flat Hut, which sits in an open and swampy tussock clearing directly below the saddle. A nice 4-bunker, but not much cop for camping. A short sharp haul up 200 m to the Little Wanganui Saddle, sprinkled with attractive tarns; 500 m/30 minutes.

Now the Wangapeka plunges 300 m down a fairly steep valley and the bush becomes more lush, though in fact you have technically been on the West Coast since the Wangapeka Saddle. After 2.5 km/1–2 hours you reach the footbridge, then it's roughish travel some 4 km/2 hours down the open riverbed through a short gorge (there's a detour track) to the comfortable Little Wanganui Hut (16 bunks) on the south bank.

The last stretch of 8 km/2–3 hours down to the carpark is a little dull. The wet weather track crosses the footbridge and the track follows through the last of the decent forest, then cutover bush and old logging roads to the carpark. Alternatively it's faster down the river and DOC has marked crossing points.

Owen Plateau

Total tramping time: 9–12 hours
Total tramping distance: 16 km
Grade: medium
Highest point: 1250 m; saddle
Maps: Kahurangi National Park 274-13;
 Wangapeka M28

The Owen Plateau is a raised platform of limestone with curious geology, old gold history and the highest peak in the Kahurangi National Park, Mt Owen (1870 m). Two huts and a variety of interesting day trips; a portable cooker is essential.

Tapawera is the closest township. From here follow the signs that indicate the Wangapeka Track: 10 km on Tapawera Road to Tadmor, then 5 km on the Bush End road and finally 6 km on the Wangapeka River road. There's a large carpark here, but a concrete ford across the Dart means that cars can usually continue 9 km to the Rolling River junction and a small 4-bunk hut. It's 3 km further to Courthouse Flat. Taxis operate from Tapawera to the road-end.

There's plenty of good camping space at Courthouse Flat but no hut. In the 1870s a courthouse and lock-up were built here but the optimism for gold was more prevalent than the gold itself and the small community soon faded.

The track starts over a footbridge at a junction with the Billies Knob track. You can either take this direct route or, alternatively, continue a short way to the Blue Creek, where a sidle track follows the creek for 1.5 km/30 minutes past old gold tailings and a large campable clearing to a junction with a side-track leading to a stamping battery and the resurgence of Blue Creek.

From this junction it is 500 m of steep track to meet the other Billies Knob track (1.5 km/1–2 hours), then a further 400 m (1 km/1 hour) to the bush edge. The tops are littered with burnt stumps and there are good views back over Courthouse Flat and the Devil's Thumb.

It's 500 m/30 minutes over a small hump down to an open saddle. Well-named the Staircase, the track drops dramatically through bush bluffs 300 m to the upper valley of Blue Creek, which is often empty of water and uncannily silent (1 km/1 hour). Follow the track upstream a short way to Taplins Hut, an historic slab and shingle-roofed hut. Useable, but only just.

The track continues up through dracophyllum forest ('pineapple tree'), then along the dry creekbed 1.5 km/1 hour to prominent forks. Coloured discs lead up the west branch, which is called Ghost Valley, and onto an alpine shrub ledge to Granity Pass Hut (6 bunks, wood stove, kero burner). Wood is scarce, so a portable cooker is essential.

There are lots of possible day trips from this hut. An easy and obvious choice is back down Ghost Valley and up the east branch to Granity Pass itself. From there you could clamber up 500 m of rock and tussock ledges onto Billies Knob, a great viewpoint (1648 m). Allow 2–3 hours return from the hut.

To reach the main Owen Plateau take the track past the toilet to the creek where snowpoles direct you onto an obvious landform nicknamed the Railway Embankment (an old glacial moraine). There's a worn trail on top and by following past the occasional cairn you emerge onto the Hay Paddock, the central basin of the plateau surrounded by peaks. The trail continues on a narrow spur which leads to the top of Sentinel Hill (1620 m; 2 km/1 hour).

For Mt Owen, drop down to the tarn saddle below and the tussock gives way to a curious and convoluted rock structure, full of 'crevasses', slumps and sinkholes; a strange, intriguing and at times difficult landscape to negotiate. It's 300 m from the saddle to the trig on flat-topped Mt Owen (2 km/1 hour), with excellent views south to the Owen River and north to Mt Arthur.

1000 Acre Plateau

Total tramping time: 15–18 hours/3–4 days
Total tramping distance: 38 km
Grade: medium
Highest point: 1100 m; plateau
Maps: Kahurangi National Park 274-13;
  Wangapeka M28; Murchison M29

The 1000 Acre (and its smaller twin the 100 Acre)
Plateau is a remarkable expanse of savanna-like landscapes edged by sharp limestone bluffs like 'lost
worlds', and dominated by the curiously named
mountains, Haystack and Needle. A good track con-
nects from Lake Matiri up to the plateau, and it is easy scrambling
up the peaks for the stunning views. Three huts and several campsites.

Turn west off Highway 6 onto Matiri River Road 7 km north of
Murchison. Follow the road to the junction and cross the bridge to
the left bank. Continue to the road-end, 15 km.

A rough vehicle track leads 3.5 km/1 hour along the left bank of
the Matiri River to the confluence of the west branch of the river.
There's a footbridge upstream. A pack-track continues across grass
and scrub flats before entering the bush, climbing 100 m and sidling
to Matiri Hut (6 bunks) situated above the lake (3.5 km/1 hour).

Soon after the hut the track drops and crosses Bay Creek (1 km/20
minutes), and a reasonable campsite can be found a little way up
this creek. On the opposite bank by the bush the track divides. Turn
left and climb up a sharp spur, then it's a 750-m plod over 3 km/2–3
hours to the edge of the 1000 Acre Plateau; there's one particularly
good viewpoint close to the top.

The track finally flattens out and crosses through a last section of
bush to break out onto the open tussocks. This is a huge upland
plain broken into two unequal halves by Larrikins Creek. The large
1000 Acre sprawls south of the creek, and the 100 Acre Plateau is to
the north. Actually, 1000 Acre is more like 1500 acres, and if you
include the entire spread of tussock and scrub highlands it's more
like 3000 acres.

View from Needle to Haystack

A poled route leads 1.5 km/30 minutes to Poor Pete's Hut, which despite its name has been somewhat improved over the years. Two bunks, and plenty of camping on a slight grass spur leading from the hut. Finding dry campsites on the 1000 Acre can be a problem at times.

The route carries on north over undulating grasslands, occasionally crossing the hard, smooth creekbeds that cut over the plateau. More like roads than rivers, these creeks often have ripple marks etched into their dry surfaces. If you follow them down (west) you reach the lip of the bluffed sides of Larrikins Creek.

There's a poled route for 5.5 km/2 hours from Poor Pete's Hut to the scrub margin where a cut track begins, then it's scrub and bush for a level 1.5 km/30 minutes around to Larrikins Creek Hut. This hut has 6 bunks, and stands beside a clearing edged with bush. A gully below the hut gives unmarked access to the head of Larrikins Creek.

Using this hut as a base, you can undertake a very good day trip over the peaks of Needle and Haystack. North of the hut, an obvious bush and tussock gully leads 500 m up onto a tarn-speckled basin below Needle. Climb 150 m onto the south ridge of Needle, avoiding the sharp-cutting spaniard plants, and it's a quick 100-m scramble to the summit (1438 m).

The conspicuous feature is the tarn-dotted 100 Acre Plateau, while the sweep of the larger 1000 Acre is visible in the distance, as is the canyonlike Larrikins Creek. To the west are the unspoiled lowland forests of the Mokihinui River.

The traverse from Needle to Haystack is almost straightforward. A couple of notches in the ridge crest have to be clambered over or around, but these are not difficult. After the Haystack (1547 m) the descent down the rock's south spur to the scrub edge can also be made without too much difficulty. Then it becomes a thrash in thicketed scrub and bush to rejoin the track. A total round trip from the hut of 9 km/4–5 hours.

Saw-Cut Gorge

Total tramping time: 4–6 hours/1–2 days
Total tramping distance: 8 km
Grade: easy/medium
Highest point: 250 m; Isolation Creek Hut
Maps: Grassmere P29

The Saw-Cut Gorge is a peculiar alleyway of stone, 50 m long, 50 m high and barely 3 m across in some places. The route up the Waima is short but has lots of river crossings (some are awkward) and it would be hopeless to attempt it after heavy rain. Some of the track entrances are easily missed, and there is some clambering over big boulders in places. A hot summer trip in low flows would be ideal. One 6-bunk hut.

Some 75 km north of Kaikoura or 50 km south of Blenheim on Highway 1 is the turnoff to the Waima or Ure River. It's 12 km of twisting metal road to the Blue Mountain Station, and the road continues right past the homestead's front door and down a steep gravel driveway to the river. There is an obvious parking place by the DOC sign, about 20 m above the river on a terrace. If you are just going to the Saw-Cut Gorge you don't have to ask permission, but please leave a note in the intentions book at the homestead.

Follow the vehicle track down to the Waima River where there's a good wide ford. The vehicle track leads across to the old homestead and yards, but the route keeps to the shingly river, crossing several times where convenient for 500 m/15 minutes past Blue Mountain Stream.

Gradually the river is squeezed between steep walls, and a trail on the north bank threads its way through boulder blocks. Where the huge limestone face of the Waima towers over the river a marked track twists in and out of scrub forest and big boulders past

Ure River canyon

Headache Stream for 1 km/1 hour.

The top river crossing is awkward, and rather bouldery, but after that a good track continues on the south bank for a short distance to where Isolation Creek enters inconspicuously (500 m/20 minutes).

Round a couple of bends in Isolation Creek and the Saw-Cut appears (200 m/5 minutes). Even by the impressive standards of the Waima Gorge this is an astonishing place. A thin slit in the band of rock, 30–40 m high and 3–5 m wide, the opposite walls are almost close enough to be touched by outstretched arms. The creekbed is shingle and it is usually easy to walk up the 50-m length of the gorge. Some hardy mosses even manage to grow in this constantly gloomy cloister (200 m/10 minutes).

At the other end, Isolation Creek winds narrowly (sometimes broken by impressive waterfalls) between high cliffs for just over 1 km/1 hour, where it opens into a wide and ugly shingle flat. The 6-bunk hut sits on a manuka terrace between the prominent forks. There are some reasonable campsites on grass flats up the Waima.

Side-trips
If you enjoy forest there is a good little side-trip behind the hut on a steep track that climbs through an open matai forest, almost 400 m

in height over 1 km/1 hour. This track eventually sidles for 1 km/40 minutes through big red beech forest around to the head of the west branch of Isolation Creek to a low saddle.

Here it is possible to bush-bash back down into the west branch, which becomes more open and scrubby, and it does not take long to get back to the hut (2 km/1 hour). Allow 2–3 hours for the complete circuit.

From the low saddle (the main track continues down into the Brian Boru) a rough route climbs up the spur onto Isolation Hill. Some scrambling is required to get to the top, but there are good views. About 3 km/2–3 hours return from the saddle.

Kowhai River and Hapuku River

Total tramping time: 10–13 hours/2 days
Total tramping distance: 20 km
Grade: medium
Highest point: 1153 m; Kowhai Saddle
Maps: Kaikoura O31

A straightforward tramp in the Kaikoura foothills between two contrasting valleys, the arid, open Kowhai and the heavier bush and closed gorge of the Hapuku. Some river crossing involved, and a bit of scrambling over the highish saddle, but generally good tracks. Two huts.

From Kaikoura township take Ludstone Road 8 km to the junction with Postmans Road. Follow Postmans Road 6 km to the carpark, picnic area and toilets. No public transport to either (widely separated) road-end, but local taxis can be hired. Otherwise leave a car or mountain bike at the other end.

From the carpark a short vehicle track goes down to the Kowhai riverbed. This is easy travel, fording where convenient through grass and scrub-forest flats, some 4 km/2 hours to a marked bypass track on the west bank. If the river is up you may have to take this route but usually the gorge will be quite straightforward as it nips around a few bends to the confluence of the Kowhai and Snowflake rivers (1 km/20 minutes).

The old Snowflake Hut has been removed, but there's still a good campsite (200 m/10 minutes up Snowflake Stream). Continuing up the Kowhai it is easy to criss-cross the shingle river, but there is actually a reliable if unmarked track on the east bank which travels through mixed coastal and alpine plants.

After 4 km/2 hours from the Snowflake Stream forks you reach Kowhai Hut, which has a sunny position on a large grass terrace. Six bunks, a fireplace and good camping on the flats.

A clear track leaves the hut, crosses the Kowhai River for the final time and climbs up a long side-creek through a jumble of rocks, alpine shrubs, small waterfalls and eventual tussock slopes. The track is generally well marked and you can see the saddle ahead, but it takes a discouraging length of time to reach it. But then it's almost a 700-m ascent over 3.5 km/2–3 hours, with wide-ranging views over both valleys from the top.

The track is poled a little to the east of the saddle down a loose scree gully and bouldered riverbed 300 m to the top Hapuku forks (1.5 km/1 hour). Here a cairned track starts on the west bank (good campsite here) and passes through interesting mixtures of bush, including some fine red beech stands; about 2 km/1 hour to recross the Hapuku by the hut. A classic 6-bunker (with open fire) occupies the far end of a river terrace, with bush around the hut and stony grass flats lower down.

Down the Hapuku the river is squeezed between valley walls and it is a boulder hop for 1 km/30 minutes until a track is marked on the north bank. It's important not to miss this track, for if you continue downriver you will emerge on a wide gravel flat above the lower Hapuku gorge, which although traversable is not easy. The track sidles this gorge.

The track climbs up 60 m on an easy grade into whiteywood (mahoe) forest for 500 m/15 minutes to overlook the top Hapuku forks. There are good glimpses over the upper Hapuku and the flanks of the Seaward Kaikouras, then the track turns downriver and wriggles down a steep face with some nice patchy podocarp forest some 150 m back out onto the end of the Hapuku gorge (1 km/40 minutes). The smooth-faced rock and canyon of this gorge are attractive and this would make an excellent lunch spot, with a couple of deep swimming holes nearby.

Immediately downstream the track disappears into a shingle bed covered with gorse, tutu, manuka and other ill-assorted scrub plants, with a few cattle tracks beaten through. Some fords of the river are required. A boring 4.5 km/1–2 hours down to a metal road on the south bank.

Mount Fyffe

Total tramping time: 6–8 hours/1–2 days
Total tramping distance: 16 km
Grade: easy/medium
Highest point: 1602 m; Mount Fyffe
Maps: Kaikoura O31

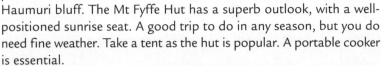

There is an aphorism that 'little mountains have big views, and big mountains have little to see'. Mount Fyffe is a little mountain with a view that includes most of the Seaward Kaikouras including the high peak of Mt Manakau, the Kaikoura Peninsula, and Haumuri bluff. The Mt Fyffe Hut has a superb outlook, with a well-positioned sunrise seat. A good trip to do in any season, but you do need fine weather. Take a tent as the hut is popular. A portable cooker is essential.

From Kaikoura township take Ludstone Road 8 km to the junction with Postmans Road. Follow Postmans Road 6 km to the carpark, picnic area and toilets.

This tramp has the easiest route description of any in this book: beyond the locked gate follow the vehicle road up to the hut, then keep following the road up to the mountain.

The first part of the road to the hut is about 5 km/2–3 hours, with a climb of almost 1000 m. It's a real sweat, but the views are outstanding and the 1970s vehicle track makes for easy walking. Take plenty of water. There's an old tarn (usually dried up) beside the roomy 8-bunk hut, and there is a water tank.

Boring people carry their cellphones up here, so to escape them follow the vehicle track up the continuing barren slopes as it rises another 500 m to the large beacon on top of the mountain (3 km/1–2 hours). Take lunch and enjoy the view before the cellphone chappie (why is it always chaps?) arrives and dials up his mum.

There's an excellent return variation if you fancy it. Only 50 m below Mt Fyffe Hut (or less) a poled track leads west down 'Spaniard Spur' to the Kowhai River — 2 km/2 hours and a 450-m descent, hard on the knees, but well signposted. Here it is easy to follow the shinglebed of the Kowhai back out to the carpark (7 km/2–3 hours).

Looking from Mt Fyffe Hut to Kaikoura Peninsula

Travers River and Sabine River

Total tramping time: 7–8 days (including Blue Lake side-trip)
Total tramping distance: 92 km (including Blue Lake side-trip)
Grade: medium
Highest point: 1768 m; Travers Saddle
Maps: Nelson Lakes National Park 273-5;
  Murchison M29; Matakitaki M30;
  St Arnaud N29; Tarndale N30

The Travers–Sabine circuit is certainly a classic tramp — two big valleys, deep gorges, with a track pushing through dense beech forest over a high alpine pass. It's big country, but not unduly difficult. The tracks are well marked, with six huts and many good campsites. Probably the biggest load on trampers is the one on their backs; you have to take a week's supply of food for this tramp. The option of going on up to Blue Lake is worth the effort.

On Highway 63 drive to St Arnaud (100 km west of Blenheim and 25 km east of Kawatiri Junction). Facilities in the small township include a garage, shop, park visitor centre, and down by the lake an excellent shelter, with campsites, toilets and picnic areas. Wasps can be a real nuisance in late summer.

(Note: another start option is to drive to Mt Robert carpark and take the west lakeside track to Lake Head Hut.)

From the lakeside at Kerr Bay a pleasant track follows left around the edge of Lake Rotoiti, past the side-track up to the St Arnaud Range. This lake is one of the two (the other is Rotoroa) that form the northern boundary of the Nelson Lakes National Park, which stretches all the way to Lewis Pass.

The lakeshore track winds through the red, silver and black beech forest across several side-streams to the jetty (8 km/2–3 hours). You can hire a water taxi to bring you across the lake from St Arnaud, saving you about half a day.

Lake Head Hut (20 bunks) lies a little further on beside a grass bank overlooking the marshy outlet of the Travers River (1 km/20 minutes).

The main track heads up the broad Travers Valley over wide grass flats for 3 km/1 hour, then enters the bush again, closing to the river near a footbridge (1 km/20 minutes).

Head up the west bank as the track wanders sedately through beech and grass clearings for 4.5 km/1–2 hours to Hopeless Creek track junction, past many good-looking campsites, with the mitre-like Mt Travers (2338 m) slowly dominating the valley. A footbridge crosses Hopeless Creek then the trail takes 5 km/1–2 hours to reach the John Tait Hut, the track staying beside the river as it chases through confined forested slopes. The large hut has room for 24 people, and there are meagre campsites in the grass clearing surrounding it.

There is another track junction 1 km/20 minutes beyond the hut; the right-hand trail leads to Cupola Basin, and the valley track crosses a footbridge over a creek notched through the rock. After 1 km/20 minutes a sign indicates a short distance (3 minutes) along a side-route to the Travers Waterfall where the river tumbles into a moss-enclosed cup of rock, almost the last word in waterfalls.

The main track continues over the Summit Creek footbridge 1 km/20 minutes from Cupola Creek, then 2 km/40 minutes further to another footbridge across to the east bank of the Travers River, and on up the shrinking valley through thick mountain beech to Upper Travers Hut (2 km/40 minutes). This is a fine spot, right on the alpine margin. The hut has 2 rooms, 14 bunks, and a convivial wood stove.

The route to Travers Saddle is profusely cairned and poled. It immediately crosses the upper Travers River and slowly climbs 450 m over tussock slopes and around small bluffs to the pass (2 km/2–3 hours). Mt Travers is a striking triangle against the sky, and a panorama of other peaks can be seen on both sides of the pass.

The descent to the Sabine River is long, steep and tedious. The first 300 m (1 km/30 minutes) crosses boulder fields and tussock to the bush edge, then briefly passes through some bush to the top of an old avalanche swathe. This is hard-packed gravel and provides uncomfortable travel for the 200-m or so descent before you re-enter

John Tait Hut

the bush and drop down to the river (2 km/1–2 hours).

A footbridge crosses the extraordinary East Sabine Gorge, a chasm barely 3 m wide yet plunging 30–35 m directly to the river. Just before this gorge there's an excellent campsite on a grass terrace.

The track eases considerably as it sidles the last 2 km/1 hour down to the Sabine Forks. Head upriver to West Sabine Hut (8 bunks) which is popular with fisherfolk, so you won't be alone, and there might even be a trout if you look especially pathetic.

If you fancy an extra jaunt up to Blue Lake allow 2 days return, or consider a long day-trip. Cross the West Sabine footbridge and continue up the confined and tree-rooted track, climbing slowly 400 m over 6 km/2–3 hours. On your way you will pass two large clearings, which were created by avalanches breaking through the forest during winter; ice debris can still linger here well into summer. The second clearing has dramatic views of the hanging rock basins below Moss Pass, with waterfalls cutting delicate trails down the cliff-sides.

From the second clearing the track re-enters the bush and rises 150 m alongside the Sabine River past an undisturbed rock glade to the beech line at Blue Lake Hut (1 km/1 hour; 16 bunks and a wood stove).

A short marked trail climbs 200 m from the hut up through alpine beech and scrub to overlook the majestic Lake Constance (1 km/1 hour). You can see Mt Franklin (2339 m), the highest peak in Nelson Lakes National Park, and from here you will also gain the best view of the startling turquoise hue of Blue Lake.

From the Sabine Forks the valley track is a good 13 km/4–5 hours downriver to the footbridge. The track stays on the west bank all the way, mostly in forest with occasional clearings (some good camp-sites), and climbs occasionally. Where the river closes in the track has to thread through a tangle of boulder slabs, and an unexpected rock bivouac provides shelter for 2–3 people.

The footbridge crosses a narrow gorge and the track highway takes 2 km/40 minutes to reach Sabine Hut beside the much larger Lake Rotoroa. There's a new 30-person hut here, with a jetty.

(Note: some keen trampers consider returning to St Arnaud via Mt Cedric and the Angelus Ridge, but the climb is formidable, and it is an exposed route along the ridge crest. Sabine Hut to Lake Angelus is 8 km/5–6 hours and a climb of 1300 m! Refer to Lake Angelus Tops, page 162, for information on the route from Lake Angelus to Mt Robert.)

The lowland track to St Arnaud has been considerably improved in recent years and has been realigned so that it doesn't do the big devi-ation via the old Howard Hut, which has been removed.

From Sabine Hut follow the lakeside track some distance to the junction, where the Speargrass Track climbs slowly at first, then smartly up to a low wetland saddle (2 km/2 hours and a 200-m climb). From the track junction with the old Howard Track the Speargrass Track starts to sidle across various side-creeks, with quite a bit of up-and-down. A huge amount of boardwalk has been placed on this track, interrupted by sections of rough tramping trail, which look like the places where the money ran out. An impressive bridge across Cedric Stream. Some 8 km/3–4 hours to Speargrass Hut (6 bunks).

From here the track crosses a footbridge and follows the bushed Speargrass valley for 5 km/1–2 hours, before slowly climbing out of the valley in a gentle grade for 1.5 km/30 minutes to reach the Robert Ridge carpark. If you have not got anyone to pick you up it's about a 5 km/1 hour walk back to St Arnaud and the first ice-cream for a week.

Lake Angelus Tops

Total tramping time: 13–16 hours/2–3 days
Total tramping distance: 27 km
Grade: medium, medium/fit
Highest point: 1814 m; Robert Ridge
Maps: Nelson Lakes National Park 273-5;
  Murchison M29; St Arnaud N29

Separating the great lakes of Rotoroa and Rotoiti is the Robert Ridge with its alpine tarns and tussock and scree slopes. On a fine day the ridge track offers one of the best short tramps in the park, but on a poor day it can be a treacherous and unpleasant place. Two shelters and a large hut at Lake Angelus. A well-marked route, but good navigation skills still needed.

Travel along Highway 63 to St Arnaud, then take the West Bay road (2 km west of St Arnaud) for 5 km to the carpark and shelter at the end of a steep zig-zag.

The beginning of the tramp is horribly steep. The Pinchgut Trail switches back for 500 m to Mt Robert (1411 m) through a burnt-off scrub face and the remaining beech forest; 1.5 km/2 hours to the Bushedge Shelter. The views are superb.

The track eases over the flat summit of Mt Robert (past the track junction to the Bushline Hut) and on to a shelter overlooking the Mt Robert skifield (1.5 km/1 hour). This club field is one of the oldest in New Zealand, and the obligatory walk in has kept the field small, isolated and almost unique. Two lodges can be seen at the foot of the basin.

The main route to Angelus follows the ridge, often skirting the highest points. Rolling at first, it becomes sharper and more broken towards Lake Angelus. In good visibility poles and a worn trail make route-finding straightforward. For 1.5 km/1 hour the track slowly climbs 150 m around the skifield basin to Flagtop (1690 m), then continues for almost 2 km/1 hour to the Julius Summit (1794 m). Wandering past some lovely tarn-filled basins the route goes a further 3.5 km/1–2 hours to a knob overlooking the Angelus upland.

This is a lovely alpine basin occupied by Lake Angelus and the

Lake Angelus

smaller and thinner Hinapouri Tarn, with other lakelets scattered around. Tussock and rock slopes sweep down from a surround of crumbled peaks, then pour steeply into the Hukere Valley. Angelus Hut stands as a bright painted dot on the edge of the lake.

The route drops steeply down scree slopes for 200 m over 500 m/15 minutes to the lakeside and around to the hut door (40 bunks and gas heating).

There are plenty of good day trips, but the most obvious is to Mt Angelus. The unmarked route simply skirts the Angelus Basin to Sunset Saddle (2.5 km/1 hour), then clambers up a crumbly rock spur 200 m to the summit (2084 m; 500 m/20 minutes). There's another knob 5 minutes away which looks suspiciously as though it might be higher. It doesn't take long to knock off. Excellent views over Lake Rotoroa and south along the main range to the rough pyramid of Mt Hopeless (2278 m).

Alternative exits

Should the weather pack up before your return trip along the Robert Ridge there are two possible options.

One alternative route in poor weather is to climb the 200 m up out of the basin, then descend to the head of Speargrass Creek. This angles north in a gentle decline and is a good deal less exposed than the ridge. It's an almost 600-m descent over snowgrass on a poled route to the bushline (3 km/2 hours) then 1 km/1 hour through untracked beech forest (following the creek) to Speargrass Flat and hut (6 bunks). A good track leads out from here to the shelter and carpark. Obviously, this alternative route can be used equally well as a way into the Angelus Basin.

The second option is to follow the cairned route down into the steep Hukere Stream, and after a 500-m descent pick up the easier bush track down to the main Travers Valley track (6 km/2–3 hours).

Waiau Pass

Total tramping time: 15–18 hours/3–4 days
   (Christopher Hut to Blue Lake)
Total tramping distance: 38 km
   (Christopher Hut to Blue Lake)
Grade: medium/fit
Highest point: 1915 m; Waiau Pass
Maps: Matakitaki M30; Lewis M31

Waiau is a high alpine pass between Nelson Lakes and Lewis Pass, and offers a challenging route down through the Spenser Mountains. It is well marked but should never be underestimated, and is only suitable for experienced parties. Only in summer is the pass free of snow and even then there can be old snow and new snowfall throughout the season. There are several huts and some fine camping sites.

Note: this description is only from Christopher Hut to Blue Lake; a total crossing from Lewis to Nelson Lakes will take anywhere from 6–9 days.

For access and route descriptions for Lewis Pass to Christopher Hut see the St James Walkway, page 172. Allow 1–2 days (22 km/8–10 hours) from Lewis Pass.

From Christopher, a large 20-person hut, follow the walkway down the Ada River for a while then cross over to the north bank keeping close to the hills on the far side as you turn the corner into the Waiau River (5 km/1–2 hours). This is all private land so take care not to disturb stock or damage fences, and keep well away from the Ada Homestead.

Round the corner pick up a four-wheel-drive track which wanders up beside the Waiau River for many kilometres, up the huge river flats with their endless flocks of paradise ducks. It's 8 km/2–3 hours from the bend to Glacier Gully. There are some reasonable campsites 500 m/15 minutes up Glacier Gully among silver beech and these offer a bold view of Mt Una, the highest peak of the Spensers at 2301 m.

Typically the travel alternates between easy river flats and hopping along scrub and grass ledges. You may prefer to criss-cross the river itself rather than stick to one side. After 6 km/1–2 hours from Glacier Gully the route rises onto an old glacial moraine scattered in park-like fashion with clumps of trees. There are nice camping spots here and a first look at the Waiau Pass ahead.

It's 3 km/1 hour on to Webber Falls on the left, then 2 km/40 minutes further to Caroline Bivouac. This is a simple 2-bunk upright hut with plenty of camping and lots of firewood.

Past Caroline Stream there is a beautiful 5.5 km/1–2 hour section of beech clearings, then over a final scree and tussock slope to the forks. There are fine established campsites in the isolated beech stand at the forks.

A narrow but well-defined trail starts from the main campsite at the forks, crosses one branch of the Waiau and wriggles up through low alpine scrub and tussock grasses, climbing a steady 200 m up beside the Waiau as it tumbles through waterfalls (1 km/1 hour). Where the last scrub ends the valley flattens somewhat and a loosely cairned trail gradually climbs up to the foot of some small cliffs just before a side-stream (500 m/15 minutes). A signpost here indicates the pass route.

The route is marked by cairns as it clambers steeply 100 m through the cliffs before emerging onto a long spur. A poled route climbs a brisk 300 m to the top of this spur with spectacular views back down the Waiau and over to Lake Thompson. The spur flattens and turns a final 30 m to a notch in the ridge (1 km/1–2 hours).

Lake Constance fills the view below with the broken top of Mt Franklin in the background. This is the main divide; the Waiau River flows to the east, the Sabine-Rotoroa-Buller Rivers to the west.

The poles lead off the pass, sidle delicately past some tarns until they reach the top of a scree slope, then it's a 300-m stumble down to the creek (1 km/1 hour) and another signpost. Follow the creek down 500 m/20 minutes over boulder-strewn tussock to the desolate but beautiful foreshore of the lake.

The route continues tightly by the west side for 1 km/30 minutes until it reaches a formidable bluff. Marker poles take the scanty track a hard 100 m/10 minutes to the top of the bluff. Once at the top follow the cairns and keep sidling high above the lake for 1 km/1 hour before dropping back towards the lake dam. It is tempting to avoid this irritating sidle by descending too quickly down to the lake, especially when the cairns peter out. However, there is a rash of bluffs below and it can take almost as long to thread a way through them as it does to persist with the high track.

Ironically, cairns abound everywhere on the rock-jumbled dam so follow them to the lip, after which a track becomes more defined. From here you can see the striking colour of Blue Lake below. There is a good track through the scrub and beech, dropping 200 m and finishing by the hut door after 1 km/30 minutes (16 bunks, wood stove).

Beside Lake Constance

See the Travers and Sabine Rivers (page 158) for route and access information on to St Arnaud. Allow 2–3 days.

Matakitaki Valley

Total tramping time: 4–5 days (Lake Rotoroa to Ada Pass Hut)
Total tramping distance: 66 km (Lake Rotoroa to Ada Pass Hut)
Grade: fit
Highest point: 1850 m; unnamed pass
Maps: Matakitaki M30; Lewis M31

A classic traverse of the northern Southern Alps via
three fine valleys and two alpine passes. A variety of
travelling from standard walkways to obscure tracks
to unmarked routes. Neither pass has tracks and
both require some stiff bush-bashing and navigation
skills. Eight huts and bivouacs and some excellent camping. Suitable
for experienced trampers only. The full trip from Lake Rotoroa to
Lewis Pass would take about 5–6 days.

Take Highway 6 to the Lake Rotoroa turnoff at Gowanbridge, then
it's 11 km down the road to the lakeside. Buses go as far as
Gowanbridge and arrangements can be made with the boat operator from Rotoroa to pick you up here. To boat up the lake is expensive, but it saves a day's tedious walk. The boat delivers you to
D'Urville Hut (10 bunks).

Leave the lake behind and follow the valley track up past the track
junction to the Sabine Hut and alongside the broad D'Urville River.
It's easy walking over river flats past the signposted Tiraumea Saddle
junction (2 km/40 minutes) and the Bull Creek footbridge 1 km/20
minutes further on, though it's even easier to stick with the river
shingle.

It's 7 km/2–3 hours to Morgan Hut (14 bunks) via beech terraces
and expansive river flats, then another 6 km/1–2 hours more of gentle valley track before it tightens into the first gorge. There are a few
good gorge views if you scramble close to the edge, then the valley
opens a little for the last 4 km/1 hour to Ella Hut (16 bunks). There
are plenty of good campsites up to here, but not much beyond.

Twisting closer to the river the track passes the Moss Pass turnoff
and footbridge (2 km/1 hour) and climbs steadily for 5 km/1–2
hours until it reaches a 2-bunk bivouac, sited just over a large open
creekbed. Just before the bivouac, David Saddle can be seen as a

Heading up to the pass from the Matakitaki River to Cannibal Gorge

distinctive notch cut into the range, nearly 900 m above you, challenging and depressing.

From the tidy bivouac a track is marked through the bush for 1 km/30 minutes to where a large side-creek joins the D'Urville. Impressive waterfalls burst down this creek.

Head up the east side of this side-creek for about 5 minutes, then clamber into a prominent dry gully that cuts steeply through the beech forest. This gives fast and direct access to the tussock. Simply sidle out of the gully once the bushline has been passed; it's a scramble of about 150 m (500 m/30 minutes).

Keeping roughly south, pick up slight tussock spurs and gullies, climbing for almost 300 m until they flatten into the top basin before the pass. In poor visibility you need to be spot on with your navigation here, and you will probably veer too far right, but the saddle's sharp notch should be an obvious landmark. There's a final 100 m of scree rock to the 1768-m pass (1 km/2 hours).

From the saddle on a fine day you can peer into the glacial swathe of the East Matakitaki River, and the vast Spenser Mountains occupy the horizon. They were named after the English poet Spenser who wrote an immensely long poem, 'The Faerie Queen', hence all the romantic names on the peaks — Mt Una, Mt Gloriana etc.

From the saddle either head down the obvious scree gully (although you will have to clamber out of it at one point to avoid a waterfall), or sidle from the pass onto the east-side spur which drops in a very steep descent down good rock alongside the gully. It's 600 m either way to the valley floor (1 km/1–2 hours), and it seems as slow going down the saddle as climbing up to it.

It's a good 8 km/3–4 hours to the East Matakitaki Hut, but the travel is generally excellent. There is no track but there are wide flats and easy beech terraces most of the way, and old deer trails can save time wherever the bush squeezes onto the riverbank. The DOC hut sits in the middle of a huge flat by a clump of beech, a cosy and usually very welcoming little 4-bunk hut with an open fire. It's almost certainly been a long day.

From here a reasonable track sidles 5 km/1–2 hours to the Matakitaki Forks, glimpsing a spectacular gorge on the way. Ignore the turnoff for the main track downstream, and follow the upper route as it turns upstream into the West Matakitaki River (1 km/30 minutes). The track drops sharply to the river where a 3-wire bridge is strung nervously across a gorge, but there is a pretty good ford downriver.

On the far side a track switches lazily uphill for 100 m before settling into a prolonged sidle of the river, and after 2.5 km/1–2 hours the track bursts out onto the top flats. Mt Maling (2127 m) is the dominant peak in a ridgeline jutted with knobs and notches. Bob's Hut is 1 km/30 minutes across the grassland; 4 bunks and a fireplace.

A track of sorts continues up the West Matakitaki River on the east side. The start is difficult to find and there are only tree blazes to follow (axecuts in the trunks). However, the track is worth persisting with because the river climbs steeply in a mess of boulders.

After 2 km/1 hour the track turns a 'corner' of the river and the bush widens into a few river flats. The first decent-sized flat is probably the best campsite (about 1 km/30 minutes from the 'corner'). From here the river flattens into tussock and gravel reaches for 2 km/1 hour before narrowing into a short gorge (500 m/20 minutes). This can be avoided by sidling high (50 m) on the north side above the bush, although you can scrape through the gorge with no real hassles.

Above the bush and around the second 'corner' the views improve. Headwalls and waterfalls loom over alpine flats as the river turns and you climb beside it slowly in good-going tussocks towards the upper basins, 3.5 km/2 hours after the gorge. The top tarns come as a sudden surprise, three of them in a row, placid in an arc of gloomy, crumbling mountains.

The position of the pass is deceptive. It is not the low point directly ahead, but rather it is in line with the three tarns (south-west) up a scree slide and final 20-m rock gut to the ridge (500 m/30 minutes). Everything becomes clear on top, at 1800 m, with great views. There is another tarn-filled basin below and 150 m of scree and grass slopes down to the twin lakes (500 m/30 minutes). A fine camping or lunch spot, and Ada Pass Hut can be seen as a speck at the bottom of the valley.

A little care is needed to get over the tip of the basin, better right or left than straight ahead. Then it's a long descent by the side of the creek, which has a pretty waterfall halfway down, though you might be too busy to admire it. It's a drop of 500 m over 2 km/1–2 hours to the bushline, then a struggle for another 1 km/1 hour through entanglements of exasperating beech until you break out to the tussock flats of the Maruia River.

A quick crossing of the river brings you to the St James Walkway, and Ada Pass Hut is a few minutes upstream, a comfortable 20-person establishment with wood stove and sun-catching verandah.

See the St James Walkway, page 172, for access and route information from Ada Pass Hut. Allow a day to get to Lewis Pass highway (12 km/6 hours).

St James Walkway

Total tramping time: 4–5 days
Total tramping distance: 67 km
Grade: medium
Highest point: 1135 m; Anne Saddle
Maps: Lewis M31; Boyle M32

The St James is the longest walkway in the country, passing through fine bush and semi-alpine country across the Southern Alps. It has graded tracks, moderate inclines and well-positioned huts to lure the tramper into these hills, but this track shouldn't be taken too lightly, and its walkway designation is possibly misleading.

Both ends of the track are on Highway 7 across the Lewis Pass. Regular bus services run along this road and these are particularly convenient for St James trampers; timetables are posted in the shelters at the track ends. Vandalism of cars at the Lewis Pass carpark has been an occasional problem and the Maruia Springs Hotel offers (or did offer) a car valet service, where they will drop you off at the track end, store your car and pick you up at the other track end at a prearranged time.

From the shelter at the Boyle Track end follow the vehicle road for 1 km/20 minutes. A track is marked off to the left, sidling the river a short distance to the footbridge over the Boyle (1 km/30 minutes), then through easy beech forest and open river flats for 8 km/2–3 hours around to a footbridge over to the east bank of the Boyle River.

You can reach Magdalen Hut by going 1 km/20 minutes downstream. It is delightfully secluded in a bush clearing; 7 bunks and character. Quite a bit of mistletoe on the beech trees.

However, the main track continues upriver from the footbridge and sidles the Boyle River Gorge. Packhorses used to wind down the gorge in the old days but the modern track stays 100 m above the river on the bush edge. Tussock flats and a short bridge lead to Boyle Flats Hut on the west bank; 20 bunks, wood stove and battered armchairs (3.5 km/1–2 hours).

Cross back over the river and follow the track up the open mountain valley 4 km/1–2 hours to Rokeby Hut, a pokey 2-bunk hut just over Rokeby Stream. Views of the exotically named Libretto and Opera Ranges continue up the valley before the forest closes in. After 4 km/1–2 hours the track sidles up 200 m over 1.5 km/40 minutes out of the valley onto bush-covered Anne Saddle (1135 m).

After an easy drop of 100 m the walkway clears the bush and reaches the spacious headwaters of the Anne River. Following cattle-grazed flats, the track stays on the south side of the river and poles, markers and cairns take the route over Kia Stream (unbridged) and down to a footbridge 5 km/1–2 hours from Anne Saddle.

On the west bank the track rambles for 2.5 km/1 hour close by the river in bush and rock to the two Anne Huts. The main hut holds 20 people; the old one is like Rokeby Hut — dirt floor and a little bit of history.

From the Anne Huts to Christopher Hut the track is entirely on grazing land, 17 km/5–6 hours all told. It swings in a semi-circle into and out of the Waiau Valley, sometimes getting monotonous, and often very hot on a summer's day.

Once over the footbridge, follow the vehicle track (marked by posts) to a track which leads to a footbridge over the Henry River. Resume the vehicle track and follow it to a junction. The markers lead tightly around the base of Mt Federation (1612 m) past thickets of matagouri into the Waiau Valley.

Ada Homestead can be seen as the track turns the corner into Ada Valley. Flocks of paradise ducks noisily greet you as you tramp upstream over huge grass flats. And there's the sheer backdrop of the Spenser Mountains to wonder at. The Faerie Queen is the twin-headed peak at 2236 m.

Christopher Hut has 20 bunks, and there's another 4-bunk hut 1 km/20 minutes above Christopher Hut, near the confluence of the Ada and Christopher Rivers. Flats turn the corner as the bush closes down to the trail, and at a huge open slip the rock faces of Faerie Queen loom 1200 m over the valley (2.5 km/1 hour).

From this open face the track cuts in and out of bush for 3.5 km/1 hour until it reaches a large alpine clearing. Cattle and semi-wild horses frequently invade the upper valley, churning the trail into a quagmire. Markers resume at the end of this clearing (1 km/20 minutes) and wander through bush and another open space to the barely perceptible Ada Pass (938 m; 1 km/20 minutes).

After crossing the upper Maruia River it's 1 km/20 minutes to Ada Pass Hut, perhaps the most attractive on the entire walkway. It has 20 bunks, a wood stove and a good view up onto the rock basins of the Spenser Range.

Below the hut the walkway crosses a footbridge over the Maruia River and slips past some pretty alpine terraces into the bush, staying firmly on the north bank for 4 km/1–2 hours down to Cannibal Gorge Hut (20 bunks).

Below the hut there have been considerable windfalls in the past and the track has to chisel through piles of dead trees completely covered with new regrowth, but in general the gorge is considerably less fierce than its name suggests. Elaborate track work has been done on this section of the walkway, steps have been cut into log bridges and a staircase leads up to a smart lookout at Phil's Knob. It's 6 km/2–3 hours down to the long suspension footbridge over the river.

Once over the bridge the trail sidles 50 m up onto a bush terrace and across two moss-sided creeks to the main highway (2 km/40 minutes). Lewis Pass itself is at 863 m and the glistening tarn is a pleasant spot to pull off those damn boots and relax. The Maruia Springs hot pools are only a short drive from the pass, and the pub will put back in what you have sweated out.

Lake Daniells

Total tramping time: 4–5 hours/1–2 days
Total tramping distance: 14 km
Grade: easy
Highest point: 562 m; Lake Daniells
Maps: Springs Junction L31; Lewis M31

A short, charming tramp to a quiet lake and a large, comfortable hut. A good 'break in' for those who haven't tramped before or are just oiling rusty legs again. This is a popular trip so those who don't fancy a crowded hut should take a tent; there are plenty of uncrowded campsites by the lake.

Drive over the Lewis Pass on Highway 7 to 5 km short of Springs Junction. Turn into Marble Hill Scenic Reserve and continue for 500 m to the road-end. There are sheltered campsites in a number of places beside the road. Springs Junction has petrol, tearooms, and an unstaffed information centre, which displays aspects of the Lewis Pass.

The signposted track commences in immaculate order for 500 m/15 minutes to the Sluice Box, a narrow runnel of rock where the Maruia River is compressed to a fraction of its usual width. Cross the footbridge and follow the gravelled and boardwalked track up the Alfred River through forest and the occasional grass clearing.

The open beech forest filters the sunlight onto the thick layer of ferns and leaf debris and the well-shingled track continues over the next 4.5 km/1 hour to the confluence of the Pell Stream. A seat is provided, and a little way up the Pell Stream a gold claim is still being worked.

After 1 km/20 minutes the track crosses a footbridge over a tiny side-creek and veers away from Alfred River to follow Frazer Stream. This stretch of the track used to be famous for its mud, but now the track has been drained, gravelled, and is like a garden path.

It's 2 km/40 minutes to the lake shore and the large hut. The hut can accommodate 24 people and was built as a memorial to two trampers killed in a mudslide in the old hut (then located further to the east) several years ago.

Calm evening, Lake Daniells

A lot of fun can be had in the rowboat (if it's useable) plying about the still waters of the lake. The lake is well stocked with rainbow trout, and the fishing season is from November to April. In the evening the rising mist, placid lapping waters and echoing bird sounds evoke a dreamy atmosphere.

Lake Christabel Crossing

Total tramping time: 10–13 hours/2–3 days
Total tramping distance: 33 km Blue-Grey return/
27 km Christabel crossing via Rough Creek
Grade: medium
Highest point: 1440 m; Rough Creek pass
Maps: Springs Junction L31; Lewis M31

A popular but long weekend trip crossing the tops to a lake at the head of the Blue-Grey River. Easy gradients in beech forest up the Blue-Grey River but a stiff pass into Rough Creek. This trip is suited to a larger party where the 'flat-walkers' can return down the Blue-Grey and drive around to pick up the 'pass-hoppers'. One hut, a few campsites.

From Springs Junction take Highway 7 towards Reefton, turning left after 3 km into Palmers Road, a narrow shingled lane. Another 9 km to the farmland at Palmer's Flat and the start of the track. The Rough Creek track is clearly signposted on the Lewis Pass Highway, 11 km before Springs Junction.

Staying on the north bank of the Blue-Grey River follow a rough vehicle track across farmland for 500 m/15 minutes until markers lead the track up onto a river-beech terrace.

For 8 km/2–3 hours the track ambles along in silver-red beech forest, gaining height very gradually. The track often keeps well away from the river, with glimpses of open river flats on the way. There are plenty of camping sites close to the river if you are prepared to investigate, especially on the opposite bank. The river is easy to ford and as blue as the name suggests.

About 2 km/40 minutes short of the lake the track does its one main climb, 150 m over the hump which forms part of the natural dam that contains the lake. Then it's an easy descent of 100 m to the gleaming Lake Christabel, bent in a long L-shape in the crook of the hills. A gravel flat is the only possible campsite here; it's obviously been used (there's a fireplace) but it hardly looks comfortable. There are no other camping spots on the lakeside till the head.

The lake track follows a well-graded bench some 5 km/1–2 hours

Lake Christabel

to the far end of the lake, where the track pops out onto a large grass flat, a good campsite, with a fine outlook over the lake and the rolling tops beyond.

A brief 2 km/40 minutes up a flat valley winding in among beech and grass flats to a good crossing to the 10-bunk hut. The bridge has gone.

For Rough Creek follow the track upstream some 4 km/1–2 hours as it swings in a half-circle, then climbs a spur to the bush edge, almost up to a low tussock saddle (500 m/1 hour). Here the track does a high sidle into the top basin of the valley, then it's a brief 1 km/30 minutes to the foot of the pass, where it is only 200 m up the steep poled route (a lot of poles missing) to the crest of the attractive pass (1 km/1 hour).

Worth lingering on top if the day is fine for it's a long descent. Not quite 300 m down to the bush edge (1 km/30 minutes), then 3.5 km/1–2 hours on the beech forest track, crossing Rough Creek several times, and a steady 650-m drop right back to Highway 7. This bush track is getting overgrown but is still discernable.

Harper Pass

Total tramping time: 5–7 days
Total tramping distance: 76 km
Grade: medium
Highest point: 962 m; Harper Pass
Maps: Lake Sumner Forest Park 274-16;
  Arthur's Pass National Park 273-1;
  Otira K33; Lake Sumner L32; Dampier L33;
  Boyle M32

A classic route from Lewis Pass to Arthur's Pass, following the Maori, explorers, gold-diggers and stockmen over the low-alpine Harper Pass. Not an all-weather trip by any means, with plenty of river crossings and opportunities to get stuck by flooded creeks, but still generally easy travel over good tracks with a variety of nine shelters and huts on the way. It's a long tramp, but could be shortened by a day if you started from Lake Sumner.

(Note: in unsettled weather some people recommend doing Harper Pass from the Otira River side first, as all the difficult river crossings — the Otira, the Otehake and the Taramakau — would then be at the start of the trip instead of the end. That makes planning more predictable and you are less likely to get stuck in the Taramakau.)

You need four topographical maps to cover the whole route so you may find it more convenient to use the Lake Sumner and Arthur's Pass maps combined.

Take the Lewis Pass Highway (Highway 7) to 7 km beyond the Hope Bridge. A sign indicates the entrance to the Hope Valley track, and a short road leads 300 m to a picnic area and small shelter. On Highway 75 over Arthur's Pass the route starts beside a DOC base hut, about 10 km north of Otira. There are regular bus services over the Lewis and Arthur's Pass highways.

The track follows a vehicle road past the Outdoor Education Centre huts at Windy Point and down over a footbridge suspended across the impressive gorge of the Boyle River. It then climbs up over farmland terraces for 2 km/40 minutes to the bush edge. The track stays in open beech for about 100 m above the river on a long bush terrace. In the 7 km/2–3 hours to Hope Halfway Hut only rarely do you see the Hope River.

The 6-bunk hut stands at the far side of the first major clearing. There is a dribbling thermal spring signposted 30 m away, disappointing if you are in search of a hot bath. The hut is sound but getting knocked around; a good lunch spot.

The track drops down to the river, and sidles through bush until it closes to the river at the foot of a large rocky slip. Another hot spring taints the air, although the seepage point is obscure. It's a short sidle through the bush, then out onto a huge grass flat covered in matagouri (2 km/1 hour from the shelter).

Marker poles lead 4 km/1 hour to the bush margin, where the Hope runs through a pretty and narrow gorge; good camping around the gorge area on both sides of the river. Follow the signs to a footbridge over this gorge, and beyond the bridge a junction is marked.

Ignore the vehicle track leading to St Jacobs Hut and follow yet more signs through 2 km/40 minutes of pleasant beech and grassland to the massive Hope-Kiwi Lodge. This is very comfortable, holds 30 people, and has good views up and down the Kiwi River Valley.

A side-track leads off up to Three Mile Stream, but the main trail continues up Kiwi Valley, skirting the cattle flats by following the beech edge. You go into the bush and it's an easy climb of 100 m to the Kiwi Saddle Track junction (5 km/1–2 hours).

One branch turns to Lake Marion and beyond to Lake Sumner. Take the other track as it follows the old pack-trail for about 7 km/2 hours in a gently sidling descent, crossing Three Mile Stream (and side-track) before reaching the wide open valley of the Hurunui. Lake Sumner stretches south, almost 10 km in length, its surface usually ruffled by winds.

Poles lead the track up the valley and along the bush margin to join a four-wheel-drive road which turns sharply south across the valley to a footbridge (6 km/1–2 hours). Cross the bridge and turn upstream through high terraces of manuka for the 1.5 km/30 minutes to Hurunui Hut (20 bunks). After all the uphill the hut doesn't have especially good views, and seems rather clumsily situated.

From here the travel on the south bank is sometimes exasperat-

Upper Hurunui and old Cameron Hut

ingly up and down. If quick, flat travel up the Hurunui River to No. 3 Hut is preferred the north bank and old vehicle trails are much easier, if the river allows it, but this description will stick to the main track.

From the hut the track drops down to a huge flat (1 km/20 minutes), and it's a plod of 2 km/40 minutes to the site of Old Springs Hut. At the bush edge the track winds across two side-creeks for 1 km/20 minutes to the signposted hot springs. These tumble from very hot vents over the track in a waterfall to the river gravel. You can have a wash here in a good-sized pool that takes 3–4 bodies.

There's a long 100-m climb after the spring through the bush, then a descent to another river flat (1 km/40 minutes). You travel along the flat briefly before entering the bush again and sidling up and down for 2.5 km/1 hour to the foot of another big flat. The route across is poled for 500 m/15 minutes until it meets a four-wheel-drive junction (signposted). Follow the road for 1 km/20 minutes to No. 3 Hut. It has 12 bunks in tiers, a large open fireplace and a lot of character.

The track stays in the bush for 1.5 km/30 minutes until it reaches the walkwire over Cameron Stream. The derelict 4-bunk Cameron Hut is 1.5 km/30 minutes further on the open flat. The track stays above and beside the shrinking flats, and the cattle become more scarce as the hills close in. At a fork 4 km/1–2 hours above Cameron Hut, there's a choice of routes.

You can criss-cross upriver to the bivouac or pick up the track as it climbs steadily through the noticeably richer bush. The trail sidles, then drops steeply to the 2-bunk bivouac which is surrounded by bright green-leafed fuchsia (1.5 km/40 minutes).

The route follows upriver 700 m/20 minutes along boulders and scrub-edged grassy flats. Where the shrunken Hurunui River turns sharply south, a sign indicates a track on the right. This rises for 700 m/20 minutes to the subtle high point of Harper Pass (962 m).

The views are limited for the track never enters the tussock and descends instead to the West Coast, crossing the dribbling upper Taramakau River and dropping quite steeply down a gully to the riverside some 450 m where it continues mostly in bush to a footbridge (2 km/1 hour).

On the south bank the route is consistently marked, winding in and out of the bush to Locke Stream Hut (called No. 4); 3 km/1 hour. This part of the route has been destroyed by slips, and any section of the marked river route could easily be washed away. The hut at Locke Stream has 12 bunks, a wood stove and a mountain radio.

There's a short track through the bush to Locke Stream. There the Taramakau opens right out, and travel is directly down open (and sometimes tedious) gravel beds. It's 9 km/3 hours from No. 4 to Kiwi Hut. At Christmas the southern rata blossoms in this valley, and the red flowers add rare colour to the dense greenery.

Kiwi Hut stands on a bush shelf well back from the river on the north bank, where cairn and markers indicate the vehicle track which cuts through bush for 10 minutes and across a clearing to the hut (8 bunks and an open fireplace). It's 2 km/40 minutes to where the Otehake River thunders out and clearly it's a good idea to ford the Taramakau River before the Otehake. Note that the footbridge across the Otehake River has been closed and may be removed.

Down the Taramakau it's 5 km/1 hour to Pfeifer Creek, where a faded vehicle track winds over stony grassland and gorse for a further 3 km/1 hour till prominent red and white markers start the final track through bracken, dead tree stumps and a little bush to the junction with the flood track.

Take the main track past the wee shelter then cut across to the Otira River. The Otira is probably the most difficult river crossing on the trip, so if the river is up, even slightly, the only alternative is to go back to the flood track and slog the 5.5 km/2 hours upstream to the Deception footbridge. This flood track is now difficult to follow and overgrown.

Otherwise after crossing the Otira line up with an obvious gap in the bushline on the far bank, a gap divided by an island-like clump of trees. Aim for the bush to the north of this gap. Beside a fenceline an old vehicle track goes past some gorse, a gate, some bush, then across open farmland to the DOC base hut by the main road (1 km/20 minutes). It's well worth finding this vehicle track, otherwise you will be blundering round in gorse for a while, not a great ending to the trip.

Kirwans Knob

Total tramping time: 12–15 hours/2–3 days (complete circuit)
Total tramping distance: 36 km (complete circuit)
Grade: easy/medium
Highest point: 1294 m; Kirwans Knob
   (1297 m; Kirwans Hill)
Map: Reefton L30

A brilliantly graded miners' pack-track leads up to a
hut on a hill, where you can see Mt Cook and a
panorama of crinkled bush tops. And it's easy to turn
this tramp into a circuit tramp, coming out past old
mining relics and alongside the wide Waitahi River.
Two huts, good camping in the Montgomerie and
Waitahi Rivers; a portable cooker is essential.

From Reefton take Highway 69 about 11 km north and turn down
Boatmans Road for 7 km to Capleston carpark. In 1877 this mining
town boasted seven pubs and 1000 people.

A vehicle track crosses farmland for 1 km/20 minutes to the bush
edge, and shortly goes through a tunnel onto a footbridge across
Boatmans Creek. After this rather dramatic start the track ambles
alongside the creek for 1.5 km/30 minutes before crossing back over
and continuing for 500 m/10 minutes to Topler Creek.

Across the creek the pack-track settles into its rhythm and zig-zags
purposefully for 8 km/3–5 hours, climbing almost 900 m to Kirwans
Knob and a short side-track to Kirwans Hut (12 bunks, wood stove).

The 'Kirwan's Reward' open-cast mine site is worth a look, along
the main pack-track and down a 5-minute signposted side-track,
and there are views of the aerial ropeway which dates from 1898.
From the hut there is another side-track onto Kirwans Hill itself,
almost 2 km/40 minutes first through stunted silver beech, then

open tussock tops with a breathtaking panorama of mountains.

The option of completing a circuit tramp is a good one, though you should get an early start if you are doing it over just a weekend.

From Kirwans Hut head down the main pack-track through several clearings and remnants of the old mine, crossing the line of the aerial ropeway twice on the long descent. There are bits of iron all through the bush, including the remains of the Lord Brassey stamping battery about halfway down. All told, at least 4 km/2 hours and a drop of 800 m into Kirwans Creek and down the marvellously worked pack-track to the Montgomerie River.

The track stays on the west bank some 4.5 km/2 hours down to Montgomerie Hut and the Waitahu River. However, the river can be crossed easily and it is just as pleasant wandering down the grass flats. The hut has 6 bunks and sometimes gets vandalised.

From here on there's a four-wheel-drive track to follow for some 14 km/3–4 hours alongside the broad Waitahu to Gannons Bridge, mostly unremarkable tramping but there are some good campsites on the way. It is also possible to cross the river and connect up with the Murray Creek goldfields tracks which link across 6 km to Blacks Point and Highway 7.

The main track finally reaches Gannons Bridge, and a signposted track climbs steeply through red beech forest onto a pine forest plateau, crosses this and follows an old road line down to Capleston (2 km/1 hour). At times this track can get overgrown, and with numerous bulldozed trails, firebreaks, and pine plantations, keeping to the route can be frustrating.

Lake Stream

Total tramping time: 5–6 hours/2 days
Total tramping distance: 14 km (Lake Stream Hut return)
Grade: medium
Highest point: 1100 m; Lake Stream Hut
Maps: Springs Junction L31

The Victoria Range is little visited and this tramp gives you a good taste of its remoteness, with a secluded track leading to a bush wetland at the head of a steep-sided valley. There's an option of a side-trip up to the tops, where you can view the tarns and narrow-gutted valleys so characteristic of the Victoria Range. There is another hard option of completing the tramp almost as a circuit, by coming out over a dramatic rocky ridge to Rahu Saddle. One small hut, limited camping.

From Springs Junction drive west along Highway 7 towards Reefton for about 11 km. Keep a sharp eye open for the Lake Stream track, which is on the north side of the road and marked by a small sign.

Once found, the track is well marked and ambles alongside the stream under a dense canopy of beech trees. The altitude at the highway is 600 m and you only have to rise 450 m over 7 km/2–3 hours to reach the hut. The track crosses the stream several times before breaking into a pretty bush clearing at the head of the valley. A run-down 2-bunk upright bivouac stands on the east side of the clearing. It's backed by beech trees which provide an ample wood supply for the wood stove. There's one good dry campsite near the hut.

From the hut a side-trip can be made up the valley. The route presses through 1 km/1 hour of bush, then scrambles 300 m over tussock and rock slopes up to the ridge crest (1 km/1 hour) and up to the sharp peak to the west. Good views all round of this glaciated country, and you might see the flighty rock-wren.

Alternative ridge traverse out to the road
It is possible to exit back to the road via the long ridge that lies on the eastern side of Lake Stream, and down to the Rahu Saddle

Tops traverse above Lake Stream

tracks. However, you need good weather, navigation skills, and to be experienced enough to handle off-track tramping.

From the saddle at the head of Lake Stream it is about 6 km/3-4 hours along the bumpy ridge, generally good travel but with one rock outcrop to turn and some struggles with alpine scrub on some steepish sections (actually the scrub is handy to hang on to). Views are superb and although the ridge never becomes knife-edge sometimes you feel it does, until at last you are looking down at the Rahu River basin, with its lovely spread of tarns.

Here you have a choice. One alternative is to drop down to the tarns (some possible campsites here) and head over to the far eastern side of the basin where an old track leads down to the valley floor itself (1 km/1 hour). There's one good dry campsite beside the swamp and tussock clearing, then it's 4 km/2 hours down the Klondyke track to the highway, a descent of 450 m.

The second option is to stay up high and traverse the tops on the western 'arm' of the ridge around the Rahu River top basin, with a solid climb of 150 m at one point, then down 300 m to the start of the good Klondyke Spur track (3 km/1 hour). This leads in a steep 2 km/1 hour to the main highway. Lake Stream track is only 3 km down the road.

Inland Pack Track

Total tramping time: 10–11 hours/2–3 days
Total tramping distance: 25 km
Grade: easy/medium
Highest point: 200 m; track
Maps: Paparoa National Park 273-12;
  Punakaiki K30

An historic, well-signposted track twisting through a landscape of sheer gorges, limestone rock forms and dense bush. No huts, but a magnificent natural rock shelter. Caves, clefts and caverns to explore. It should not be attempted in wet weather, as river levels can rise quickly and dangerously. There are a lot of fords in the Fox River and Dilemma Creek, so make sure you get good weather information from the visitor centre at Punakaiki.

From Greymouth travel 54 km north along Highway 6 to the Fox River bridge. This is 48 km south of the town of Westport. A sign and information boards on the north bank of the river indicate the start of the Pack Track 500 m ahead at the end of a short road. At Punakaiki (the 'pancake rocks') there is a good visitor centre, cafe and craft shop, and a DOC-run motor camp.

The marked track follows scrub flats and riverbed for 1.5 km/30 minutes, crossing two bush spurs via old miners' cuttings. Where the shingle bed narrows a track sign indicates a division of the route. Either cross the river to join the well-benched south bank track (which continues most of the way to the Dilemma Creek confluence; 2.5 km/1 hour) or continue along the north bank to the Fox River Caves. If you have the time this is the preferable route; the caves are easily accessible and an unmarked side-trail drops back to the river so you do not have to retrace your steps.

The north bank track is benched most of the way until it abruptly turns uphill after 2 km/40 minutes. The side-trail down to the river starts here. Drop your pack and scramble up a slippery rock track, dodging the ongaonga (stinging nettle), to the entrance of the first cavern, a vault of rock and hanging vines bevelled out of the cliff face.

The only safe cave to enter is up on the left-hand corner. Step blocks have been laid to its entrance, and inside some of the floor has been paved with stones. You do not have to go in far (100 metres and a dead-end) to appreciate the stalagmites and stalactites in the cold, complete darkness. Only experienced cavers should enter the lower Fox River Caves.

Return to your pack then drop down the side-trail for 100 m/5 minutes beside a thick moss-covered stream to the Fox River. You can either cross and scramble up the other side to the south bank track, or continue wading upriver. If you do not mind a few deep fords this is a pleasant option.

The Fox Gorge is striking, especially with the sun illuminating one face and darkening the other. Every twist in the river breaks open new angles of rock and light. Sometimes the deep green pools may have to be scrambled around, but the side bush is usually no problem.

It's 1 km/30 minutes upstream to the confluence of the Dilemma Creek. Here the rock walls have formed a sharp prow, splitting the two rivers. Keep to the main Fox River and travel another 1 km/30 minutes upstream to the high natural rock shelter nicknamed The Ballroom.

This is a massive overhang which curves over a grassy flat, making it a unique and dry campsite. You could fit a few houses under here comfortably. Wood is a bit scarce so a portable cooker is essential. There is some graffiti on the walls, but this can't mar the impressiveness of this solid cavern. Toilet provided.

Return to the Fox–Dilemma confluence. Up the Dilemma Gorge the creek cuts tightly back and forth between the rock sides. These are easy fords and you have plenty of time to gaze at the towers of sculptured limestone. After barely 2.5 km/1 hour Dilemma Creek balloons out into a wide gravel- and gorse-covered flat and meets Fossil Creek. Signs indicate the route up Fossil Creek, and there is a small campsite by the confluence, but there are better campsites on grass flats 100 m/5 minutes further up Dilemma Creek.

Follow Fossil Creek upstream, travelling past quiet pools and under a canopy of bush. After 1 km/30 minutes a cairn and sign will indicate the start of the Pack Track. There is reasonable camping on a small flat just above the sign on the left bank of the creek.

The track meanders for 4 km/1–2 hours in a variety of rimu, beech

Lower Fox River

and manuka forest, with quite a lot of mud, though by now it might be boardwalked or gravelled. It crests a small ridge before it touches the farmland at Bullock Creek. Between 1860 and 1910 this was the main route up this part of the West Coast, but there are few traces of its historic past. Several footbridges are now in place over the main creeks.

The track skirts the farmland for 1 km/20 minutes and joins a farm road; the route through the farm is signposted. All gates on the farm must be left as found, and stock should not be disturbed. Follow this vehicle track to a ford over Bullock Creek, and along to a crossroads (1.5 km/30 minutes). Campsite here.

Follow the signposted road (straight ahead) as it climbs 500 m/10 minutes to a small crest, where a sign marks the resumption of the track. Once past the cut-over bush the track winds through forest rich in mature rimu and beech trees standing above an abundance of tree ferns. Sinkholes, cracks, and deep shafts are dotted beside the track so the warning signs ('Beware of holes') should be heeded. Keep to the trail unless you fancy some unexpected caving.

The track wanders along this karst landscape for 4 km/1–2 hours, dodging the various geological obstacles to the Pororari River. Across the lovely ford there's quite an attractive campsite beside the still river, and it's a short distance to a prominent track junction. A signposted, well-graded track goes down the Pororari Valley for 3.5 km/1 hour, offering an easy and probably more convenient exit.

However, the main Inland Pack Track climbs 150 m easily up a benched grade to a low saddle, and then descends to the Punakaiki River (2.5 km/1 hour). Nikau palms are everywhere, and an old farm road leads to a broad ford.

On the other side a gravel road leads under limestone bluffs some 1.5 km/30 minutes to the main highway, where you are 2 km/40 minutes south of Punakaiki settlement and visitor centre.

Croesus Track

Total tramping time: 6–8 hours/1–2 days
Total tramping distance: 20 km (including side-trip
  to stamping battery)
Grade: medium
Highest point: 1220 m; Mt Ryall
Maps: Ahaura K31

Following the goldminers' footsteps, the Croesus Track crosses the southern Paparoa Range from Blackball to Barrytown. The forest is strewn with history in the shape of stamping batteries, mine sites, collapsed aerial gantries and, not least, the smoothly graded pack-track itself. One new hut, two old huts.

From Greymouth take Highway 7 to Stillwater, cross the Buller roadbridge and continue upriver to the old town of Blackball (25 km). From the township head 1 km on the Roa Road then turn onto the Blackball Road, which winds through forest for 4 km to the Smoke-Ho! carpark. The road-ends may make it more convenient to use only the Blackball access, where the historical remains are more accessible and the track easier than the steep climb from Barrytown.

From the Smoke-Ho! carpark there's a coal-smeared track that leads quickly to a trail-bike bar and a visitors' book, then it's 500 m/10 minutes down an easy grade through manuka to a track junction.

The 'Gorge Track' drops to Blackball Creek after crossing the Smoke-Ho! Creek and follows the river upstream past the two Minerva Mine Sites. The First Site has good camping space; the Second Site is the actual mine entrance, with nostalgic goldminers' bric-a-brac. This track then meets up again with the main Croesus at the large grassy clearing of the First Hotel Site. Either way 1 km/30 minutes.

Over the footbridge at Clarke's Creek the Croesus holds to a steady gradient for 2 km/40 minutes, across another footbridge then up to Mulcares Track junction. The side-trail involves a boulder-hop across the Blackball Creek to Perotti's Mill site, which offers a bush-sheltered camping spot. The main track carries on smoothly past the

Goldminers' stamping battery

toetoe-fringed Second Hotel Site (camping here also) and on up past a couple of long zig-zags to the Garden Gully junction (2.5 km/1 hour). The rimu-kamahi forest has changed to silver beech, and changes again further up to rata and mountain neinei ('pine-apple tree') forest.

There's an interesting side-trip along the Garden Gully track as it crosses a subtle bush saddle 500 m/10 minutes down to the old Garden Gully Hut by the Roaring Meg. (Four sacking bunks, an open fire, and plenty of camping on flats around the hut.) This track continues upriver, crosses a footbridge and turns into Dugout Creek where it climbs up to an impressive stamping battery and further on the site of the old quartz reef mine (1 km/20 minutes).

The main Croesus Track continues from Garden Gully junction in lazy loops upwards, finally breaking out of the bush after 3 km/1 hour into a burnt-off area of stumps and flax. Top Hut has 3 sacking bunks and a fireplace but has been superseded by the Ces Clark Memorial Hut a minute further on. Dedicated to a ranger who died on the track, this is surely the only mountain hut to be opened by a prime minister (David Lange, August 1986). Spaces on platforms for

16 people, wood stove, sunny verandah and fine views over the Grey River.

The Croesus continues immediately into wide tussock basins, sidling underneath and around Croesus Knob (1 km/20 minutes). It is well worth doing a brief jaunt up onto Croesus Knob itself, with the remains of the aerial cableway for the Croesus Mine and views of Mount Cook on a fine day.

Leaving the pack-track, the Croesus follows a line of snowpoles around the easy ridge (past one or two tarns) onto Mt Ryall (1220 m; 3 km/1 hour).

It's almost an 1100-m descent from Ryall to Barrytown. The track is fairly basic for most of the way down this long bushy spur, and although a miners' track lower down flattens out some of the steep parts, it's a long, knee-jerking descent to the main road (5 km/2–3 hours). But there is a pub opposite when you meet the highway, so it's not all bad.

Lake Minchin

Total tramping time: 20–23 hours/3–4 days
Total tramping distance: 51 km
Grade: medium/fit
Highest point: 1082 m; Minchin Pass
Maps: Arthur's Pass National Park 273-1;
Otira K33; Dampier L33

An east-west traverse trip across Arthur's Pass National Park, with extensive river travel to a lake deep inside the Park. Solid route-finding skills are required, and expect some scrub-bashing off Minchin Pass down into the Taramakau River. Three huts and two shelters.

For access and route description to Casey Hut see Binser Saddle, page 197. From Andrews Stream road-end and shelter to Casey Hut is 14 km/7–8 hours.

Opposite and slightly upstream of the hut a large marker indicates the start of the track, which leads over a bush tongue and cuts through windfalls to the Poulter River, about 1.5 km/30 minutes. Follow the track through forest then drop onto salubrious flats and wander upriver for 3.5 km/1 hour to the Trust/Poulter Hut.

This warm hut has 6 bunks, an open fire and a fine outlook. The Poulter River is a typical eastern divide river, its bed filled up with shingle debris from the eroded tops. Flocks of paradise ducks are often present in this valley, flying in pairs and honking in mournful circles over intruders.

The Poulter River swings left around a big corner. Follow this upstream over gravel beds for 3 km/1 hour and cross over to the flats beside the Minchin Stream confluence. A track on the east bank of the stream ambles for 2.5 km/1 hour in bush to Lake Minchin, a large and placid lake.

The track continues around the east side of the lake to a big shingle river flat (1 km/30 minutes). Cross this (some fine-weather campsites here) and after 1.5 km/30 minutes the river divides. A track is marked on the west bank of the main Minchin Stream, and you certainly want to pick it up as the stream goes through a short gorge. The track climbs 100 m briefly, then drops 50 m, re-entering Minchin Stream just before Linwood Creek (1 km/30 minutes).

Easy travel from Linwood going north up the main stream for 1.5 km/30 minutes, crossing where necessary on gravel flats to the upper Minchin forks. A 2-person bivouac ('dog kennel' type) is obviously sited between the two creeks. Keep going north from the bivouac, and sidle up the snowgrass valley 100 m to the obvious low point of Minchin Pass (1.5 km/30 minutes).

Impressively jagged ridges and rock faces fall off into the Townsend Valley and this hardly looks a promising route. Access to this creek is not obvious, and apart from a few cairns the route is not marked. Make sure you have plenty of time in hand to get down to the Taramakau River as there are no real campsites in the Townsend gorge, and some parties misjudge the distance and have an unpleasant 'benightment'. Also, don't continue if it has been raining for any length of time; the Townsend quickly becomes impassable.

From Minchin Pass drop through tussock and a little scrub into the main creek, some 100 m. For the next 150–200 m of descent travel in the scrub edges of the creek. Generally, there is a worn and noticeable trail on the west side of the stream, where people and deer have broken through. It's a scramble, but it is easier than it looks.

After about 2 km/1 hour the creek reaches the bush edge, and here it becomes open and possible to travel in. Big boulders, tight bends and a continuously steep descent through the confined gorge completes Townsend Creek, a steady 450-m boulder bash over 3 km/1–3 hours down to the welcome spaciousness of the Taramakau River.

(Note: times can vary considerably down Townsend Creek depending on the experience of the party. Also, if doing the trip in reverse you need to be careful not to go up the wrong creek.)

For access and route description down the Taramakau River see Harper Pass, page 179; 15 km/5 hours to the Otira River and Highway 73.

Hallelujah Flat and Binser Saddle

Total tramping time: 18–21 hours/2–3 days
Total tramping distance: 44 km
Grade: easy/medium
Highest point: 1085 m; Binser Saddle
Maps: Arthur's Pass National Park 273-1;
    Dampier L33

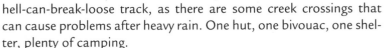

A circuit tramp that stays fairly low most of the time, so it is suitable for modest trampers, though it's still a bit of a leg-stretcher, particularly if you are trying to do the whole circuit in a weekend. Three days is better for less fit trampers. And it's not a guaranteed all-hell-can-break-loose track, as there are some creek crossings that can cause problems after heavy rain. One hut, one bivouac, one shelter, plenty of camping.

From Highway 73 turn off onto the Mt White road, 2 km north of Cass bridge (about 22 km short of Arthur's Pass village); after 1 km cross the Mt White bridge over the Waimakariri River and head straight across the large river flat (past the Hawdon River road) some 4 km to Andrews Stream picnic area, campsite and shelter on the other side. The track starts beside the enclosed shelter.

Right at the beginning you have a choice. On a fine summer's day it is very pleasant to get to Hallelujah Flat by splashing up the Andrews Stream. An old and marked track criss-crosses the stream for some 7 km/2–3 hours to meet the track at the start of the large flat. Good campsites here.

But if the stream is up, or wet feet are not your thing, then the track climbs from the shelter a stiff 200 m up a bush spur through old windfalls (1 km/1 hour), where it settles into a long meandering sidle some 5.5 km/2–3 hours to Hallelujah Flat. The stream route is probably an hour quicker than the track for agile trampers.

It's 3 km/1 hour over the huge golden clearing of Hallelujah Flat and over shingle beds to the next flat at Casey Saddle (777 m). A sign points to a small 2-bunk bivouac 100 m up the slope on the east bank, but there are good campsites all round here.

Across the grass flat of Casey Saddle the track eases into Surprise

Keeping boots dry!

Stream, 1.5 km/40 minutes to the point where the track climbs out of the stream. Climbing some 200 m and sidling for a good 2 km/1–2 hours, the track finally drops 300 m down an easy open beech spur for almost 2 km/1 hour to Casey Hut (12 bunks, mountain radio, wood stove and several campsites near the hut).

Only a few minutes down from the hut to the wide Poulter River, and an obvious vehicle track turns the corner and heads south over grass flats, then dodges up onto a back terrace to an attractive pond (3 km/1 hour). A pleasant spot for an evening camp.

The track drops down to Rabbit Flat where an old vehicle track leads 4 km/1 hour across Mt Brown Creek, then another 6 km/2 hours on to Pete Stream. Good views down this stretch but it does get a bit monotonous. The old hut at Pete Stream has gone and the track to Binser Saddle starts from the top of steep terraces across the stream from the old hut site.

It's almost 600 m up an easyish bush spur 3 km/2 hours to the welcome clearing on the top of Binser Saddle (1085 m). There are a few small tarns here so this could be a great place to camp, though wasps can be really bad in late summer.

A romp of 4 km/1–2 hours down through the beech forest some 600 m back to farmland and the Mt White road, and a stroll of 2 km/40 minutes up to your car at Andrews Shelter.

Tarn Col (Edwards River to Hawdon River)

Total tramping time: 12–15 hours/2–3 days
Total tramping distance: 32 km
Grade: medium/fit
Highest point: 1368 m; Tarn Col
Maps: Arthur's Pass National Park 273-1;
    Otira K33

An alpine route over three distinct passes between the valleys of the Edwards and Hawdon Rivers. Straightforward valley travel, some river crossing, plenty of waterfalls and two huts. Good navigation skills essential to negotiate the passes. A popular route but not to be taken lightly, and you need good weather to make the trip enjoyable. Some people reckon the Edwards Valley is the prettiest in Arthur's Pass, and they may well be right. Worth going to even if you don't fancy the complete Tarn Col circuit.

On Highway 73 stop at Greyneys Shelter, 5 km south of Arthur's Pass township. There are good campsites here, and regular bus services on the highway, crossing daily between Christchurch and Greymouth.

From the shelter, cross the road and railway and follow the short vehicle track to the Bealey–Mingha confluence; 700 m/15 minutes. Head up the gravelled Mingha River for 1 km/20 minutes to where the Edwards River emerges to the east. A short track on the south side of the Edwards avoids a brief gorge, and travels for 1.5 km/30 minutes through bush to a long gravelled flat.

Continue over the easy flats for 2.5 km/1 hour to the junction of the east branch of the Edwards River. A track begins between the forks, 50 m up the east branch, marked by a large rock cairn. This climbs for 100 m onto a scrubby terrace, and smooth rock outcrops give views of the Edwards Valley (10 minutes).

For most of the distance to the hut the track sidles up and down through beech forest well above the main river. After 1 km/30 minutes there is a view of the Edwards waterfall. Further along two

Looking over Taruahuna Pass

cables have been strung to assist trampers. The first cable goes down a steep slope, the second one acts as a guide rail over a slippery creekbed.

After another 1 km/20 minutes the track leaves the main forest behind and closes with the river, following the east bank over boulders, tussock and scrub for another 1 km/30 minutes to Edwards Hut. This is a spacious hut with a wood stove and bunkrooms for 16 people. The porch faces towards Williams Saddle (1327 m), a low tussock pass dividing the Edwards from the Mingha Valley.

Travel up the Edwards is either in the riverbed or on well-worn trails on the banks. It's attractive, open tussock travel, with occasional wetland ponds. After 4 km/1–2 hours you reach a prominent fork, and Amber Col (1631 m) can be seen at the head of the east branch.

A further 1 km/20 minutes up the Edwards the river becomes too narrow to walk, and a cairned and worn trail leads for 2 km/1 hour to Taruahuna Pass (1252 m). Many years ago a huge mass of rock, disturbed by an earthquake, split from Falling Mountain (1901 m) and filled the pass. Only now have lichens and a few small plants begun to take hold on this jagged rubble.

To reach Tarn Col sidle east from the pass to the foot of the obvious notch. After 150 m of steep scrambling through scrub and tussock you suddenly reach the col itself, with its big gleaming tarn. An excellent lunch stop (700 m/1 hour).

Keeping above the stream which flows from the tarn, follow the north side down, dropping 300 m over 1.5 km/1 hour, until you find yourself on a slight spur which drops down to the stream. Occasional cairns help with the route-finding. Then it is barely 500 m/20 minutes of boulder-hopping to the upper forks of the East Branch of the Otehake.

(Note: this junction is particularly important if you are doing the trip in reverse. The Otehake Hut logbook is full of people who have come from the Hawdon River, over Walker Pass and continued happily down the East Branch of the Otehake, completely missing the turn west to Tarn Col. It seems a surprising error but there it is. If you do end up in Otehake Hut it is far easier to either retrace your steps, or go direct to Taruahuna Pass up the West Branch of the Otehake, which is not especially difficult (5 km/2–3 hours). The lower Otehake track is overgrown, and sidles high to avoid the gorge, a hard route.)

From the junction head up the East Branch over snowgrass and alpine scrub for 1 km/40 minutes to the obvious low-lying Walker Pass (1095 m), with its large, attractive tarn. Pass the tarn and keep to the north of Twin Falls Stream, and after a gentle 100-m descent over 1.5 km/30 minutes a track starts on the scrub edge quite close to the stream. This track sidles around waterfalls and makes a sharp descent of 200 m to the broad Hawdon Valley (1 km/30 minutes).

The track emerges amid tree stumps in a thick bed of shingle, and it's slightly more than 1 km/20 minutes down wide flats, through a short defile, to Hawdon Hut on the west bank (16 people, wood stove and radio). If you've come all the way from Edwards Hut that day then you definitely deserve a rest.

After the hut follow a good worn trail on the same bank (or follow the river) to the East Hawdon confluence (3 km/1 hour). Then it's a dull 6 km/2 hours over gradually increasing amounts of gravel to Hawdon Shelter, which is up a short bush track on the east bank above the river.

Mingha River to Deception River

Total tramping time: 9–12 hours/2–3 days
Total tramping distance: 27 km
Grade: medium
Highest point: 1070 m; Goat Pass
Maps: Arthur's Pass National Park 273-1;
Otira K33

A popular weekend trip which crosses from the gentle moss-carpeted beech forest of the east coast over the Main Divide into the entangled rain forest of the West Coast. Two huts, one bivouac, one shelter; you will need a portable cooker for Goat Pass Hut and if you camp at Lake Mavis. For many people the Mingha–Deception is *the* Canterbury weekend trip, but be warned, there's lots of river crossing involved in this tramp and every year people get stranded by heavy rain. Check the weather beforehand. Since the Coast-to-Coast runners use this track in February you might want to avoid that particular weekend.

Travel to Greyneys Shelter, 5 km south of Arthur's Pass village. There are regular bus services on the highway, crossing daily between Christchurch and Greymouth.

From the shelter, cross the road and railway and follow the short vehicle track to the Bealey–Mingha confluence (700 m/15 minutes). Head up the wide gravelled Mingha Valley for about 4 km/1–2 hours, and where the river narrows take the signposted bush track on the west bank and climb onto a bench track above the Mingha Gorge.

The track wanders through mixed beech and podocarp forest for 1 km/30 minutes to a clear area called Dudley Knob, then crosses two side-streams in the next 2 km/1 hour (lots of boardwalk) before closing to the Mingha River by a grass river flat and a tiny 2-person bivouac.

Above here the route follows flats on the west bank for 1 km/30 minutes to a fork. It's a pleasant stretch and you pass the ribboned Kennedy Falls (150 m) cutting down the cliffs. A marked track begins on the east bank of the dwindling Mingha, and zig-zags up onto the soft tussock expanse of Goat Pass. Much of this track is board-walked for its 100-m ascent over 1.5 km/ 30 minutes. The 20-bunk Goat Pass Hut (mountain radio) is tucked on the Deception side of the pass. No cooking facilities.

If you want a good side-trip, climb 500 m east up steep tussock faces to the turquoise Lake Mavis (1 km/1–2 hours one way), which is an excellent place to camp, but you'll need a portable cooker.

From Goat Pass Hut a short track leads down a dry,

Boulder hopping, upper Deception River

rocky gully to the headwaters of the Deception River (500 m/20 minutes). Then it's slow travel among substantial boulders dropping 300 m over 2 km/2 hours to the 6-bunk Deception Hut.

There are occasional bush trails on the banks but they are not always easy to find or consistent, so it is usually easiest to bash down the river. The amount of river crossing often surprises people.

Keep to the riverbed for 1 km/30 minutes until you reach the Doreen Creek confluence, where the Deception River swells into a wide gravel valley, and it's straightforward travel for 7 km/2 hours to a somewhat mysteriously placed footbridge. Sulphur wafts through the air but it's hard to find the source.

It's another 6 km/1–2 hours of gravel and grass flats to the Otira River, where a fixed footbridge takes you back to the main highway.

Carroll Hut and Hunt Creek

Total tramping time: 9–12 hours/2–3 days
Total tramping distance: 20 km
Grade: medium/fit
Highest point: 1400 m; Kellys Range
Maps: Arthur's Pass National Park 273-1;
  Otira K33

A short, sharp tramp up to the alpine Carroll Hut, then along the Kelly Range to Hunt Saddle, along to Hunt Hut, and back down to the highway. A good circuit with alpine tarns, fault scarps and two huts. Good route-finding skills required and some scrub-bashing down to Hunt Saddle. Primus essential.

From Highway 73 turn left after the Kellys Creek bridge 3 km north of Otira, into the picnic area and shelter. Camping here.

Walk over the flats and past a small side-creek to where a sign indicates the beginning of the bush track to Carroll Hut (500 m/10 minutes). It is a steep climb of almost 700 m through thick rainforest to where the track levels out at the bushline (1.5 km/2–3 hours). On the way up there are a couple of excellent viewing points over to Hunt Saddle and the Barron Range.

The track continues by sidling upwards for 100 m, entering a layer of alpine scrub and crossing two dry gullies. At the snowgrass the track flattens and reaches a basin where Carroll Hut stands (500 m/30 minutes). The hut has 10 wide bunks, a portable cooker bench (no wood stove) and double-glazed windows, but it can still get perishingly cold. It's at an altitude of 1113 m and looks straight up the Otira Valley to the zig-zag road winding up to the pass.

A quick side-trip to Kellys Saddle and on to Kellys Hill is a possibility; it's a 200-m climb over 1 km/40 minutes and gives fine views to Mt Rolleston and Tara Tama.

For Hunt Saddle head to Kellys Saddle then wind westwards, climbing slowly past marker poles 200 m along easy tops, some 2.5 km/1 hour towards the twin 1400-m mounds and large alpine tarns. The marker poles turn away here, down to the bushline and the start of the Seven Mile Creek track.

Hunt Saddle

The range, however, stays easy for another 3 km/1 hour over small bumps and tarns, but gradually dropping 150 m or so to where you can look right down on Hunt Saddle. Study the route carefully, as it is possible to avoid most of the scrub. It's a 400-m descent to Hunt Saddle (1 km/1 hour), passing a small tarn basin about halfway down. Some scrub-bashing is inevitable, but how much is dependent on your skill.

On the track you have a choice. If you head south over Hunt Saddle and along a well-marked track in alpine forest for 2 km/1 hour you reach the 6-bunk Hunt Hut, situated at the start of a long tussock valley.

Otherwise from Hunt Saddle follow the track into Kellys Creek which is a gentle descent of 7 km/2–3 hours back to Kellys Shelter by the main highway. This track suffers from periodic wash-outs and slips, and can be slow going after any recent flood, but since the track follows the creek pretty closely all the way you should be able to pick it up fairly quickly again. There are at least a couple of sections of boulder-hopping, as well as one place where the track goes inland to avoid a short gorge.

Avalanche Peak

Total tramping time: 9–11 hours/2 days
Total tramping distance: 18 km
Grade: fit
Highest point: 1833 m; Avalanche Peak
Maps: Arthur's Pass National Park 273-1;
  Otira K33

A weekend tramp over a prominent peak in Arthur's Pass. Open river travel, a companionable hut and a close look at the Crow Face and icefall of Mt Rolleston. The track is not marked all the way, and good navigation skills are required.

From Christchurch take Highway 73 to the Klondyke Corner turnoff, 1.5 km past the Waimakariri bridge. There are sheltered campsites at the road-end, and regular bus services over Arthur's Pass between Christchurch and Greymouth.

Travel up the wide-shingled Waimakariri is straightforward, but generally it is easier to keep to the north side of the river. Two crossings should be enough to reach the large grass flat before the Crow River confluence (5 km/1–2 hours). Anti-Crow Hut can be seen on the opposite bank of the Waimakariri.

A trail has been worn over the flats and a short track is marked through a tongue of bush to the Crow River (2 km/40 minutes). The low peak of Rolleston (2212 m) is an imposing backdrop as you travel up the Crow Valley, and after 2.5 km/1 hour of shingle flats the river narrows. On the west bank a track scrambles between beech and large boulders alongside the Crow as it tumbles down a short rapid, then the river widens and smooths into flats again; Crow Hut is located on the left (2 km/1 hour). This is a cosy hut which holds 10 people.

An hour's side-trip to the head of the valley brings you underneath the blunt triangle of Crow Face, and the scoured rock and icefall of the Crow Glacier.

The route to Avalanche Peak is not direct. Some large cairns stand on the east at the foot of a big scree slide, 1 km/30 minutes above the hut. This slide leads to the top of the ridge, but keep to the edge of the scree where the rocks are more firmly held together. It's a 500-m climb to a saddle, which is marked by a cairn and pole (1 km/1–2 hours).

(Note: clearly this junction is crucial if you are coming in reverse over Mt Avalanche and into the Crow, and misty weather can make navigation difficult here. It's definitely easier navigationally doing the trip from the Crow to Avalanche.)

From the saddle the route turns south along the ridge, and since the rock is crumbly it is

Looking down into Crow Valley from near Avalanche Peak

easier not to keep exactly on the ridgeline. After 1.5 km/1 hour and a height gain of 150 m, Avalanche Peak (1833 m) is reached. It takes longer along the ridge than you might think, and again in misty weather it can be confusing, though there are cairns along the way.

There is plenty to see from the top of Avalanche Peak, Mt Rolleston in particular, as well as Mt Phipps (1965 m), Aicken (1858 m), Bealey (1836 m) and Arthur's Pass village itself, with the thin highway wriggling over it.

The two routes off Avalanche follow spurs which enclose Avalanche Creek basin like two arms. In mist the northern route is preferable because it follows an obvious ridge north-east from the peak, and a noticeable trail has been worn on the ground; 1.5 km/

1 hour and a 500-m poled and cairned descent to the bush edge. The bush track is called Scotts Track and takes about 1.5 km/1 hour and still another 300-m drop before it emerges out on the main road just north of the township.

The southern track is also cairned and poled (not always reliably) to the bush edge but it is a steeper drop through the bush. For the last 300 m it closely follows Avalanche Creek as it leapfrogs dramatically down several high waterfalls to the Bealey River. This track comes out behind the DOC visitor centre (3 km/2 hours).

Three Pass Trip

Total tramping time: 24–27 hours/3–4 days
Total tramping distance: 57 km
Grade: fit
Highest point: 1753 m; Whitehorn Pass
Maps: Arthur's Pass National Park 273-1;
   Kaniere J33; Otira K33

A classic Canterbury trip, crossing from Arthur's Pass to the West Coast via three impressive passes, Harman, Whitehorn and Brownings. It's usually done as a three-day tramp, but it is by no means an easy jaunt. Strong navigation skills are required as this trip is suitable only for experienced trampers. A good tent and portable cooker are essential. Five huts and several good campsites.

(Note: Whitehorn Pass has a permanent valley of snow, which although not steep might still require the use of an ice-axe and even crampons. This is the only tramp in this book where a route crosses a permanent snowfield and it is advisable to have at least one member of the party with snow experience. Brownings Pass is a steep scramble in any weather and unseasonal snow can make it impassable.)

From Christchurch take Highway 73 to the Klondyke Corner turnoff 1.5 km past the Waimakariri bridge. There are sheltered campsites at the road-end, and regular bus services over Arthur's Pass between Christchurch and Greymouth.

From Klondyke Corner to Carrington Hut up the Waimakariri River is about 15 km/3–4 hours whichever way you choose to do it. If the river level is normal you can cross freely just about anywhere and many people opt for a straightforward gravel grind taking the straightest route. Anti-Crow Hut can be seen on the far side after 5 km, but Greenlaw Hut has gone.

Peaks jostle around the top forks, giving you a taste of the large mountain country coming up. Carrington Hut is slightly up the White River along a bush track. It's unlikely you will walk past it — it's a big hut, holding 24 people in two bunkrooms; mountain radio.

Ariel Tarns on Harman Pass,
looking towards Whitehorn Pass

Plenty of campsites here.

The route to Harman Pass is up the White River, a milky glacial river not always particularly easy to cross. Upstream 1 km/20 minutes is the Clough Cableway if the White is too high. Virtually opposite the cableway on the north bank is the Taipoiti River, a steep bouldery stream that tumbles off Harman Pass. Despite its cliff-like appearance the travel is reasonable in the rock-choked riverbed, criss-crossing as necessary for some 2 km/1 hour to where a large waterfall blocks the stream. A cairned track starts on the east bank, climbs around the waterfall on smooth rocks and up through the rock and tussock 1 km/30 minutes to the pass.

Now the route turns sharp west past the lovely Ariel Tarns (excellent campsites) and up towards the obvious Whitehorn Pass. It's 3 km/1–2 hours from Harman to Whitehorn, rock-hopping up a valley some 400 m across a permanent and gentle snowfield to the top (1753 m). On either side are the romantically named sisters Isobel (2036 m) and Rosamund (2186 m).

It's a steeper descent of 300 m off Whitehorn Pass into Cronin Stream (1 km/1 hour), then the valley eases somewhat and it is a rather uninspiring 3 km/1 hour round the corner to the first of the scrub. A track takes you 1.5 km/40 minutes down to Park Morpeth Hut (6 bunks), which sits on the edge of a grass flat beside the Wilberforce Valley.

With two down and one to go the route turns up into and crosses the Wilberforce River, with some 2 km/1 hour to the Clough Memorial. From a distance the famous 'zig-zag', the remnants of the goldminers' track of the 1860s, is clearly visible, but up close it seems to disappear. It is not really followable, and the best way to tackle the pass is to aim dead north up the obvious face direct to the pass, cutting across the zig-zags. Cairns get demolished every year by avalanches so there may be few markers.

Towards the top the rock gets quite steep and loose, but it's a mistake to veer too much left or right. After 1 km/1–2 hours and 500 m of climbing you reach the abrupt lip of the pass and Lake Browning.

The views are great: Popes Pass to the east, Hall Col to the west, Canterbury behind you and the West Coast opening up in front. In fact all the hard tramping is behind you now and it's 1 km/20 minutes around the lake and across the surprisingly flat pass to the lip of the Arahura River. The old miners' pack-track is easy to follow now as you plunge down past the cascades of the upper Arahura, cross the top forks and sidle up high across screes, before dropping down to the bottom forks; 1.5 km/1 hour and a descent of 350 m.

The pack-track disappears for a while and the route boulder-hops down the west bank 1.5 km/40 minutes to where cairns lead up a rocky stream gully and pick up the pack-track again. An easy 1 km/20 minutes to Harman Hut (6 bunks and a wood stove).

The track down the Arahura is the 1860s highway, which first crosses a pretty gorge over a long footbridge then sidles for 3 km/1 hour past tussock slopes then thick alpine shrub forest to the junction with the Styx track.

For access and route information down the Styx River see the Arahura Valley, page 212. Allow one day's tramping to the road-end (18 km/8–9 hours).

Arahura Valley

Total tramping time: 17–20 hours/2–3 days
Total tramping distance: 41 km
Grade: medium
Highest point: 770 m; Styx Saddle
Maps: Otira K33; Kaniere J33

The beauty of this tramp is that it generally follows easy pack-tracks most of the way, and stays below the bushline, so it is suitable for newer trampers. However, it takes longer than you might think, parts of the pack-track have slipped away, and the track-marking is a little unclear in places. It would be a long weekend tramp and is best suited to three days. Excellent forest, three huts and some good campsites.

From Hokitika follow the road towards Lake Kaniere about 19 km, and turn off down the Milltown Road some 11 km to the Arahura River bridge. You will probably have to organise a car at the Styx road-end, which is only 10 km from the Milltown junction past Lake Kaniere.

A good vehicle track starts the way up the east bank of the Arahura, then deteriorates, dips down to the river, climbs up and follows a boggy terrace to a signposted track leading to the footbridge (4 km/1–2 hours).

Once across The Cesspool gorge the track turns the corner, crossing various side-streams, and heads upvalley 4 km/1–2 hours to where it drops into the river by a large bouldery flat. This stretch has some good pack-track sections, and is generally well-marked, but it keeps you sharp.

The boulder flat has some obvious green-hued stones that belong exclusively to the Maori owners of the Arahura riverbed. After the flat 1 km/20 minutes the next part can be a mite confusing as there are still remnants of a pack-track up on the bank. Stick close to the river and boulder-hop round the corner to regain the obvious main pack-track again (500 m/15 minutes).

Only another 500 m/15 minutes to the Lower Arahura Hut (6 bunks, open fire) which sits on a tus-sock terrace quite high above the river. Good lunch spot.

The track upvalley passes the lower foot-bridge and unexpect-edly heads up a rocky streambed 150 m to regain the washed out pack-track after 1 km/1 hour. At last

Styx–Arahura junction

the travel is clean and the pack-track ambles some 5 km/1–2 hours upvalley, crossing some slippery side-streams (one of which must be spring-fed) around to the head of Third Gorge Creek.

Here the pack-track has been washed out, so the route drops down into the creek for 20 m, then climbs back up steeply to the other side (100 m/10 minutes). (The route down Third Gorge Creek carries on over Newton Saddle into the Taipo Valley.)

The main pack-track continues smartly for 2 km/40 minutes before a marked track leaves the old pack-track and scrambles down 200 m onto grass flats beside the Arahura River (500 m/15 min-utes). Mudflats Hut (6 bunks, wood stove) is across the bridge, past the old ruined hut and up a last steep climb (200 m/10 minutes). Good views from the well-placed hut.

For the route upvalley go back across the bridge, then follow south pretty close beside the west bank of the Arahura through the lanky tussocks to where track markers re-emerge on trees again. This section is poorly marked (500 m/15 minutes). The track dodges alongside the river, then clambers up a streambed and back to the main pack-track (1 km/40 minutes).

A rollicking pace can be set for 3.5 km/1 hour round to the Styx Saddle junction (just past an old hut site, a good possible campsite). For route information to Harman Hut and Browning Pass see Three Pass Trip, page 209, otherwise cross the obscure open tussocky and swampy clearing of the Styx Saddle for 1 km/30 minutes to the bush edge.

From here a much better track is marked down the attractive upper valley of the Styx River, crossing several side-streams before emerging onto the big grass flats at the head of the Styx (2 km/1–2 hours), and an easy 300-m descent. The track crosses the Styx River and goes to the roomy 6-bunk Grassy Flats Hut (500 m/15 minutes).

The main Styx track heads downriver from the hut across the flats for 1 km/20 minutes and fords to the pack-track on the other side, and from here on it stays on the north bank. It's 3 km/1–2 hours to the signposted Mid Styx Hut junction, then a further 4 km/1–2 hours to where the farmland starts. This is pleasant, relaxed travel, and the old pack-track is in generally good condition, with only one or two slips to mar progress.

Another 2 km/40 minutes down to Mount Brown Creek and track junction, then a drop through a cutting onto the farmland proper, around some daunting gravel cliffs, then rather a dreary vehicle track for 2.5 km/1 hour to the Lake Kaniere road. This farm road is notoriously boggy and it's doubtful you will be able to get your car far from the public road.

Cedar Flats

Total tramping time: 8–10 hours/2 days
Total tramping distance: 17 km
Grade: easy/medium
Highest point: 440 m; Cedar Flats
Maps: Kaniere J33

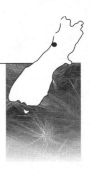

A short, easy tramp to a lush upper valley that boasts a good hut, a neat gorge and hot pools. What more could you ask? Plenty of potential side-trips so although you can tramp to Cedar Flats as a weekend trip you can easily spin it out to a three- or even four-day sojourn.

From Hokitika drive inland to Kokatahi 14 km, then 11 km to a road junction, where you should turn south over the Kokatahi River bridge about 3 km to the road-end beside the Toaroha River.

The first part of the track is a bit messy, and follows an old tramway for 2.5 km/1 hour through cut-over bush alongside the Toaroha River. Because the river has cut into the bank the track climbs very high above bluffs before dropping back down to the river again. Then the route boulder-hops along the riverside for 1.5 km/1 hour past two side-creeks to Macmillan Creek.

Here a well-marked and graded pack-track starts to climb steadily for 2 km/1–2 hours up to a sort of saddle on a spur. This is some of the most luxuriant vegetation in the world, and the slow 350-m ascent gives you time to appreciate it.

After this first haul it's a relief when the pack-track flattens out considerably for the next 2 km/1 hour to Cedar Flats. The pack-track was built to avoid the Toaroha Gorge and to provide easy passage for early tourist excursions to the hot pools, which by now you might have caught a whiff of.

Cedar Flats is a large grassy flat, and a footbridge takes you across to the 6-bunk hut on the west bank. However, the hot pools are actually on the east bank, another 500 m/15 minutes along the Toaroha track and up Wren Creek a short distance. You might need the hut shovel to dig them out, but they are pretty well guaranteed to be hot if it hasn't rained for a couple of days.

Spur overlooking Cedar Flats

Several side-tracks go up from Cedar Flats to Squall Peak (3 km/3 hours one way), Adventure Ridge bivouac (3 km/2–3 hours one way), and Yeats Ridge Hut (3 km/2–3 hours one way). Plus there is the main Toaroha Valley track and the pretty little gorge just up from Wren Creek, which often has a pair of blue ducks dabbling about.

Frew Saddle Circuit

Total tramping time: 4–6 days
Total tramping distance: 48 km
Grade: medium/fit
Highest point: 1308 m; Frew Saddle
Maps: Kaniere J33; Whitcombe J34

A landscape of gorges, broken tops and luxuriant rain forest, coloured by a history almost as rich as the plant life. Nine huts and bivouacs connected by a well-marked system of tracks. Many of the side-creeks can flood rapidly and dangerously, so be prepared to take some extra food and allow a spare day for poor weather. Some of the highest rainfall in New Zealand has been recorded in the catchment of the Whitcombe River. DOC Hokitika can help with up-to-date track information.

Drive 40 km east of Hokitika through the locality of Kowhitirangi to the road head by the Hokitika River. There is no public transport, although a minibus can be hired from Hokitika.

Where the metal road peters out, follow the rough vehicle track for 3 km/1 hour to the run-down hut and cableway by the Hokitika River. Ignore this cableway, drop down to the river and boulder-hop 500 m/40 minutes to the start of a bush track. Follow for 2.5 km/1 hour along easy bush terraces to the second cableway. Once across the swaying cage it is only 500 m/15 minutes to Rapid Creek Hut (4 bunks).

From the hut, boulder-hop along the riverside to Rapid Creek; 500 m/15 minutes. This creek floods easily causing delays, which is why it is better to do the tramp from this road-end. Frews Hut logbook is full of entries about hungry trampers watching the interminable rain.

After Rapid Creek pick up a track across the flats for 1 km/30 minutes, then follow the slow bush-tangled track beside the Collier Gorge till it swings across a spectacular bridge where the (now) Whitcombe squeezes through a narrow gap in the rock; 3 km/1–2 hours. Tramp a further 2 km/1 hour close beside the river, boulder-hopping apart from a short section of track to Frew Hut (6 bunks).

Lunch on a huge rock, Whitcombe River

From Frew Hut climb inland steadily up a track that follows Frew Creek for 2 km/1 hour then there's a climb of 250 m to Saddle Creek and the first of three 2-wire bridges. These are testing affairs, but you generally have no choice, as the scramble in and out of the creek hardly looks more palatable.

Another 500 m/20 minutes and 200-m climb to the second 2-wire bridge, then 1 km/1 hour to the third. There's a campsite by the top bridge, almost the only good one on the climb to the saddle. The track continues by following the upper creek a short way, then snowpoles lead through the tussock to the 'dog kennel' biv (2-person); 2.5 km/1 hour. It's 200 m/10 minutes short of the saddle itself, a total climb from Frew Hut of 850 m.

From Frew Saddle (1308 m) the well-poled route drops 200 m steeply down a slippery tussock face to the upper Hokitika Valley (500 m/20 minutes).

The route follows the easy river and occasional marker poles downstream over tussock banks for 3.5 km/1–2 hours until it picks up a good track on the west bank. This sidles through alpine scrub, avoiding a gorge which plunges the Hokitika 450 m down to the Mungo River.

It's approximately 2 km/1 hour to Bluff Hut (4 bunks), magnificently sited on rock outcrops by the forest margin. You can see Toaroha Saddle through the window, and if you walk above the hut you can see the full sweep of the Hokitika Valley curving to the coast.

Watch out for crevasses in the rock. Good sunsets here.

Below the hut a track drops dramatically to the valley floor. It's 500 m down a continuously steep spur, via two ladders when the angle gets too extreme. Fortunately there are plenty of trees to hang on to (1 km/1–2 hours). A footbridge has been slung across large boulders over the Hokitika, and the track heads upstream and follows a slow bank track for 2.5 km/1 hour to the old-style Poet Hut. Cosy 4 bunks and fireplace.

The trail continues for 500 m/30 minutes past the Poet footbridge and across Beta Creek, to the foot of a narrow spur. It's a vigorous 500-m climb to the scrub edge, where poles lead over tussock to the tarn, saddle and splendidly exposed 2-person upright bivouac (1.5 km/2 hours). Good camping and superb views.

The track down to Top Toaroha Hut is well marked but complicated. From the biv follow poles down into a creek, then boulder-hop downstream for 15 minutes or so until marker poles (don't miss these!) lead the trail steeply out of the creek and onto a tussock shoulder, then drop into another creek. The route follows this creek for a short time, then side-steps into another branch of the same creek and travels down this until a good track cut through the scrub takes you down to the wide snowgrass basin at the head of the Toaroha, all told 2 km/1–2 hours.

The 6-bunk hut is comfortable and there are some reasonable campsites by the lake. The main track swings west around the lake and sidles through scrubby terraces a while before closing to and boulder-hopping along the Toaroha River to the crossing point (1 km/30 minutes). Crossing is okay at average flow, but after rain can prove a real problem.

The east-bank track down to Cedar Flats is slow up-and-down work, and poorly marked as it edges past slips and side-creeks beside the plunging Toaroha; 3 km/2 hours to opposite Mullins Creek. Then another 2 km/1 hour to the Yeates Track junction.

Across Esma Creek is another junction, where a side-track goes off up to Adventure Ridge. Dip over Median Creek and swing left, then cross a footbridge over a smooth-walled gorge to Cedar Flats and the 6-person hut (1 km/30 minutes). Hot pools up Wren Creek.

For access and route information down the Toaroha Valley see Cedar Flats, page 215. Allow half a day's tramping (8 km/3–4 hours).

Whitcombe Pass

Total tramping time: 5–7 days
Total tramping distance: 63 km
Grade: medium/fit
Highest point: 1239 m; Whitcombe Pass
Maps: Rakaia J35; Whitcombe J34
  (optional Kaniere J33)

One of the big east-west crossings, not especially difficult as there are well-marked tracks and plenty of
huts, but the transport hassles and river crossings
often put people off. Snowmelt and high rivers can
be a problem in spring and early summer. Big moun-
tains, big rivers and big on solitude. It would be a surprise if you met
anybody, so you have to be well-organised and self-contained. If the
side-creeks come up you could be stuck for a while. Although the
tracks are generally well-marked, slips can make them rough in
places, and it's by no means a fast track.

For access and route information to Louper Bivouac see Rakaia
River, page 239. Allow one long day's tramping for the 23 km/7–8
hours from the Glenfalloch Station road-head.

From Louper Biv it's 1 km/10 minutes on gravel flats to where
Louper Stream comes out inconspicuously, then 5.5 km/2–3 hours
up this gentle valley on tussock and scree to the low-lying
Whitcombe Pass. It seems strange to have such a low pass (1239 m)
among such towering peaks, which go up to 2400 m on either side.

Travel 3.5 km/1–2 hours down the other side, crossing the river as
it suits, eventually picking up the track on the east bank. Another 2
km/1 hour down to Neave Hut (6 bunks), situated in an open, sunny
site beside the Whitcombe River, with the Katzenbach Ridge rearing
up over it.

A well-marked track stays on the east bank and tumbles through
bush (past Cave Camp rock bivvy, comfortable for 3–4 people)
down to the footbridge across to Wilkinson Hut (6 bunks); 3
km/1–2 hours. The main track stays on the east bank and sidles
some 5 km/2–3 hours in a messy bit of travel, with slips and wash-
outs down to Prices Hut. Think of poor Whitcombe and Lauper

struggling down here in 1863 without a track.

Prices Hut has 6 bunks and sits on a terrace overlooking the much older Prices Flat Hut, an original slab-built and hand-adzed hut dating from the 1930s.

From here it's 6 km/1–2 hours on another messy bit of track down to the Vincent Creek foot-bridge, then 1 km/20 minutes on to the Cropp bridge, then 2.5 km/1 hour around to Frews Hut (6 bunks).

For access and route information down the Whitcombe

Whitcombe from the Rakaia

River to the Hokitika road-head see Frew Saddle Circuit, page 217; 13 km/6–7 hours.

Welcome Flat Hot Pools

Total tramping time: 12–15 hours/2–3 days
Total tramping distance: 30 km
Grade: easy/medium
Highest point: 180 m; Shiels Creek
Maps: Mt Cook & Westland National Parks 180;
  Mount Cook H36

This is a moderately easy trip to the steamy hot pools at Welcome Flat. It also forms part of the Copland Track, the classic route between Mt Cook National Park and the West Coast. It's a well-marked and graded track with flood-bridges over most side-streams, however it takes longer than most people realise. Hut and rock bivouac.

From Fox Glacier township travel 25 km down to the Karangarua River bridge where there's a large signpost indicating Copland Valley. Shelter here. Regular bus services between Fox Glacier and Wanaka over the Haast Pass.

It's 200 m down the road to a carpark and intentions book. A memorial stands to Charlie Douglas and his persistent and courageous explorations up many West Coast valleys. He first discovered the hot pools at Welcome Flat in the 1890s. There is plenty of camping space at the road-end and loads of firewood, but the mosquitoes are fierce. There's only scratchy camping from here to Welcome Flat.

Cross Rough Creek directly to the marker pole. There's a flood-bridge 30 minutes upstream, but if you have to use it you should consider whether to continue at all. The track sidles through bush a little way till it breaks out onto a river flat, where marker poles lead across to the bush again (2.5 km/1 hour).

Staying in dense forest now, the easy-graded track goes through tall rimu and totara for 2 km/1 hour to a viewpoint side-track. This looks up the vast valley of the Karangarua River.

The track turns into the Copland Valley itself and drops to the river, travelling underneath sheer fern-clad river terraces for 1 km/30 minutes. Here you boulder-hop along the rocks by the deep-blue Copland River for about 1 km/30 minutes until a prominent marker

Weka after food, Douglas Rock hut

leads the track back into the forest again.

Beyond an unnamed creek (flood-bridge) the track sidles gently for 2 km/40 minutes to McPhee Creek and another flood-bridge. It's a further 1 km/30 minutes to Architect Creek, the rough halfway point of the trip. This is a big river with a long footbridge slung across it. After ambling along for a few minutes on the other side you reach a pleasant grassy area with a rivulet, a nice lunch halt.

From Architect Creek the track climbs very gradually as the river narrows. It's 2 km/1 hour to Palaver Creek (flood-bridge), and from here you should catch a glimpse of The Punchbowl falls on the opposite bank, and higher up, silver threads of waterfalls cutting down the tall bluffs.

A short 1 km/20 minutes to Open Creek (flood-bridge), after which the ascent becomes more noticeable. From the flood-bridge it's a climb of 1.5 km/1 hour to Shiels Creek, an open gash of rock with a footbridge spanning it. After a short zig-zag you reach the highest point of the track, which then leisurely descends through ribbonwood, mountain holly and fern forest for about 1 km/30 minutes to the hot pools at Welcome Flat.

These pools are in a bush-surrounded open space facing the bluffs underneath Mt Glorious, and wisps of steam hang over the green-gold algal flats. The pools are dug out, with channels between them, and the temperature of the pits varies. The thick sediment of mud on the bottom is not as unpleasant to sit in as it sounds. Take some sandfly repellent, ahhh …

Welcome Flat Hut lies about 150 m further upstream. It has space for about 30 people, and it is advisable to bring your own portable cooker. There is an excellent rock bivouac tucked behind the pools via a short track, and there are campsites on the old airstrip between the hut and the river, or upstream 10 minutes off the flats across the footbridge. Mozzies can be bad if you are camping.

There are excellent mountain views, particularly from Welcome Flat itself, of Sefton (3151 m), Footstool (2764 m) up the Copland Valley, and evil-looking side-peaks like Fang (2081 m) at the head of the Darkwater Stream.

The track continues upstream to Douglas Rock Hut, a worthwhile day trip although the going is rougher and steeper, and most of the side-creeks are unbridged (including Scott's). It's about 8 km/2–3 hours one way. From Douglas Hut it is only 15 minutes until you are out onto the alpine tops with good views to the head of the Copland Valley.

The Paringa Cattle Track

Total tramping time: 9–12 hours/2–3 days
Total tramping distance: 35 km
Grade: easy/medium to Maori Saddle;
  medium/fit to Waita River
Highest point: 650 m; Chasm Creek
Maps: Haast F37; Landsborough G37

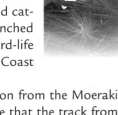

This track follows the historic Paringa–Haast Cattle Track, used by the early goldminers, settlers and cattlemen until as late as 1959–60. A carefully benched track with three huts. Dense bush and rich bird-life complete this route through a slice of West Coast history.

(Note: although the track is in good condition from the Moeraki end to Maori Saddle the latest reports indicate that the track from Maori Saddle down to Coppermine is in poor condition, overgrown, with some slips. Only experienced trampers should attempt the full crossing.)

The northern end of the track starts on Highway 6, 75 km south of Fox Glacier township. Haast is 48 km south of the track. Regular bus services run between Fox Glacier and Haast. All services, petrol, food, accommodation etc. at both Fox and Haast.

At the Moeraki track end a big sign by the main road marks the start, though you could easily miss it. The track ambles off from here for 3.5 km/1 hour across side-streams and closes to the Moeraki River.

Just before the Moeraki or 'Blue' River you pass a track junction leading up the Moeraki Valley and continue on to the footbridge spanning the Moeraki. A few minutes upstream to another junction, and Blowfly Flat Hut is only 200 m further. It has 8 bunks and a large gear porch.

From Blowfly junction the track starts its slow perambulations up to Maori Saddle, some 10–11 km/3–4 hours when all the kinks are included.

The forest is rich in rimu, with thick silver beech and fuchsia further up, entwined with ferns and the tramper-snaring bush lawyer.

The bird life is equally profuse. Kereru (wood pigeons) erupt over-head with a frantic wing-beating; tomtits, fantails, bellbirds and the distinctive creaky-door cry of the kaka add sound to a rarely silent forest. Occasionally, old totara posts on the trackside indicate the telegraph line (there are even some insulators remaining). Also evi-dent are the flat stones in the creeks laid to make the passage of the cattle easier.

After 1 hour you reach a campsite perched on the narrow Whakapohai Saddle, and a little while later there's a side-track (which may be signposted) to the mica mine, some 400 m up above the bushline on the Mataketake Range. The main track climbs steadily and meanders on past several side-creeks (Thompson, Stormy, and finally the Whakapohai itself), then descends a little to the spacious hut at Maori Saddle.

This hut stands in a cleared beech glade. It has 12 bunks in 3-tier fashion, a large wood lobby and a wood stove. A short side-track goes up 100 m to the private little bush pond of Lake Law.

A better side-trip is to bash up through the open forest onto the tops of the Mataketake Range some 500 m to the gleaming Lake Dime. There's no marked route though a bush bash should bring you to the tussock in about 1 hour. From here you have views over miles of tussock ranges, deep clad valleys and the whole curve of surf-edged coast from Paringa to Jackson Bay, and Mt Cook in the distance. Allow 3–4 hours for this return side-trip.

From Maori Saddle the overgrown cattle track climbs a little and slips neatly through two pretty waterfalls at Chasm Creek. It then loses height steadily past Sundown and Summit Creeks. A washout forces an annoying diversion at 21 Mile Creek, then the track resumes, zig-zagging sharply down to the open grass slopes and scree cliffs at Robinson Creek (7 km/2 hours).

A slip here forces a 50-m descent to forks, then you have to scout around for markers climbing some 30 m back onto the old track line. This section is getting messy, with thick toetoe on the roadline mak-ing it slow going at times.

Still descending, the overgrown track continues past more side-streams for some 5 km/2 hours until it strikes a four-wheel-drive road. It's a good walk 2 km/40 minutes down the road to open farmland at Coppermine Creek. The first two huts are private (beside

Morning mist near Paringa Cattle Track

each other), but the third is across Coppermine Creek 1 km/20 minutes further and is a pleasant DOC hut (6 bunks).

Cattle were taken in mobs of about 200 from the South Westland river valleys like the Arawhata and Cascade, mustered along the beach to the Waita River, and brought to graze near Coppermine Creek Hut. In the predawn they were broken into smaller mobs to stop them bunching on narrow parts of the track, and pushed over the saddle to be corralled at the Moeraki River, near Blowfly Hut.

The next day involved getting them across the river and onto the road-head at Paringa. At the turn of the century, before the road had got that far south, it took two weeks to take the cattle from the Cascade Valley to the Whataroa yards. The last mob was driven through in 1961, and then cattle were trucked out over the newly completed Haast Pass road. In 1965 the main highway down the coast was finally put through.

DOC has marked the next 4 km/1 hour route across the scrubby farmland from Coppermine Creek Hut to the Waita River, but the trail is getting vague. From a junction just before Coppermine Creek Hut follow markers down the flat and across the creek into a stand of young kahikatea. Old markers (permolat/venetian blind type) lead you to a four-wheel-drive road down the west bank of Coppermine Creek and across the Waita River, about 100 m below the Coppermine Creek and Waita confluence.

Keep to the Waita River downstream, crossing over easy cattle flats and the shingly river where appropriate, some 4 km/1 hour to the main highway. Should be easy going but there might be some deep fords. The last ford can be thigh-deep across to a short four-wheel-drive road on the west bank which leads the last 100 m to the main highway. You may have to bush-bash on the north-east side to get to the highway if the river is up, though pray you don't have to because it's horrible work.

The Coast (Barn Bay to Martins Bay)

Total tramping time: 4–5 days (Cascade River to Martins Bay);
  7–9 days (Hollyford road-end)
Total tramping distance: 70 km (to Martins Bay);
  126 km (Hollyford road-end)
Grade: medium
Highest point: 100 m; Sandrock Bluff
Maps: Cascade E38; Lake McKerrow D38, D39

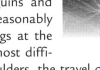

A wild, wilderness stretch of coast, some 50 km of rugged headlands, deserted beaches and spray-soaked shoreline. Fiordland crested penguins and seals can often be seen. The route is reasonably straightforward, with the big river crossings at the Cascade and Gorge Rivers providing the most difficulty. Since about half this route is on boulders, the travel can get ankle-wrenching at times. Three huts.

From the Arawhata river bridge a shingle road goes up the Jackson River, over the Martyr Saddle and down to the Cascade River flats to finish beside the homestead. Some 20 km. Access to Martins Bay is by walking along the Hollyford Track (see page 280) or by arranging a pick-up by plane or jetboat through the Hollyford Guided Walk company.

From the road-end follow the four-wheel-drive track 4 km/1 hour to the crossing point. Probably the most difficult part of this tramp is getting across the Cascade River; it's wide and deep, and clearly after rain it would be impossible.

From here the route follows the line of an old bulldozed track, which is still employed as a just useable but rugged four-wheel-drive 'road', some 14 km/3–4 hours to the private hut. Parts of the track get horribly muddy, and the route isn't always clear. Buoys and other markers help to indicate the route. From the private hut the route drops into the riverbed (occasional crossings as needed) for 1.5 km/30 minutes to Barn Bay, and a private house and airstrip just inland.

From the attractive high curved beach at Barn Bay, cross the Hope River (you may have to bush-bash across the tongue here) and

An evening stroll

follow the coastline south. It's not all pleasant seaside sauntering, and in places the boulders are hard work, as the noted explorer Charlie Douglas commented:

'... it can't be called good walking by any means, the beaches are steep slopes of boulders about the size of sixty-four pound shot and move down in an aggravating way when walking ... The boulders are interesting for their variety and hardness, Olivine Jasper, granite, serpentine & porphyry are all to be found, and they would have been splendid ammunition for an ancient catapult ...'

This describes the travel exactly. It's 7 km/2 hours slowly down to Sandrock Bluff, where an old bulldozed trail (becoming overgrown and harder to find) climbs 100 m over the bluff and down to Callery Creek. From here to the Gorge River the travel is quite good, particularly at low tide. Another 2 km/40 minutes down to Spoon River and some possible campsites, then 3.5 km/1 hour round to Cutter Rocks, and 4 km/1 hour to the Gorge River. There's a useful bivvy rock about 1 km before the Gorge River, near The Steeples, which can house 4–6 people.

At high or mid-tide the Gorge River is deep and can be difficult to cross, a swim in fact. Usually there's a gravel bar near the bluff that enables a thigh-deep wade across a deep pool, but if the river is up you may have to head a considerable way upstream for a while, or alternatively catch the eye of the Long family who live in a private hut on the south bank, and they might row you across. There's a cosy 6-bunk DOC hut just south of the Long house and beside the airstrip.

The 4 km/1–2 hours to Longridge Point are a boulder slog, then travel perks up with a brisk 8-km/2-hour trot down to the Hackett River, and some good campsites just up the Hackett on the east bank. Any bluffs that are marginal to get around will usually have a rough route marked over them, often with buoys.

Around Awarua Point to Big Bay is all slow going. Big, slippery boulders for 14 km/3–4 hours, and the beach at Big Bay is a joy to reach. Two large bulldozers were driven from Barn Bay to Big Bay in about 1973–74, trundling steel sledges with accommodation huts and fuel behind them. They took about five months to get to the Pyke River, and the displaced lines of boulders can still be seen in many places on the coast.

The DOC hut is 1 km/15 minutes along the beach, tucked amongst the sand dunes. Some good campsites here, and quite a few whitebaiters' baches. This place booms when the whitebait season gets going, approximately September–November. It's also a record den for sandflies — you have been warned.

More than 5 km/1–2 hours down Big Bay beach sands (an airstrip at low tide) to the rocky coast again. Initially you can follow an old bulldozed line in the scrub for a while till it reaches a private bach, then it's back to boulders — 9 km/2–3 hours along tidal rocks to the penguin colony at Longridge Point. This stretch is best done at low tide. Around the point it's 1 km/20 minutes along the track to a 16-person hut with a wood stove.

For access and route description down the Hollyford River to Hollyford road-end see Hollyford Track, page 280. Allow at least three days' tramp to reach the Hollyford road-end, still some 56 km away.

Jollie Brook

Total tramping time: 10–12 hours/2–3 days
Total tramping distance: 26 km
Grade: easy/medium
Highest point: 750 m; Gabriel Stream Saddle
Maps: Lake Sumner Forest Park 274-16;
  Boyle M32; Waikari M33

An unfrequented corner of Lake Sumner Forest Park with well-marked tracks and two huts. Lots of river crossing involved, so it's a summer and fine weather tramp. Features of this circuit tramp are the broad river terraces of the Hurunui, the delicate beech forest of Gabriel Stream, and the open river travel of the Jollie Brook.

From Highway 2 turn off at Waikari and drive 8 km to Hawarden then about 26 km on the signposted Lake Sumner road over Jack's Pass to the Sisters footbridge carpark. This twisty road closely follows the Hurunui River, with several fords of side-creeks.

From the beech-shaded carpark a marked trail drops down to the Hurunui River and the Sisters footbridge. The poled track turns upstream through matagouri clumps for about 1 km/30 minutes, then it noses into a scrub gully and tops out 30 m onto a terrace to avoid a river bluff. Back down to the river the track ventures onto a series of broad terraces. Alpine spaniard, snowberries and gentians suggest that these low-lying river flats must get extraordinarily cold in winter.

Poles follow close to the hillside and after 6 km/2 hours (with glimpses of Lake Sumner) the trail enters a manuka/kanuka forest and quickly reaches old Gabriel Hut. Sited in a modest clearing, well populated with bellbirds, the hut has 4 sacking bunks, open fire, and a slightly run-down appearance, which can be improved with a fierce manuka fire in the grate.

It is well worth crossing Gabriel Stream and following the side-track 1 km/20 minutes to have a look at Lake Sumner. It was once called the Greenstone Lake but its usual colour is a blue-grey, with plenty of whitecaps on a blustery day.

From Gabriel Hut a sign indicates the gently graded track through mountain beech up beside Gabriel Stream. It's a 200-m climb in all (3 km/1 hour) to the peaceful saddle, and 1 km/20 minutes downhill to meet the Jollie Brook River (100 m descent).

The track turns downstream on beech terraces, and crosses the Jollie Brook to the hut, situated on a generous river flat edged by bush (1 km/20 minutes). The hut has a pleasing, roomy design, and despite its size has only 7 bunks; wood stove.

The last lap of the tramp stays with the Jollie Brook. Because of the numerous river crossings and this river's tendency to flood and discolour quickly, some care should be exercised. The first 1 km/30 minutes hops back and forth on a good track either side of the river, then the valley swells out and the route is a random 4 km/1–2 hours through shingle and grass flats to the forks with Cold Stream. At one point a track climbs over a low spur some 30 m to avoid a waterfall in the river.

A further 1 km/20 minutes of wide shingle flats before the river wiggles through a short, easily forded gorge to The Forks. The next 5 km/1–2 hours involve some river crossing with occasional vague tracks on either bank interrupted by short well-marked sections through the beech forest.

At last the beech trees are left behind and the trail enters the Hurunui valley. You should resist the temptation to ford the Hurunui as it is always a big river, never much rising or falling because of its even flow from Lake Sumner.

A good track leads up the east bank of the Hurunui to the Sisters swingbridge (3 km/1 hour), or alternatively a track enlarged by cattle follows down beside the Hurunui for 1 km/20 minutes to the Jollie Brook bridge, with a 4 km/1 hour road-bash back to the Sisters carpark.

Wharfedale Track and Black Hill

Total tramping time: 7–9 hours/2 days
  (including Black Hill 8–11 hours)
Total tramping distance: 25 km
Grade: easy/medium
Highest point: 1335 m; Black Hill
Maps: Puketerakai L34

The Wharfedale Track follows the sinuous route of an old road put through in the 1880s to the Lees Valley, and makes for a lazy weekend tramp. However, if you include Black Hill Hut in the weekend, you get some leg stretching and splendid views of the Waimakariri back country. Three huts.

The township of Oxford is 45 km from Christchurch on Highway 72. From the town travel west 3 km on the main highway and turn into Woodstock Road. After another 10 km turn into Perhams Road and continue past two fords to View Hill carpark (6 km). The other end of the Wharfedale is reached from Oxford by taking the Ashley Gorge road 6 km then turning into the Lees Valley Road. This is a twisting scenic road through the upper Ashley River gorge. After about 20 km, and 1.5 km past the Lees Valley bridge, is a signposted four-wheel-drive road, close by the Mt Pember Station.

View Hill carpark sits on a tiny saddle between farmland and forest at about 600 m, and the trail heads gently uphill 1 km/20 minutes to meet the Coopers Creek side-track. The 'road' becomes a track and after two more quick junctions (the first to Ryde Falls, the second to Mt Oxford) settles into an easy, meandering rhythm.

The forest is a rather lovely and unexpected mixture of beech interspersed with the occasional rimu, matai and totara. After passing a number of inconsequential side-streams, the Wharfedale arrives at a first bush saddle (9 km/2–3 hours).

The descent to the second bush saddle is 1.5 km/30 minutes; here is the side-track to Black Hill, but the main track follows beside the Dobson Stream for 3 km/1 hour to Wharfedale Hut (8 people). Down by the stream itself there is an old fireplace and some excellent campsites.

A good track carries on down 2 km/40 minutes to Townshend Hut (8 bunks), but if you do not mind wet feet you can take the old track instead, which criss-crosses the river through clearings of grass flats among the beech. Several camping spots.

From Townshend Hut a four-wheel-drive track travels 9 km/2–3 hours out to the Lees Valley Road. It crosses the river at two points, which in normal flow will be easy, but if it's in flood an emergency flood-track is marked.

Cup of tea

Black Hill

From the Wharfedale Track at the bush saddle follow the up-and-down track through open beech forest as it climbs for 5.5 km/2–3 hours along a ridge, past the track down to Townshend Hut and on to Black Hill Hut (6 bunks). A total climb of 600 m.

It's worth going above the hut the 1 km/20 minutes to Black Hill itself (1335 m), which looks out over the remote backblock country of the Waimakariri gorge. On the return take the alternative track down to Townshend Hut (5 km/1–2 hours).

Cass Saddle and Lagoon Saddle

Total tramping time: 13–16 hours/2–3 days
Total tramping distance: 33 km
Grade: medium
Highest point: 1360 m; Mt Bruce sidle
Maps: Wilberforce K34

This well-developed track comprises two passes over 1200 m and three bush-clad valleys. Quiet, attractive rivers with grass flats and sharp-sided gorges. An abundance of six huts. It is a fairly long weekend tramp, and the less fit might consider an easier three-day option.

The track starts 500 m short of the Cass River bridge on State Highway 73, 40 km north of Springfield. The other track exit is at Cora Lynn some 11 km on towards Arthur's Pass. Most people park a car at the other end as well, or secrete a mountain bike in the trees. There's a daily bus service along the highway between Greymouth and Christchurch.

Cross the stile and follow poles over the farmland to Cass River. Head upstream over the broad gravel flats for about 6.5 km/2 hours to where the river narrows and winds past rock pools to the McLeod Stream junction. The signposted bush track starts on the south bank of the Cass River.

The trail climbs sharply through beech forest until it's about 100 m above the river, then sidles 2 km/1 hour steadily uphill another 200 m, crossing two open creekbeds, and returns to the river at a log bridge by a grass clearing, a pleasant snack spot. The track continues uphill, climbing 100 m over 1 km/1 hour, through mountain beech and glades to a cosy 3-bunk hut.

Just on from the hut is the open tussock, and a poled route leads 1.5 km/1 hour to Cass Saddle (1326 m), a climb of 200 m. From here there are views to Hamilton Hut and of the broken-topped Craigieburn Range.

After a short sidle from the pass to the bush, the track falls 300 m down a narrow-edged spur into the Hamilton Valley (1.5 km/1 hour). Then a more gradual descent past several pretty side-creeks

Flurry of snow, Lagoon Saddle

(and some devastated bush from a large slip) to the lower river flats (3 km/1 hour). A short walk of 500 m/15 minutes to Hamilton Hut, easily seen on a river terrace.

Spaciously designed, this hut has 20 bunks, a wood stove and a sunny verandah. Located midway along the Cass-Lagoon Track, it is the obvious place for a night's stopover if you're doing the trip in a weekend.

Downstream from the hut it's 500 m/15 minutes to the Harper-Hamilton forks. Although there is an emergency 3-wire bridge, you will find it easier to ford the Hamilton Creek. The track cuts the confluence corner to a footbridge across the Harper River (700 m/15 minutes), and from here winds upstream, occasionally sidling, for 4 km/1-2 hours to the old West Harper Hut (6 bunks) standing in a peaceful clearing. Good campsites on the way to the hut.

Above the hut 700 m/15 minutes the river passes through a short steep-faced gorge. This is an easy and pretty alternative to the track, which clambers up and down 100 m to avoid the gorge (1 km/50 minutes). From here the Harper widens into a gravel flat where

Doubtful Creek, Mangos Creek and Long Creek enter it (1 km/30 minutes).

Where the gravel narrows a sign indicates a flood-track on the east bank. It's a short walk past the Long Creek forks, where signs and cairns lead up the Harper River. Criss-crossing at first the track gradually climbs above the gorgelike river for 3.5 km/1–2 hours to an A-frame bivouac sitting nicely in a tussock clearing. The bivouac holds a wood stove and a bunk. There's also the old 3-bunk hut awkwardly placed on the opposite bank of the river.

The track avoids Lagoon Saddle and climbs gently past the bush edge onto a snowgrass bench (1 km/30 minutes). From here you overlook the large tarn on the saddle. Mt Bruce is worth a quick ascent, for though it's a small peak (1630 m), it has a great view of the jumbled mountain terrain of Arthur's Pass.

Following snowpoles, the route sidles for 2 km/1 hour along a tussock bench with some boardwalks, then it drops 200 m back to the bush edge through lines of pine trees. Once in the beech again, the track broadens and steadily drops in zig-zags 400 m to Bealey Hut (6 bunks); 2 km/1 hour.

A four-wheel-drive road goes down past the Wilderness Lodge and Cora Lynn station to the carpark, where a short gravel road leads out onto Highway 73.

Rakaia River

Total tramping time: 20–22 hours/3–5 days
Total tramping distance: 52 km (Lyell Hut return)
Grade: easy/medium
Highest point: 1276 m; Meins Knob
Maps: Arrowsmith J35

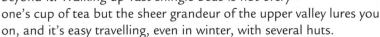

This huge valley penetrates deep into the Southern Alps, and at its head are clusters of 2000-m peaks, with their associated icefalls, glaciers and terminal lakes. Samuel Butler walked up this valley in the 1860s and set his book *Erewhon* in the remote passes beyond it. Walking up vast shingle beds is not everyone's cup of tea but the sheer grandeur of the upper valley lures you on, and it's easy travelling, even in winter, with several huts.

The turnoff for the upper Rakaia Valley is 3 km south of the river bridge along Highway 72. It's approximately 45 km along this metalled road to its end, about 2 km past Glenfalloch Station. Ring Glenfalloch beforehand for access permission.

Walk along a vehicle track over a low saddle between the Whaleback Hill and the main Palmer Range to the banks of Lake Stream (4 km/1 hour). This stream flows out from Lake Heron at a steady rate and can be difficult to cross after rain, but once over it head upriver diagonally across the gravel flats to the edge of Prospect Hill (3 km/1 hour).

The Rakaia can be a problem to ford in spring, with rivers flushed with snow melt, but later in summer, autumn and winter it should be OK. Keep more to the south bank for 3 km/1 hour until you are opposite Thompson's Hut, which can be seen in a scrub thicket over to the left in Washbourne Creek. This hut is just useable, but there's precious little firewood around it.

Good travel on grass and matagouri flats 3 km/1 hour to Banfield Creek; Banfield Hut is tucked away up on the south bank of Jagged Stream about 500 m/15 minutes away. It's rather run-down; 6 bunks, mountain radio.

The pointed backs of the Arrowsmith Mountains are impressive as you cross Jagged Stream onto Washbourne Flat, and after following

'Celmesia Flat', looking up the Rakaia River

the hillside for 3.5 km/1 hour you should reach the old slab-built 4-bunk Washbourne Hut shaded in bush. Quite a characterful place, with clay stopped into the walls.

If the matagouri is starting to get too thick on Washbourne Flat you may have to follow around the edge from Jagged Stream out onto the river gravels, and pick up the four-wheel-drive track that leads direct to Washbourne Hut.

A vehicle track continues on across the flat for 2 km/30 minutes to the corner at Bull Spur Stream, where it's only another 3 km/1 hour to Reischek's Hut. Tucked behind a small promontory, Reischek's Hut is a comfortable 8-bunk hut managed by the New Zealand Deerstalkers' Association.

The dot opposite Reischek's on the Rakaia's north bank is 2-bunk Louper Bivouac, a misspelling because the Swiss explorer's surname was actually Lauper. He and Henry Whitcombe were the first Europeans to traverse Whitcombe Pass in 1862.

It's 3 km/1 hour of open flats to the foot of Meins Knob from Reischek's Hut; Reischek's Stream can flood easily. You can investigate the edge of the Ramsay Glacier and terminal lake by taking the track around the base of Meins Knob some 1 km/20 minutes to a footbridge across the Lyell River. However, this is not the best way to reach the top hut in the Rakaia, Lyell Hut, because you have to recross the Lyell again, and without the benefit of a bridge this can be rather difficult. It's a deep glacial-fed torrent, with lots of boulders and holes between them.

But a rough track starts at the base of Meins Knob and negotiates a way up through the scrub 300 m or so onto the top (1 km/1 hour). It pays to pick your way carefully as it can save you a great deal of scrub-bashing. There are tarns on top, a great campsite and an excellent view of the valley and Whitcombe Pass.

For Lyell Hut the route is not obvious, but look out for occasional markers. From the tarns drop down approximately north-west, and perhaps slightly to the north through scrub and scree runnels about 300 m to the riverside (500 m/20 minutes). Then bash along the boulders to the track markers which take you immediately to the 6-bunk army-built hut; 1.5 km/1 hour. It can get really cold here.

If you've come this far it's well worth heading up to the Lyell terminal lake and the impressive views of Rangitata Col (2–3 km/1 hour).

Mount Somers Walkway

Total tramping time: 8–10 hours/2–3 days
Total tramping distance: 16 km
Grade: easy/medium
Highest point: 1180 m; saddle
Map: Methven K36

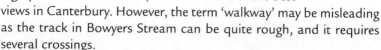

A popular tramp around an old, isolated volcanic dome. Well-marked tracks, unusual rock formations, waterfalls and canyons — the Mt Somers walkway has it all. Two huts, and one of them has a sauna! There is also plenty of opportunity to do side-trips, including up to Mt Somers itself, which has one of the best views in Canterbury. However, the term 'walkway' may be misleading as the track in Bowyers Stream can be quite rough, and it requires several crossings.

Mount Somers township is 100 km from Christchurch; the best access is Highway 1 south to Rakaia, then turn onto Thompsons Track. From Mt Somers township take the Ashburton Gorge Road (to Erewhon) and after about 10 km turn off down a signposted and quite rough gravel side-road 3.5 km to the Coalminers Flat picnic area and campsite. For Sharplin Falls road-end turn right at Mt Somers and follow Highway 72 some 7 km to Staveley, then follow the signs 3 km to Bowyers Stream carpark, shelter and toilets.

From Coalminers Flat follow along the Black Beech Walk for 10 minutes through black and silver beech; the track follows beside Woolshed Creek then picks up the old jig road to the foot of the jig railway incline. Full 4-tonne hoppers of coal would plummet down from the mine, and the empty hoppers would be pulled up by means of a self-acting ropeway. Inevitably a few hoppers ran off the rails and there is a good example of a mangled hopper at the foot of this incline (1 km/30 minutes).

The Miners Track zig-zags up the jig incline for a steep 500-m/30-minute sweat to the bare bleached site of the Blackburn Coal Mine. About a 150-m climb. From the mine site a well-poled track sidles in tussock gullies, along the edge of Woolshed Creek canyon, eventually climbing to Trig R, a splendid viewpoint (1.5 km/1 hour).

Waterfall, top of Woolshed Creek

Looking west to the Southern Alps you can see the 3000-m Mt Arrowsmith massif and the distant headwaters of the Rangitata River. The poled route nimbly descends past a rocky lookout and drops right down to the gouged and twisted canyon at the head of Woolshed Creek. The track easily fords the dainty upper stream and leads directly to the former musterers' hut (1 km/30 minutes). This accommodates 8 people comfortably in the trampers' section, and there is a sauna hut further upvalley.

The headwaters of both Woolshed and Morgan Creeks have a fascinating array of rock outcrops, watercaves, waterfalls and deep crystal pools. A poled track goes from the hut downstream into the Woolshed Creek canyon, zig-zags neatly under and around bluffs, and drops right into the base of the roaring canyon itself, a very worthwhile 10-minute side-trip.

From Woolshed Hut follow the vehicle track over the small saddle to Morgan Stream and as it climbs slowly and surely up to the main saddle at 900 m (4 km/1–2 hours). The route follows the vehicle road until it runs out then a poled track twists in and out of tussock gullies beneath weathered towers of rock, down into the head of

Bowyers Stream some 2 km/1 hour to the 20-bunk Pinnacle Hut. This is an attractive and well-situated hut.

The track continues by dropping quickly 200 m into Bowyers Stream and wandering some 4 km/2 hours downriver, occasionally crossing, with some boulder-hopping involved. There's a pretty part where the track goes underneath a small waterfall.

The track then climbs up out of the stream and over Duke's Knob (lookout side-track here) then you have a choice of two tracks down to the carpark — steep or easy. Either way you drop down some 200 m to Sharplin Falls carpark (1.5 km/1 hour). It's well worth following the boardwalks back to have a gander at the falls themselves.

Arrowsmith Approach

Total tramping time: 9–12 hours/2–3 days
Total tramping distance: 39 km
Grade: medium
Highest point: 1300 m; Cameron Hut
Map: Arrowsmith J35

The Arrowsmiths are a huddle of peaks offset from the Main Divide by the long trench of the Rakaia River. They have a sharp, harsh character of their own, and the popular approach to them is via the Cameron River, a simple one-route tramp to the hut and upper valley. From here you can venture closer to the icefalls and glaciers.

From Mt Somers township (about 100 km from Christchurch) take the Ashburton Gorge Road inland towards Erewhon. After 20 km you reach the Hakatere Station and road junction. Turn north towards Lake Heron and follow the road through bronze hummocks to the lakeside picnic area. It's 5 km further to a broad, flat tussock plain where you can see the Cameron Valley entering on the left. A faint four-wheel-drive track goes across the 1-km flat to the Cameron Valley but for an ordinary car it is better to stop by the main road.

The route up the Cameron River stays entirely on the west side and you should hardly need to get your feet wet. After 2 km/40 minutes over the flat, the travel settles into an alternating pattern of gravel stretches of river, scattered sheep and cattle trails, and tussock flats. Early on there are clumps of matagouri and briar but these thin out and the landscape becomes solely alpine. Mt Arrowsmith (2781 m) looks temptingly close, but it is almost 19 km away.

It is 8 km/2 hours to Highland Home, a 4-bunk musterers' hut on the other side of the river, and a useful shelter in poor weather. About 3 km/1 hour from here the Cameron closes into its only 'gorge'. This can easily be followed close by the river (though a loose rock slip is a bit nasty), but it is probably quicker to grunt up 30 m or so onto the obvious grass shelf and follow this for 1 km/30 minutes down to the river beyond the gorge. Good stock tracks on the

Heading down Cameron Valley

west bank make short work of the 2.5 km/1 hour of the upper Cameron Flats to where Spean Creek bustles in.

Though not an obvious route, the best way to avoid the central mass of river moraine is to stay well on the west side, climbing gradually on a low tussock spur dotted with pine trees. Slowly a worn foot-trail emerges and nips around the back of the moraine past cairn markers to arrive unexpectedly at the hut (2 km/1 hour).

The hut has a great view of the shattered peaks of the Arrowsmiths. It has 9 bunks, but no wood of course, so a portable cooker is crucial. Upvalley from the hut is a noticeable 'tramway' of moraine which slopes up to a viewpoint overlooking the icefalls of the Cameron and Arrowsmith glaciers.

Mueller Hut

Total tramping time: 6–9 hours/2 days
Total tramping distance: 9 km
Grade: medium/fit
Highest point: 1780 m; Mueller Hut
Maps: Mt Cook & Westland National Parks 273-10;
    Mt Cook H36

A short trip in Mt Cook National Park to the superb vantage point, Mueller Hut. Impressive views of Mt Cook (Aoraki), the Hooker Glacier and the Mt Sefton arc of peaks and icefalls. It's a fair slog up a steep hill, and this is a summer trip only. In winter you would need ice-axe and crampons.

Mueller Hut has a mountain radio installed and every party is required to 'check in' each evening. You should therefore register your intentions at the park headquarters before you leave. This keeps the rangers informed of who is where in the park and provides information on hut usage.

From Highway 8 take Highway 80 to the park headquarters and Hermitage Hotel. There are regular bus services between Christchurch and Queenstown to the Mt Cook village. The track starts from either the Hermitage or the White Horse camping area.

From the Hermitage the signposted track skirts an incongruous field of lupins (brilliant in season) then passes through a patch of alpine scrub onto grass flats, past Foliage Hill (793 m) to a track junction (2 km/30 minutes). A well-screened camping ground with toilets and a shelter has been provided under White Horse Hill.

The track re-enters the alpine scrub and at a second junction climbs fiercely through rock outcrops and snowgrass to the twin Sealy Tarns; a height gain of 500 m over 1 km/1–2 hours. Here there

Mt Cook Lily

are quiet, reflective pools among alpine plants, one tarn capturing an image of Mt Cook. They also provide the only water on the climb, although you might be wise to carry your own, as people swim in the tarns.

The slope eases a little for the next 300 m, and slight tussock and rock basins and a roughly cairned route give way in the last 150 m to a loose crumble of rock and gullies. Most of these can be scrambled up easily, though they get progressively steeper if you move south. The easiest route is slightly north and out onto the end of the Sealy Range as it falls to the Mueller Glacier; 1.5 km/2 hours to Mueller Hut.

The hut sits at 1780 m in a tangle of rocky bulges on top of the ridge, very close to the long drop back to the Hooker Valley. It is possible to 'lose' it in the mist, though there are several prominent cairns and obvious worn trails on the ground. The hut has 18 bunks, and not surprisingly is very popular.

The site is magnificent. From here you have striking views of Mt Cook, the toy-like village, and the icefalls off Mt Sefton, pieces of which frequently avalanche to the valley floor. If these sights wear thin, the kea will amuse or infuriate you, depending on whose gear they are ravaging.

There is a quick rock scramble up to Mt Ollivier (1933 m), the peak immediately behind Mueller. However, you don't see much more up there than from the hut itself. Beyond that is Mt Kitchener at 2042 m, a higher and harder clamber. From here you can see the permanent snowy blanket of the Annette Plateau and further around the pointed top of Mt Sealy (2627 m), the highest peak of the range.

Remember on your return to drop into the park headquarters to register your exit and pay hut fees.

Huxley Valley and Brodrick Pass

Total tramping time: 16–18 hours/3 days
Total tramping distance: 31 km
Grade: easy/medium
Highest point: 1640 m; Brodrick Pass
Maps: Landsborough G37; Tasman H37

The Huxley's intimate bush-clad valley holds its own amongst such giant southern valleys as the Landsborough, the Hopkins and the Rakaia. It is easy to approach, with good tracks through beech forest and tussock terraces. Four huts, excellent camping, and the chance on a fine day to reach a Main Divide pass.

On Highway 8, 14 km from Twizel and 16 km from Omarama, there is a signposted turnoff to Lake Ohau. Travel about 50 km along this road past Ohau Lake, Maitland and Temple Stream bridges, to a carpark by the massive shingle bed of the Hopkins River. The upper Hopkins Valley road has been prone to wash-outs and slips. Four-wheel-drive vehicles can be taken onto the riverbed a further 2 km to the picnic area and Monument Hut (6 bunks).

A track sidles from the hut through the beech (past a shy waterfall) and back to the Hopkins River flats (1 km/20 minutes). It's 1.5 km/30 minutes of easy travel to a prominent sign, where a bush track goes inland and climbs a low saddle to drop down beside the Huxley River and footbridge. In normal flow it is easiest to ford the river underneath the bridge, but if you are determined to keep dry feet cross the bridge and follow the track upstream to where it emerges onto grass flats.

About 6 km/2 hours of pleasant terrace travel to the Forks Hut; a 6-bunk hut and a small upright 2-bunk bivouac. Good camping all around the Forks area which is an attractive parkland of forest and flat.

A short distance up the North Branch of the Huxley is a footbridge. The track crosses this and gradually sidles upriver through intermittent bush and bare avalanche gullies. Brodrick Pass is seen regularly as the track stays high above the river, eventually passing alpine shrub and herb fields before closing back onto the river again in a

Huxley Forks Hut

pocket of scrawny mountain beech. A brief riverside track then a final 50-m climb up through the bush to the hut door (4.5 km/2–3 hours).

Brodrick Hut has 6 bunks and a wood stove. There are some campsites on the alpine terrace and fine views into the serrated upper valley of the North Huxley.

Brodrick Pass is a popular day trip. The unmarked route crosses a tussock plain (cut by deep gullies) for 1 km/20 minutes to the foot of the 600-m climb to the pass. On the right an obvious tussock spur can be followed, or alternatively a rough unmarked zig-zag trail cuts through the scrub belt and onto the upper tussock slopes. From here you make your own route up to the flat, gravelly top of the pass (1.5 km/1–2 hours).

The views are a bit disappointing, the Landsborough River being mostly hidden, though a walk up to the snowline of McKenzie gives a better prospect. There are plentiful tarns and stony camping spots on the pass itself.

Dasler Bivouac

Total tramping time: 7–9 hours/2 days
Total tramping distance: 18 km
Grade: easy/medium
Highest point: 1300 m; Dasler Biv
Maps: Ohau H38; Tasman H37

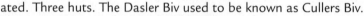

A short trip to a bush-edge bivouac. Impressive mountain views over the massive Hopkins Valley and the Main Divide peaks. The Hopkins River has to be crossed and should be treated circumspectly; there is also a tricky rock slab on the biv track to be negotiated. Three huts. The Dasler Biv used to be known as Cullers Biv.

On Highway 8, 14 km from Twizel and 16 km from Omarama, is the turnoff to Lake Ohau. Travel approximately 50 km along the mostly metal road to the carpark by the Hopkins River. Frequent washouts along the last 7–8 km of this road at times makes access problematic.

From the carpark it is a half-hour walk up the dizzying expanse of the Hopkins riverbed to Monument Hut. Four-wheel-drive vehicles and some sturdy cars can be taken this far. Monument has 6 bunks, and there's camping in the surrounding open beech forest.

A track sidles from the hut in bush for about 1 km/20 minutes then drops onto the flats. Alternatively plough straight on up the riverbed, though this will mean a crossing or two of river braids. After 2 km/1 hour of salubrious travel on grass flats (past the Huxley Track sign) you reach the forks of the Huxley and Hopkins Rivers.

The Dasler Pinnacles are very impressive from the Huxley forks, and you can fix the rough position of Dasler Biv, which is sited on the spur below the Pinnacles with the prominent 'plateau' on it. If you count the side-valley opposite the Huxley River then the biv track is just after the third side-valley.

You cross 4 km/1 hour of the Hopkins Valley, mostly shingle beds and straightforward fords of the many-channelled river (river flows are lowest in late summer, autumn and winter). Big flats on the far side are welcome after the gravel slog and a busy creek runs out of the third side-valley, collecting shingle around the beech trees. The

Hopkins Valley

track is on the far side of the creek and a bit vague at first, but becomes strongly marked immediately it starts to climb.

About 300 m up to the rock slab (500 m/1 hour). This looks rather daunting, a 7-m stretch of smoothish rock with a big rope dangling down. However, there are good footholds on the rock and the rope is reasonably well secured, and as there are no alternatives it's better to tackle the obstacle before you get too nervous.

After the slab the track winds up a graceful beech spur for about 250 m then sidles into a small valley and across an open mountain stream to the bivouac (500 m/1 hour). The biv has 2 bunks and an open fire. Camping is tight but possible.

The biv is sheltered and sunny but the views are restricted, so climb up 50 m or so onto the tussock plateau. Great views over the Hopkins Valley and up the splintered spurs of the Dasler Pinnacles. It's a pity the name is not spelt 'dazzler'; it would be appropriate.

A variation on the return would be to stay on the east bank of the Hopkins and amble through the grass and matagouri terraces down to Red Hut, a roomy 12-bunker. From here cut across the shingle desert to Monument Hut and carpark (10 km/3 hours).

Gillespie Pass

Total tramping time: 16–19 hours/2–3 days
  (assuming jetboat to Kerin Forks)
Total tramping distance: 37 km (assuming jetboat to Kerin Forks)
Grade: medium
Highest point: 1600 m; Gillespie Pass
Maps: Mt Aspiring National Park 273-02;
  Wilkin F38

A tramp that is becoming something of a classic, up the Siberia branch of the Wilkin over Gillespie Pass and down the Young River. Well-marked tracks, two good huts and excellent scenery, including an option of a splendid side-trip to a lake called The Crucible.

However, although this track is becoming popular with overseas backpackers, it shouldn't be treated as a doddle. Gillespie Pass is steep, it is a difficult journey in poor weather, and crossing the Makarora at the Young–Makarora confluence can be problematic at the best. Fortunately there is now a phone shelter here, and by pushing a button you can speak directly to DOC or the jetboat operator at Makarora. There is an airstrip in the Siberia and quite a few groups are flying in direct from Makarora — the so-called Siberia Experience. The Siberia Hut can get busy so a tent is useful, and a portable cooker is handy for the Young Hut.

Travel along Highway 6 to Makarora, 60 km north of Wanaka. Jetboats can be hired from here to take you up the lower Wilkin to Kerin Forks. At $40 (1998 prices) one way they are not cheap, but they do save a long 16-km slog over river flats and an awkward (not to say downright difficult) crossing of the Makarora River. If you have not been on a jetboat before it's an exciting ride, and you will be amazed at their manoeuvrability. No doubt the driver will throw in a spin or two. Arrangements can also be made for a jetboat pick-up at the Young–Makarora confluence, thereby avoiding all the dodgy river crossings.

Assuming you catch the jetboat you'll be landed on the north bank of the Wilkin River, just downstream from where the Siberia Stream comes in. The 10-person hut at Kerin Forks is visible on the south bank of the Wilkin. The section of track between the Wilkin and Siberia Hut is currently being upgraded to a benched path.

The track starts by ambling along the grass and bush terrace for a while then abruptly follows an old

On the way up to Gillespie Pass

cattle trail that zig-zags laboriously some 300 m up a steep beech face (1 km/1–2 hours). You are nicely warmed up by the time the rough track starts to sidle and turns into the Siberia valley, travelling 3 km/1 hour down to the edge of the vast flats that characterise Aspiring rivers. Mount Awful lives up to its name. Another 2 km/40 minutes over the extensive flats to Siberia Hut — 20 bunks, and a fine outlook up the valley.

For Gillespie Pass it's 3 km/1 hour of easy meandering upvalley following a good trail over grass flats to the junction with the Crucible track. There are a couple of popular campsites just where Gillespie Pass track enters the beech forest.

At first the track is steep but roughly graded, as it zig-zags to avoid the waterfall in Gillespie Stream and climbs first a sharp 200 m then a more gradual 100 m as the track flattens, crosses a couple of side-creeks and turns into an upper basin on the bush edge (2 km/1–2 hours). Good camping here, or a pleasant rest-up spot. Fill up on water as the tops tarns are not reliable.

Track markers lead straight up through the last of the bush and scrub and orange poles take you on a rather circumlocutory tour of the tussock basins, gradually climbing some 500 m onto the ridge-line itself. Great views, and some small tarns might have water for a lunch stop (2 km/1–2 hours). Note that the metric map shows the track following a wrong line, and with some poles missing this track could be confusing in misty weather. Poles continue along the ridge and down to the pass proper, where the track sidles onto a spur and commences a long zig-zag into the Young River.

This is definitely the steeper side and isn't a piece of cake, particularly if it's wet. However, a good trail has been etched into the ground now, so you are generally walking on earth and rock rather than greasy tussock. The track crosses to another spur and finally cuts down through light alpine scrub to the valley floor. All up a descent of 1 km/1–2 hours, and a vertical drop of 600 m.

A great place for a breather, and you could camp here on alpine flats with a stunning backdrop of huge slab rock walls, but otherwise mosey down an easy well-worn trail (occasionally cairned and poled) that leads down the west bank some 1.5 km/1 hour to the well-positioned hut; 10 bunks, wood stove.

Now it's 7 km/2–3 hours of tramping along a track down the north bank of the Young to the bottom forks. First back up to the footbridge then down through scrub, then bush slopes to the main river. From here on the track generally stays a little above the river to the cute bridge over Stag Creek, then sidles awkwardly around several slips (some with huge house-sized boulders poised above you) and climbs around a deep gorge with some impressive cataracts buried in it. It finally descends sharply to the grassy flats and confluence of the North and South branches of the Young River.

About 500 m/10 minutes upstream is the footbridge, and a little further is a rather exposed campsite with a toilet and shelter. However, there are other campsites around these huge flats that might be more salubrious.

After the footbridge the track becomes easier, and after the first 3 km/1 hour climbs 15–20 m above the Young and gently sidles 7 km/2–3 hours down to the Makarora River. The track gets very cruisy lower down the Young so if you are coming up the river be warned that the track gets noticeably rougher the more upvalley you go. There is a phone shelter by the forks and you have a choice of buttons — one to call DOC, one to call the jetboat operator.

If crossing on foot check that the river levels are normal; they can fluctuate quickly and easily become uncrossable. The Makarora is normally in two streams, but the deepest crossing is usually the last one.

At present the route crosses the Young River first, then follows markers diagonally downstream over Courtneys Flat. There is rather an oversupply of markers at times but you roughly aim for the orange triangles on the far side, crossing both branches of the Makarora to arrive at Sawmill Flat (1.5 km/1 hour). If at all in doubt go back and hit the button.

The Crucible side-trip

A good day trip from Siberia Hut is to the lake called The Crucible. There's a signposted turnoff from Gillespie Pass track after 3 km/1 hour, then follow the poles across Gillespie Stream and the Siberia Stream 1 km/30 minutes upvalley, picking up a steep bush track on the north bank of the Crucible Stream. The track climbs up beside cataracts for 300 m to the first basin, then crosses the stream and a good worn trail (marked with cairns) leads the way through open grass and ribbonwood country to the top basin. The trail gets lost among the final alpine flats and rocks leading to the dramatic lip of Lake Crucible (3.5 km/2 hours).

The perfectly round lake is often clogged with ice-lumps that refuse to melt in this deep dark valley, and the rock faces of Mt Alba (2360 m) regularly send down small avalanches of scree and ice.

Wilkin Valley

Total tramping time: 10–12 hours/2–4 days (Kerin Forks return)
Total tramping distance: 36 km (Kerin Forks return)
Grade: easy
Highest point: 600 m; Top Forks hut
Maps: Mt Aspiring National Park 273-02;
   Wilkin F38

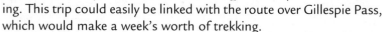

One of the great valleys in the Southern Alps, with a good track leading through super scenery to the fine upper forks. Extensive grass flats, with huge mountains and glinting icefalls. Several good day trip options from Top Forks Hut, and lots of good camping. This trip could easily be linked with the route over Gillespie Pass, which would make a week's worth of trekking.

Travel along Highway 6 to Makarora, 60 km north of Wanaka. Jetboats can be hired here to take you up the lower Wilkin to Kerin Forks, and they do save a long 16-km slog over river flats and an awkward crossing of the Makarora River. The times and distances in this description are based on the assumption that you catch a jetboat both ways. If you choose to walk add at least 2 days to your overall time.

There is a 10-person hut at Kerin Forks, a handy place to sort out gear and have a brew. A clearly marked track travels up beside the Wilkin River in a leisurely fashion for 8 km/2–3 hours to Jumboland Flats, a gravel flat where Wonderland Stream joins the Wilkin.

From here it's 2 km/40 minutes through bush to the vast top flats, and so begins a series of tussock terraces for 6 km/2 hours to the expansive Top Forks Huts.

There are warden's quarters in the old hut, and 10 bunks in the modern one. The latter has a pot-belly wood stove and window views of the ice-twins Mts Castor (2518 m) and Pollux (2536 m). There are good campsites on the beech margin.

Day trips
Lake Diana and Lucidus Lake — 8 km/3–4 hours return
There is a good side-trip to Lake Diana, which sits out on the flat

Loading the jetboat, Makarora

under the headwall of Pollux. From the hut head north across the flats, cross the Wilkin and follow a good track up alongside the east bank of the North Branch of the river. A 200-m climb through the bush for 1 km and you reach the bushline and alpine scrub which backs onto Lake Diana. A fairly awesome place. Another 1 km across the tussock and swampy flats to Lake Lucidus.

Waterfall Face — 12 km/5–6 hours return
Might as well find out what all the fuss is about. A track has been cut up the south bank of the Wilkin and stops at the scrubline on Waterfall Flat. It starts right behind the hut, sidling the river above Snow Bridge Gorge for 500 m over 3.5 km. At the tussock, the valley flattens and curves around 2 km to the base of the waterfall face. The waterfall leaps in two goes, 90 m and 35 m. A fine alpine basin, and you can usually pick out the odd snowpole which indicates the improbable route up the face, but only experienced trampers should try it on. See The Waterfall Face and Rabbit Pass, page 260.

The Waterfall Face and Rabbit Pass

Total tramping time: 19–22 km/3–5 days
  (Kerin Forks to Matukituki Valley)
Total tramping distance: 46 km (Kerin Forks to Matukituki Valley)
Grade: fit
Highest point: 1400 m; Rabbit Pass
Maps: Mt Aspiring National Park 273-02;
  Wilkin F38; Matukituki F39

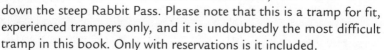

A hard, classic trip in Aspiring National Park. Impressive terrain through two alpine valleys surrounded by ice-clad peaks. Excellent tracks and huts in the valleys but a notoriously difficult passage between them over the infamous waterfall face, and down the steep Rabbit Pass. Please note that this is a tramp for fit, experienced trampers only, and it is undoubtedly the most difficult tramp in this book. Only with reservations is it included.

The waterfall face is a short, extremely steep and unprotected face, with little to hold on to. It is recommended that you only attempt the tramp going up the face; the descent is much more difficult. Some parties coming from the Matukituki have looked down the waterfall and decided to retrace their steps, other parties have used ropes to belay down it. In wet conditions it is especially dangerous. You get the idea?

For access and route information to Top Forks Hut see Wilkin Valley, page 258; allow one tramping day for the 16 km/6 hours.

A track has been cut up the south bank of the Wilkin and stops at the scrubline on Waterfall Flat. It starts right behind the hut, sidling the river above Snow Bridge Gorge for 500 m over 3 km/2 hours. At the tussock, the valley flattens and curves around 2 km/1 hour to the base of the waterfall face.

DOC has issued stringent warnings about the route up the waterfall face; they once even printed a little map which showed the precise route up. Too much deviation left or right gets you into serious problems. Some snowpoles mark the route. The first 50 m up a fan is not too bad, but the next and steepest 150 m is the crunch. The rocks are loose and the tussock short. Toeholds in the hard gravel

The Waterfall Face

give some grip but out of necessity the climb is over quickly, and after an unnerving grovel you arrive on a thin ledge which sidles around to the flats above the waterfall (1 hour).

Picklehaube (2165 m) stabs high into the air and Pearson Saddle (1409 m) is the low pass to the right. There are reasonable campsites opposite Pearson Saddle. It's 2 km/1 hour over grassy flats to Rabbit Pass, and on the pass there is a large tarn and an exposed campsite looking down to the East Matukituki River.

Rabbit Pass also needs some careful navigation, although it is snowpoled. Turn east uphill for 200 m over 700 m/20 minutes along the lip of the headwall. A large cairn stands at the head of a steep gully at 1600 m which is the way down, not a very pleasant way.

The rock is unstable, sliding easily. About 30 m down a small ledge angles down across the steepest part, and you may have to lower your packs first. This is the crunch though, and from here it is straightforward, following snowpoles and descending rock and snowgrass spurs to the scrubline and top flats. A 500-m drop over 2 km/1–2 hours.

Down on the valley floor it's easy going along the river flats for

5 km/2 hours to the broad Ruth Flat. The route continues 2.5 km/1 hour downstream on the east bank over grass terraces to where the river closes into Bledisloe Gorge. A poled track is marked from here at the bush edge.

For 1 km/30 minutes it sidles low in the bush to a side creek, then climbs steeply, switching back 200 m or so onto a high terrace (1 km/1 hour). It levels out, and runs a little through alpine bush to break out onto the tussock, a good 400 m above the gorge (1 km/1 hour). Mt Aspiring sticks out over the Kitchener Valley like a needle.

The track contours over snowgrass past thickets of scrub before dropping back to the bushline and descending 550 m to Junction Flat (2 km/2 hours). Ford the river, and there are excellent campsites on this pretty flat.

If you have the time, Aspiring Flat and Rock of Ages Bivouac is a marvellous place to visit. There is a good track there up the south bank of the Kitchener River. Otherwise the main route crosses Kitchener River and picks up this track as it turns downstream and sidles for 4.5 km/2 hours through forest to the grazing land. There's a footbridge over the Glacier Burn if you need it.

It's 3 km/1 hour over huge flats past the old homestead. The river should not be difficult to ford at the last 1 km/20 minutes to Cameron's Flat and the road, but there is a footbridge upstream some 30 minutes if you need it.

A minibus/taxi service operates a regular timetable from Wanaka during the summer months and a private taxi can be hired out of season. Otherwise during the weekends there should be plenty of cars to hitch a ride from if you get stuck.

Matukituki Valley

Total tramping time: 4–6 hours/2–4 days (Aspiring Hut return)
Total tramping distance: 17 km (Aspiring Hut return)
Grade: easy
Highest point: 460 m; Aspiring Hut
Maps: Mt Aspiring National Park 273-02;
  Aspiring E39

James K. Baxter set a poem in this magnificent high-walled alpine valley. Although a popular access for climbers to Mt Aspiring, tramping is limited and best done as day trips from a base valley hut or camp. Exploring the upper valley and the striking hut vantage points is substitute enough for the restricted scope of the tramping.

From Wanaka travel 54 km up the Matukituki Valley to the road head at Raspberry Creek carpark. There are some 13 fords and ditches on the last 8 km which can flood badly after heavy rain. A minibus/taxi service operates a regular timetable from Wanaka during the summer months and a private taxi can be hired out of season.

From the Raspberry Creek carpark (there's a footbridge across Big Creek) follow the poled tracks for 1 km/20 minutes to the Matukituki River. A track junction leads to a footbridge which crosses the Matukituki for those who want to go into the Rob Roy Valley. This is a lovely side-trip and the alpine flowers and glaciers at the head are memorable.

The main valley track follows a vehicle track for 3 km/1 hour across easy flats towards the gushing Brides Veil Falls. Thwarted by a bush outcrop the track climbs up and over the bluff and fords Red Rock Stream, then there's a short dash across a matagouri flat to Cascade Hut (2.5 km/1 hour).

Cascade Hut is a quixotic affair of two tiny huts sharing a wooden porch. In 1932 the recently formed Otago section of the New Zealand Alpine Club bought two Department of Works huts from Dunedin and formed Cascade Hut. One side is locked and for the exclusive use of New Zealand Alpine Club members. A cosy home,

Matukituki Valley

with Sharks Tooth dominating its view down the valley.

The much larger 30-bunk Aspiring Hut is 2 km/40 minutes further up the valley, and is managed by DOC. Built in 1949, it commands a fine outlook to Mt Aspiring. For many years its existence has been threatened by a huge shingle slip. A warden is on duty during the summer season, advising travellers and collecting hut fees for all huts in the valley.

Either Cascade or Aspiring Hut makes a good base, and there are also one or two nice campsites between them beside two small side-creeks. There is further sheltered camping upvalley among the beech and grass terraces.

Day trips
Above Aspiring Hut the track eases west (past good sheltered camp-sites) and around through bush to a footbridge over Cascade Creek. It then climbs out of the creek and back into the spacious flat until it meets the bush edge again (1.5 km/30 minutes).

Back into the beech forest the track crosses another footbridge over Rough Creek then gains a little in height before emerging onto the expanse of Shovel Flat (1 km/20 minutes). You are in the thick of typical Aspiring country, with waterfalls and big-walled mountains all around, and good outlooks back towards Shotover and Cascade Saddles.

It's 2 km/ 30 minutes over Shovel Flat to a brief bush tongue gaining access to Pearl Flat. The Matukituki River lingers in some lovely deep pools and sculptured rock just by this bush tongue, though you have to bash off the track a little way to appreciate it. Pearl Flat has some good campsites, particularly by Liverpool Stream where another footbridge can be used to avoid the rocks (1 km/20 minutes).

There are two good side-trips from here. The first goes to French Ridge Hut. A track is marked on the east bank, just above the outlet from Gloomy Gorge. Climb a sheer 600 m (hand over fist stuff), up steep gullies and hanging on to tree roots to the tussock line (1 km/1 hour). Then continue a further 1 km/30 minutes along the edge of a spur to the hut (12 bunks).

The huts command a circle of views, from the edge of the Breakaway, to an icefall from the Bonar Glacier, past Rob Roy (2644 m) then over to the graceful Mt Liverpool (2482 m), Barff (2252 m) and the shadowed cliff headwalls of the upper Matukituki. Here you will experience a rare silence, broken mostly by the raucous kea clattering on the hut roofs, in Baxter's apt words 'the carrion parrot' of the Alps.

A second side-trip is to Liverpool Bivouac, and the track junction is just above where Liverpool Stream enters. If anything, the track is steeper than French Ridge, particularly on the open tussock, but the ascent is shorter. You climb 300 m through bush, then a steep scree and scrub face for 150 m, following cairns and poles to where the spur flattens.

The trail takes you almost 50 m above the bivouac, which can be seen to the south, but do not be tempted to try and cross direct the first time you see the biv. The slopes are very steep, and there has been a fatality from attempting this. The track does a short sidle around and down to the bivouac (1.5 km/2–3 hours).

The bivouac holds 8 people, and is perched like a doll's house in this place of giants. Mt Aspiring (3033 m) is vividly close. Be careful and sure-footed on the return; at some points there is bugger-all to hang on to.

Rees Valley and Dart River

Total tramping time: 4–6 days
Total tramping distance: 67 km
Grade: medium
Highest point: 1471 m; Rees Saddle
Maps: Mt Aspiring National Park 273-02;
  Aspiring E39; Earnslaw E40

Two valleys joined by a low saddle in the heart of massive mountain country. High peaks, glaciers, stark bluffs and rich bush are the daily stuff of tramping in this area. Good trails, four huts, several rock bivouacs and lots of opportunity for camping. Quite a few trampers choose the Rees–Dart as a quieter alternative to the Routeburn or Kepler, but the tracks are a bit rougher, and the distances can deceive.

From Queenstown take the dusty road to Glenorchy, 47 km. Then it's another 19 km to the Muddy Creek carpark up the Rees Valley, with a couple of fords on the way. Various bus companies run daily services to the track ends during the summer season, and a local taxi operates from Glenorchy to either the Rees or the Dart road-end, and will pick you up as arranged.

The track plunges across Muddy Creek and follows a four-wheel-drive road down easy cattle flats to the private Arthur Huts (2 km/30 minutes). Ford Falls can be heard roaring as you cross Arthur Creek and wander for 4 km/1 hour to 25 Mile Creek. There's a good campsite here.

Alternatively, climb 50 m up the track to 25 Mile Hut which sits on an open grass shelf. You can't see the hut but the shelf is plainly visible as you come upvalley. A cosy 4 bunks, with stone fireplace. Worth investigating is the deep creviced gorge just behind the hut where the thundering 25 Mile Creek cuts through to the Rees River.

Head casually upstream from 25 Mile Creek 3.5 km/1 hour along poled river flats, crossing where convenient, and always under the looming shadow of Earnslaw's East Peak (2830 m). Where the flats end (campsites here) a track cuts through the bush 1 km/20 minutes to a footbridge, crosses to the other bank of the Rees and follows gentle gradients and back-gullies to the meadowlike clearing at Clarke's Slip (1.5 km/40 minutes). Impressive views all round. Large boulders dot the slip, which is 1 km/20 minutes long, with the track winding between them and across to the far bush edge.

It's a gentle 100-m climb over 2 km/1 hour through beech forest to the old hut site, now a good camping spot, with a fine upriver view. For 1.5 km/30 minutes as it heads upstream the track bustles in and out of avalanche slips

Crossing the Rees River, Mt Earnslaw behind

(these can require care), stunted beech forest and alpine shrubbery dotted with Mt Cook lilies in season. Then it closes back to the river, crosses a footbridge and shortly arrives at the charming Shelter Rock Hut (20 bunks).

This hut sits in a tussock flat with a calm pond below it. Camping between here and the Dart Hut is discouraged due to the fragile nature of the subalpine zone.

The track continues upvalley by tripping around the rock-river edge for 1 km/20 minutes, then gradually sidles through tussock and low alpine scrub for 3 km/1 hour to the top tussock flat. It's a make-your-own route up the head valley for 2 km/40 minutes to the final 'step' of 100 m to the Rees Saddle, which is poled. You pop up suddenly into views up and down the Snowy River.

From the saddle a good poled route drops a sudden 100 m to a lovely cluster of tarns, a good lunch site. Then the track sidles the deeply gutted Snowy Gorge for 2 km/1 hour, abruptly descending to a footbridge then as sharply climbing above it. The bridge is reduced to 4 wires during winter to minimise avalanche damage. Not far from here you are suddenly confronted with a dramatic view of the Dart headwaters and glaciers.

Picking a delicate route through rock and scrub, the track descends almost 500 m over 2 km/1 hour to the lower footbridge. From here it's a few minutes to the Dart Hut (20 bunks).

Down the Dart River the track sidles uninterestingly past the Whitbourn Bridge junction to the vastness of Cattle Flat, a gradual descent of 300 m over 6 km/2 hours on an easy trail. For 3 km/1 hour the track vaguely ambles along the flat till a sign indicates a rock bivouac 5 minutes up the hillside. This is an established affair with a stone fireplace, and can easily accommodate 4 people.

Cattle Flat continues another 2 km/40 minutes, then enters the bush via a gate. The track becomes wide, wet, stony, and graded for cattle. It's 2 km/40 minutes to a 2-person rock bivouac, then a steady descent over 2 km/40 minutes brings you to the first open clearing at Quinns Flat. There is a bit more bush before reaching Daley's Flat, with a hut (20 bunks) visible on the far side (1.5 km/30 minutes). Plenty of campsites.

After this the track closely follows the river, easing along bush shelves and small grassy flats, many of which are fine for camping, with views of the craggy peaks of the Barrier Range. It's 6 km/2 hours to Sandy Bluff, which has a ladder and overhang as track hazards.

Continue for 10 km/2–3 hours along beech and grass terraces, crossing 2 footbridges over the Bedford and several unnamed streams. The Dart runs close and blue to the shoulders of bush and Mt Nox (1940 m) is impressive as you approach Chinaman's Bluff, and if you look back Pluto (2480 m) sticks up from the Earnslaw Massif.

A neat track cuts under Chinaman's Bluff to where yet another rock bivouac (about 10 people) is signposted. Then it's a long inland haul over a rough four-wheel track to the carpark at Mill Creek where the gravel road begins (9 km/2–3 hours).

Cascade Saddle, route from Dart Hut to Cascade Saddle and Matukituki River

An attractive, but in places steep, connecting route between the Dart River and the Matukituki Valley. The descent down the Cullers Route into the Matukituki should be treated with caution, and in wet or snowy conditions it's best not even to attempt it.

From Dart Hut the track leads 7 km/2 hours up alongside the upper Dart River to the foot of the moraine. There are some good campsites along the way. At the moraine the track squirms up the east side for 3 km/1 hour before climbing out and sidling around to Cascade Saddle itself (1524 m). About a 450-m climb from the river.

But that's not the end of the climbing for there's another 200 m up onto the Cascade basin, a beautiful place of tarns and tussock with rave views of the mountains (1 km/40 minutes).

To reach the Matukituki follow the marker poles through the Cascade Basin, and up onto the ridge some 250 m to the drop-off point to the Cullers Route (2 km/1 hour). The descent is really steep and slippery, especially in wet conditions. A poled route wriggles almost 500 m down over steep snowgrass, short rock steps and scree slopes to the bush edge for 1 km/1 hour, then with the worst of the scrambling over with, the track still has 3 km/2 hours to get down some 700 m to the Matukituki Valley floor.

Routeburn Track

Total tramping time: 11–14 hours/2–3 days
Total tramping distance: 32 km
Grade: medium
Highest point: 1277 m; Harris Saddle
Maps: Routeburn/Greenstone Track 335-02;
   Milford D40; Eglinton D41; Earnslaw E40
(See *New Zealand's Top Tracks* by Mark Pickering for
a more detailed description of this track.)

This is one of the most famous and popular tramps
in New Zealand. It is a true alpine walk, with deep
valleys, bracketed by bluffs and waterfalls, opening
out to steep tussock tops and dramatic views of the
Darran Mountains.

Some warning notes. The stretch of track between Falls Hut and
Mackenzie Hut is open and exposed, and bad weather can easily
delay you. The track varies between an easy country walk and a standard tramping trail; although always well graded, it can be rough
underfoot.

Huts and campsites have to be booked. The four huts range from
20–60 bunks each, with gas cookers, wood stove (for heating only),
toilets, water supply and a warden on duty throughout the summer
season. Camping is allowed only at the three designated campsites,
which also have to be booked. Finally, if you want a get-away-from-
it-all holiday, with uncrowded tracks and empty huts, go somewhere
else.

Drive from Queenstown to Routeburn via the Dart River bridge, 78
km to the track end. Alternatively, drive from Te Anau to the Divide
shelter (85 km). There is plenty of public transport to either track
end during the summer season, and round-trip transport packages
are offered.

From the Routeburn shelter walk back along the road a few minutes to the start of the track. It crosses a footbridge, winding in
leisurely fashion through stately red beech forest to Sugar Loaf
Stream (1 km/20 minutes).

The track slowly climbs 250 m to negotiate the Routeburn Gorge;

the Maori name is Te Komana. After 1 km/1 hour the track comes to a bridge over the fine and fast-running Bridal Veil Falls Stream, then it closes on the gorge where the high walls trap the sounds of the water and squeeze out the sun.

After another 2.5 km/1–2 hours you top out into the upper valley and cross a footbridge, gradually meeting the extensive tussock flats that give their name to the hut 2 km/40 minutes further on. There are 20 bunks and a camping area 5 minutes down a side-trail.

For Routeburn Falls return to the junction and sidle 2 km/1–2 hours through red, silver and mountain beech, climbing 250 m across Emily Stream to Falls Hut (48 bunks). This is a grand spot for relaxing, sunbathing, eating and diary-filling.

This is the crunch day for most walkers, and the most spectacular. Almost immediately behind Falls Hut the Routeburn gushes over a variety of rock ledges before the main falls themselves. The track, marked by poles, threads past the falls and emerges into the lower Lake Harris basin. The track can be seen well ahead, delicately cut and graded around the snowgrass slopes of the basin.

It's 3 km/1–2 hours to Harris Saddle over tussock decorated with daisies, gentians and hebes, a 200-m climb all told, with the deep-centred blue of Lake Harris dominating the valley.

An emergency shelter sits just on the other side of Harris Saddle, and the Darrans are a glittering jostle of peaks, quite stunning when you first come over the lip. Madeline (2536 m) is the large, flat-topped peak to the north, Tutoko (2723 m) is the highest, a little behind its sister peak. A side-track offers a jaunt to Conical Hill, a 250-m climb that's thoroughly worth the effort, providing 360 degrees of marvelling.

The main track descends a stony gully 150 m off the saddle, then turns and sidles along for 7 km/2–3 hours to the Mackenzie Hut. After 1 km there's the alternative exit of the cheerfully named Deadman's Track, which is not much used now but offers a frantic 900-m descent into the Hollyford Valley.

After another 2 km there's a signpost down to an emergency rock bivouac, and on a clear day you can see Lake McKerrow and the coastline at Martins Bay. The trail turns into the Mackenzie basin the last 1 km and does two long, lazy zig-zags down a steep face above the lake. It's a 300-m descent to the lakeside, the last 50 m in bush.

Key Summit tarns

The double-storey Mackenzie Hut has 48 bunks, and a designated campsite. It's a nice walk to the head of Lake Mackenzie beneath Emily Peak. Swims in the lake are exhilarating and hasty.

The main track continues across a small tussock flat past a private walkers' hut, enters the bush and climbs steadily for 150 m to a bridge over Roaring Creek. It stays at this height along the bush margin through tussock, mountain beech and tarns in a park-like setting beside The Orchard (2.5 km/1 hour). For the next 2 km/1 hour the track wanders around Sunny Creek to the foot of Earland Falls, with a semi-permanent rainbow, a fine munch spot.

From here a forest rich in ferns and understorey shrubs encloses the track as it drops to Lake Howden (3 km/1 hour). Howden Hut is a large split-level hut with 28 bunks, and you can camp at the far end of the lake, 20 minutes away along the first part of the Greenstone Track.

A short track climbs 100 m from the hut round the flanks of Key Summit up to the track junction (500 m/15 minutes). The 30-minute side-track to Key Summit climbs up to tarns and alpine shrubbery delicately poised on this historically and geographically significant hill. The mountain panorama is breathtaking on a clear day, and the great slabs of these Fiordland peaks can seem almost too close for comfort.

Back on the main track it's a descent of 300 m to The Divide, and this last bit of track passes though silver beech forest with ribbon-wood and fuchsia (2 km/1 hour). At The Divide carpark there's a large shelter and toilets, and all the shuttle buses stop here.

Greenstone Valley and Caples Valley

Total tramping time: 4–6 days
Total tramping distance: 71 km (total circuit from The Divide)
Grade: easy/medium
Highest point: 976 m; McKellar Saddle
Maps: Eglinton D41; Queenstown E41;
   Routeburn-Greenstone 335-02

A satisfying and popular circuit tramp along two spacious South Island valleys. People often choose the Greenstone–Caples as an easier and less crowded alternative to the Routeburn. With six huts, big open flats, a tarn pass, several short impressive gorges, and lots of beech forest, the Greenstone–Caples is easy going through big mountains, with plenty of camping opportunities. There's a good escape option to the Greenstone carpark for people with limited time.

Drive from Te Anau 85 km to The Divide shelter where the Routeburn Track starts. The access via Kinloch is about 18 km from Glenorchy. Transport options are good during the summer, and various bus companies operate regular bus services to both The Divide (on the Milford Sound road) and the Greenstone road-end.

From the carpark at The Divide (shelter and toilets) take the Routeburn Track as it winds 1.5 km/1 hour up through rainforest to the side-track to Key Summit. It is well worth the short detour to the Summit as the views range over the Darran Mountains and the three great catchments of the Hollyford, Greenstone and Eglinton Rivers. There is a mountain-finder table and tarns on the Summit. Please keep to the track because the alpine plant communities are easily damaged.

The main track sidles 500 m/10 minutes easily down to Howden Hut (28 bunks) and to the start of the Greenstone Track. Follow along beside the pretty Lake Howden to the clearing at the far end (1 km/20 minutes), and the closest campsite to the lake, then the track wanders over the subtle Greenstone Saddle 2.5 km/1 hour through beech and tussock down to Lake McKellar and the track junction to the Caples River.

Greenstone Valley

A slowish sidle of the lake for 4 km/1–2 hours brings you round to McKellar Hut (20 bunks) in a large, grassy glade. Across the footbridge the track keeps to the bush, avoiding the leasehold grazing land. The tendency of the track to stay in the bush can get irritating as it travels 13 km/3–4 hours downvalley to Steele Creek, though there are some occasional good views of the big mountains either side. At one point there are some rocky mounds and a pretty tarn which makes a welcome lunch stop.

About 1 km before Steele Creek the Greenstone River drops sharply through a short gorge. The track keeps away from the edge, but it's worth a closer look. After the gorge there's a junction with the Steele Creek track, then a bridge over the incised Steele Creek itself, and a steepish walk up past the private palace by the river terrace to the DOC hut on the hill 1 km/20 minutes from Steele Creek.

Mid-Greenstone is adroitly placed, with a grand outlook up the valley and a sunny verandah to laze about on (12 bunks).

From the hut the track drops gradually through beech forest to the river flats and follows along the Greenstone River as it begins to swing round the corner (4 km/1–2 hours). The marking becomes vague, but towards the end of the grass flats look for a small scree slide and a worn trail up it. This turns into a broad and stony cattle track that is easy to follow as it sidles up and down alongside the Greenstone River, which is now bustling through a deep, invisible gorge.

After 1 km/20 minutes there's the side-track to the Mavora Walkway. This crosses a short sharp gorge and climbs up only 10 minutes to the well-situated Slyburn Hut (4 double bunks/8 people in all; you need a portable cooker as there is no wood stove or fire-place).

However, the main Greenstone track travels 2.5 km/1 hour down to Slip Flat. Excellent camping here. There's a poled route past an attractive series of big grass hummocks, but you will have to keep your eyes sharp to spot the discreet Slip Flats Biv, which is high up at the back of the flat and cosy for 2–3 people.

Through Slip Flat the track climbs back into the bush after 1 km/20 minutes, and another 1.5 km/30 minutes on there's the track junction to Elfin Bay and Lake Rere. Continue on the main trail as it sidles steadily 2 km/1 hour past two side-creeks (with a waterfall apiece) into the Caples Valley, and crosses a footbridge to the east bank of the Caples and a track junction.

The exit via the Greenstone is only 1 km/20 minutes further, sidling through bush to the carpark and picnic area at the road-end, and if blisters are your lot then this might be the time to consider that option.   .

It's about 7.5 km/2–3 hours up the Caples valley, keeping as always to the bush most of the way, and passing the old Birchdale homestead across the river. Where the Caples River gets compressed into a short gorge the track climbs onto a terrace and crosses the footbridge over this spectacular defile to Mid-Caples Hut (12 bunks) in a bright open position.

Up the valley the track stays on open tussock terraces for much of the 7 km/2–3 hours alongside the Caples. Where it finally enters the bush the beech forest is high and lovely, and it's only another 1 km/20 minutes past the two Steele Creek track junctions to the 20-person hut. Like all the huts on the Greenstone–Caples Track it is well situated, in this case in a private sunny glade. Side-tracks lead over the bridge to Fraser Creek and Kay Creek tracks.

Upriver the main track slowly climbs 300 m through bush for 5 km/2 hours, then crosses the upper Caples for a last steep burst of 150 m through the alpine shrubs to the tussock edge across over McKellar Saddle, which is a broad and boggy alpine basin (2 km/1 hour). Much of this stretch has now been boardwalked. On the pass itself there are some damp campsites and excellent mountain views, and a peaceful lunch spot with tarns and a chance to admire Lake McKellar below.

The track down to the lake is slow, boggy, and gouged out in places, probably the roughest part of the entire Greenstone–Caples circuit. It's about a 300-m descent to the valley floor and up to the Greenstone Track junction (2 km/1 hour).

Mavora Walkway

Total tramping time: 11–14 hours/3–4 days
  (Mavora to Greenstone junction)
Total tramping distance: 40 km
  (Mavora to Greenstone junction; to Greenstone carpark 50 km)
Grade: easy/medium
Highest point: 740 m; Pass Burn saddle
Maps: Walter Peak E42; Queenstown E41

A long but easy traverse through tussock grasslands from the Mavora Lakes to the Greenstone track. Four huts dot the length of a trail that does not get heavily used at all, and wanders up a typically vast high country landscape. Alpine lakes, beech forest, bush birds and tussock wetlands are some of the sights. However, cattle flats and plains of tussock are not everyone's cup of tea, and transport to the track is a pain. The walkway is closed between May and October (the winter months).

This is a track that could easily be linked into the Greenstone Track, providing a satisfying 4- to 5-day tramp — with hardly anything called a hill to climb.

From Highway 94 about 30 km west of Mossburn, follow the dusty unsealed road for 45 km to the North Mavora Lake. The road stops just at the start of the lake, and you really can't go further without a proper four-wheel-drive. There are many DOC camping and picnic areas, with toilets and barbecue sites at both the South and North Mavora Lakes. People with four-wheel-drives can go as far as Boundary Hut. For the Greenstone road-end there are regular bus service pick-ups during the summer months.

From the carpark a four-wheel-drive track rambles alongside the North Mavora Lake for 3 km/1 hour through open beech forest with a healthy variety of bush birds, including riflemen, parakeets, the yellow-breasted tomtit and the ever-inquisitive robin. Then it's 7 km/2–3 hours on tussocklands round to Careys Hut (8 bunks). Despite the closeness to the road it's in good condition, with a wetback and shower, though you'll need to bring your own firewood.

The four-wheel-drive track persists upvalley 1 km/20 minutes to

Wide open spaces, Mavora Walkway

the head of the lake with good views from a highish shoulder, then drops into the Mararoa River 5 km/1 hour to Boundary Hut. Like the other huts it has 4 wide bunks, which can accommodate 2 people each. No cooking facilities so a portable cooker is essential.

Across the footbridge the poled track wanders in vast flats upriver, picking up old vehicle tracks for some of the 13 km/3–4 hours to the Taipo Hut. The track stays on the west bank all the way though some of the poles have fallen over (maybe the cattle rub their itches on them?) so at times you need to have sharp eyes to spot the next pole. Away from the four-wheel-drive track there's very little of a worn trail as the tramping use is not great, and there are attractive patches of red tussock, sphagnum moss soaks, and wetland ponds invariably tenanted by a couple of paradise ducks.

After about 9 km from Boundary Hut the Mararoa River goes through an obvious gorge and the poled route does a rather odd circumlocutory route alongside it. There's an alternative short-cut if you take the four-wheel-drive track straight over the terrace, and you are also rewarded with a magnificent sweeping view of the upper Mararoa forks. The Taipo Hut is marked in the wrong place on the metric map, right by the top forks when in fact it is 1 km up the main Mararoa River. Keep well to the west side of the valley and the poles will march you to the well-situated hut beside the footbridge (4 double bunks).

Next the Mavora Walkway heads up the delightful Pond Burn, with poles guiding you through snow tussock and over damp oases of wetland plants, then round the toe of a hill some 3 km/1 hour to the top pond. There's an old 4-bunk musterers' hut in the bush terrace on the west bank overlooking the pond, which is private and belongs to Elfin Bay Station.

There's a choice of two routes from the top pond. The official poled route climbs up onto a terrace just beside the old hut, then steadily sidles through the beech forest for 5 km/1–2 hours over the barely noticeable saddle. Windfall is cluttering this track. Eventually it cuts across the Pass Burn from the west bank to the east and meets the wide cattle track.

The cattle track provides a more scenic alternative from the top pond, and although not marked it is easy to follow as it rambles down one long, extensive clearing of tussock and bog pine for 5 km/1–2 hours, when it meets the walkway again. Probably the cattle track is slightly quicker, though either way the birdlife is excellent over the pass, with kaka and falcons being seen here.

From the junction of the cattle track and walkway a good track ambles about 2 km/1 hour through bush and clearing down to the well-located Slyburn Hut (4 double bunks). The hut sits on a sunny terrace, 500 m/10 minutes above a pretty cleft in the Greenstone River and on to the track junction with the Greenstone Track.

For access and route information either down or up the Greenstone River see Greenstone Valley and Caples Valley, page 273; 10 km/2–3 hours to Greenstone carpark.

Hollyford Track

Total tramping time: 6–8 days
Total tramping distance: 112 km
Grade: easy/medium
Highest point: 143 m; Little Homer Saddle
Maps: Hollyford Trackmap 335-03; Milford D40;
   Lake McKerrow D39

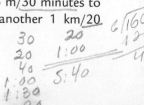

An historic track on the northern edge of Fiordland National Park, penetrating extensive bush to the remote coast at Martins Bay. Rich plant life and bird sounds contrast with marine fauna, seals and penguins on the coast. If bush and coast is your thing then you will enjoy this track, but some trampers find it monotonous, particularly when the rain sets in. The 'Demon Trail' section is not really deserving of its name, but it is slow compared with the rest of the pack-track.

The Hollyford is a very long track, and the times and distances given above are for the outward and return journey. Many people prefer to walk one way only, then jetboat or fly out. Transport arrangements can be made with Hollyford Valley Walks at Te Anau or Invercargill (or at the private Martins Bay Lodge itself during the summer season).

Travel from Te Anau 87 km on Highway 94 to the junction by the Hollyford Road, then 16 km to the end of the road. DOC Te Anau has an up-to-date list of transport operators. Gunn's Camp is halfway down the Hollyford Road. It's a cosy place to stay and the museum is well worth a visit.

From the carpark the graded and gravelled pack-track leaves the Hollyford River and cuts inland past a verandah bolted into the rock, which overlooks a quiet backwater. It's barely 1.5 m/30 minutes to a substantial footbridge over Eel Creek, then another 1 km/20 minutes to a bridge over Swamp Creek, the track passing close to several silent and dry river channels.

After 2 km/40 minutes past the large kahikatea clearing the Hollyford River swings tightly into the hillside, and an elaborate track gallery negotiates the bluffs for 30 m, and overhangs the slick dark waters of the river. Five minutes further there is a decent break in the bush canopy, with memorable views up to the splinter peaks of the Darran mountains.

After this the track wanders in rich vegetation to a glorious view of the thundering falls at Hidden Falls Creek (3 km/1 hour). Cross the footbridge and walk a few minutes to the 12-bunk hut. The large grassy flats offer plenty of camping space, and you also get kiwi here. It is surprising to realise that you are barely 100 m above sea level, even though there is still another three days of walking to reach the sea, some 60 kilometres away.

From the hut the benched track meanders under a tall bush canopy, then climbs up to Little Homer Saddle (4 km/1-2 hours); at 143 m this is the highest point of the track. The descent is a bit steeper, dropping 100 m over 1 km/20 minutes down past the pretty Little Homer Falls.

It's about 1 km/20 minutes to the bridge over Rainbow Creek, then the track closes to the sluggish Hollyford and ambles along its banks 3 km/1 hour past a couple of grassy clearings (the second has a private hut and a good view of Madeline).

After crossing a bridge over Chair Creek the track passes the suspension walkway over the Pyke and continues for 1 km/20 minutes to the smooth, milky Lake Alabaster and the lakeside hut (16 bunks).

Across the Pyke footbridge there's a brief gallery, then the track cuts under the bluff for 1 km/20 minutes before turning west. For 5 km/1-2 hours it's buried in deep podocarp forest with abundant bird life (kaka, tui, bellbirds) heard more often than seen, except for the flurrying wood pigeons. Eventually the track rejoins the Hollyford River and follows along its side for 1.5 km/30 minutes to a track junction for McKerrow Island Hut.

This hut is reached by crossing the obvious side-channel of the Hollyford then following a track across the island to the 12-bunk hut; 1.5 km/30 minutes. There's no bridge, so if it rains you'll be nicely stranded.

Hollyford River mouth

Continue along the main track to a clearing on the old McKerrow Hut site, the start of the Demon Trail as it sidles the huge Lake McKerrow. Stony, muddy, rambling up and down in an irritating fashion, occasionally unclear — in fact just an ordinary tramping track. Although there are many 3-wire bridges across the side-streams on the Demon Trail, even the smallest unbridged stream can get choked with rain and become impassable. The Trail is not as fierce as its name, but it can get tedious. Think of the MacKenzie brothers driving their cattle along here in the 1880s.

It's approximately 3 km/1 hour to Demon Trail Hut, over two 3-wire bridges. The hut sits on a sunny terrace and has 12 bunks, a wood stove and a pleasant view over the lake. Continue along the undulating track for 10 km/3–4 hours to Hokuri Hut (12 bunks). This is perhaps the dullest stretch with only occasional lake views and a glance to the mountains beyond. There are three 3-wire bridges to cross; at last you've broken the back of the Demon Trail.

After this the track continues for 1 km/20 minutes to a junction. The main route follows the shoreline and the flood-track goes inland to a 3-wire flood-bridge over Hokuri Stream and a shorter 3-wire bridge over an unnamed side-creek before rejoining the lake track. Follow the shoreline if you can, it's nicer. There are campsites on the flats by Hokuri Stream.

The lakeside track is pleasant, easy travel along gravel beaches but it's only thinly marked. Continue 1 km/20 minutes into Gravel Cove and on to the site of Jamestown, now utterly overgrown. This was a settlement established in 1870 and lasted barely 5 years.

About 1.5 km/30 minutes on, just past a large fan-creek, the lake comes right up to the bush. There's a poorly marked and boggy track tucked in behind the margin of flax, then after 100 m the beach resumes for 1 km/20 minutes to a signposted turnoff.

The trail swings inland along a well-drained benched track, twisting back and forth in heavy forest for 2.5 km/1 hour before breaking out onto the airstrip clearing. Poles lead across grass and buttercups for 1 km/20 minutes, past a sign indicating the private Martins Bay Lodge. If you wish to fly or jetboat out, this is the place to contact. They take Visa (just joking! Actually they probably do.)

Re-enter the bush for 1 km/20 minutes to Jerusalem Creek, an easy ford, then the track scrambles among matted forest and coastal scrub, crossing two side-streams. Sudden views of the Hollyford mouth and the 16-bunk hut after 2 km/40 minutes.

Around the corner of Long Reef Point there is a fur seal colony, where you can watch them sleep, snore and squabble among the boulders. Fiordland crested penguins can often be seen hopping over the rocks.

For access and route information to Big Bay and onto the Cascade River see The Coast, page 229.

(Note: to continue around the Hollyford 'loop' via Big Bay, Upper Pyke, Lake Wilmot and Lake Alabaster entails another 4–5 days. Although the route is roughly marked some parts are badly overgrown, and the main rivers (apart from the Awarua and Olivine) are not bridged. There are no huts except at Big Bay and the Olivine River and there are no plans to develop the 'loop' further. For information, contact DOC Te Anau. This route is only suitable for experienced parties.)

Milford Track

Total tramping time: 15–18 hours/3 nights, 4 days
Total tramping distance: 48 km
Grade: medium
Highest point: 1073 m; Mackinnon Pass
Maps: Milford Track 335-01; Milford D40;
    Eglinton D41
(See *New Zealand's Top Tracks* by Mark Pickering for
a more detailed description of this track.)

The Milford is the most famous track in New
Zealand. It penetrates the sheer walls of the
Fiordland mountains in a remarkable trick of track
engineering and opens up vistas of alpine tops,
waterfalls (the world's sixth highest), lakes and bush-
carpeted valleys. Most superlatives have been wasted on the Milford
and there's little need to add more. Take a good raincoat and don't
expect an easy country ramble and you will have a satisfying and
memorable tramp.

For 'independent walkers' (as opposed to those who pay for a
guided trip) the Milford is a managed track. You can only walk in one
direction, take only three nights and four days, and stay only at spec-
ified DOC huts. Camping is not allowed. If the regulated aspects of
Milford Track bug you then do another tramp. Many trampers who
have done both tracks think the Routeburn is just as good, if not better than the Milford. This account is written for the 'independent'
walker.

You can buy a total transport package through DOC (PO Box 29,
Te Anau), where for about $200 (1998 prices) you get both launch
trips (Te Anau Downs to Glade Wharf, and Sandfly Point to Milford
Sound), transport from Te Anau to Te Anau Downs, and transport
from Milford back to Te Anau, plus 3 nights' DOC hut fees. This is a
convenient package, since most of these costs are obligatory anyway.
Food and hostel accommodation at Milford is extra, and the hostel
needs to be prebooked. The booking system has the merit of elimi-
nating overcrowding on the track; the quietest times are pre-
December and post-February.

After all the palaver of getting out of Te Anau the 30-km/1-hour boat trip up the immense Lake Te Anau is relaxing. The Milford Track starts quietly, following an old vehicle track up beside the Clinton River. It is 1 km/20 minutes to Glade House (for guided walkers only) and then 4.5 km/1-2 hours to Clinton Hut. The track ambles through beech forest with one good view back to Dore Pass.

Turning inland up the west branch of the Clinton the track potters through silver beech forest for 7 km/2 hours to the old Six Mile Hut, used in packhorse days. It's 2 km/40 minutes to the Prairies, the first open grasslands on the track, with a tantalising distant view of Mackinnon Pass. A side-track goes to Hidden Lake, a good lunch spot.

It is 3 km/1 hour further to Bus Stop Shelter and Marlene's Creek, which floods badly in wet weather. Past the Pompolona Hut the valley walls loom oppressively above the track as it crosses many old avalanche paths on its steady 200-m climb over 4 km/1 hour to Mintaro Hut, where there are good views. Lake Mintaro is a blue gem, reflecting at various angles the bush and mountain surroundings. The hut is the standard 40-bunk model.

If you get to Mintaro Hut the evening before and the weather is fine, it's not a bad idea to take advantage of it to walk up in the afternoon/evening to Mackinnon Pass. Take a torch, and tell the warden. The evening light can be memorable, and you might avoid disappointment the next day if the cloud comes down.

After 1 km/20 minutes up through the last of the alpine bush the track lazily zig-zags 350 m up over 3 km/1-2 hours to the narrow rock ridge that is Mackinnon Pass, at 1073 m.

On top there is a scatter of tarns and a 4-m-high memorial to Quintin Mackinnon, who discovered the pass. There are superb views down both valleys, with an even better outlook as you climb toward the lunch shelter and the romantic shape of Mount Balloon.

Descend gradually off the pass for 1 km/20 minutes. The track then takes a steeper dive, crossing the Roaring Burn and dropping more easily, a drop in altitude of over 800 m in 5 km/2 hours.

Don't miss the Sutherland Falls, or as the Maori more poetically called them, Te Tautea, 'The White Thread'. There is a day shelter at Quintin where independent walkers can drop their packs and take the side-track (1-2 hours return) to the base of these 580-m falls.

Kea

You can wonder at the redoubtable William Quill, who made a hair-raising ascent beside the falls in 1890 to reach the feeder lake that bears his name. In any weather this waterfall is a tremendous sight.

Downstream from Quintin Hut the track ambles 3 km/1 hour to Dumpling Hut, the final night's stay on the track. The next 18 km out to Sandfly Point has to be covered in a quickish day if you are planning to catch the 3 pm bus back to Te Anau in the afternoon. The launch leaves at 2 pm so you will have to leave early. There is another launch at 3 pm for those staying at Milford or catching the 5 pm bus out.

Leaving Dumpling Hut behind you, follow the track as it closes on the Arthur River and after 6 km/2 hours reaches the guided walkers' boatshed, then crosses the Arthur on a long footbridge. Shortly over Mackay Creek there's a 500-m/10-minute side-track to the bursting Mackay Falls and the unusually eroded Bell Rock. The track follows the river closely now, crossing side-streams and climbing onto a rock shoulder with good views before easing down to Giant Gate Falls (7 km/2 hours).

There is a shelter and toilet here, and a fine lunch and swimming spot. It might be more sensible to wait here and give yourself time to wander down the last 6 km/2 hours to the jetty, to avoid the sand-flies at Sandfly Point.

Slipping out into Milford Sound on the launch beneath the awesome shining circle of peaks gives a satisfying crowning touch to the walk, perhaps the 'finest in the world' after all?

Kepler Track

Total tramping time: 3–5 days
Total tramping distance: 67 km
Grade: medium
Highest point: 1270 m; Luxmore Saddle
Maps: Kepler Trackmap 335/9; Manapouri C43
(See *New Zealand's Top Tracks* by Mark Pickering for
a more detailed description of this track.)

This circuit track has rapidly become one of the 'big' tramps in New Zealand, and there are no hassles or costs involved with boat transport. The Iris Burn has lovely beech forest and the Luxmore tops splendid views. However, the alpine section is a full day and should not be taken lightly. There are two emergency shelters on the tops, and the three huts have gas cookers, wood stoves (for heating only) and a warden on permanent duty throughout the October–April season. A Great Walks pass is required for huts and campsites.

Transport to the track must be the easiest anywhere. You can walk 5 km from Te Anau to the Control Gate Bridge (this is to control water, not people!), or catch a shuttle bus to here or the Rainbow Reach start point which is about 14 km from Te Anau, down the Manapouri Road, turning down a steep shingle road to the footbridge across the Waiau River. You can also arrange a water-taxi from Te Anau to Brod Bay to cut out a couple of walking hours, if you are tackling the Luxmore climb first.

From the Rainbow Reach carpark the track crosses the footbridge, turns south and follows the Waiau River downstream in the fertile river terraces. Red beech with a thick carpet of crown ferns make up the forest, as the track wanders around Balloon Loop, a side channel of the Waiau. The track crosses the Forest Burn over a footbridge and climbs to an attractive sphagnum moss swamp and lake. It's about 4 km/1–2 hours from the carpark to the junction with the Shallow Bay side-track.

(It's a few minutes down to the tranquil shoreline of Lake Manapouri, where reflections of the typically heavy Fiordland clouds

Iris Burn waterfall

roll out over the surface of the lake. Shallow Bay hut is 20 minutes along the beach and track, a cosy 6-bunker with fireplace.)

On the main trail it's only 2 km/40 minutes to Moturau Hut, a 40-bunker with a warden's hut next door and a fine outlook over the lake.

The track from Moturau Hut continues around the lake for a short distance (2 km/40 minutes), then turns up the Iris Burn, staying on the north bank all the way. The climb upvalley is gradual, peaceful and mostly unremarkable for its 15-km distance, and it emerges from the thick, mossy forest in only two places. At Rocky Point, roughly the halfway point up the Iris Burn, there is a private track maintenance hut.

About 12 km/3–4 hours above Moturau Hut comes the second clearing, the Big Slip, which was caused by a rock avalanche in 1984, and underscores how unstable some of these mountain slopes are. From the Big Slip there's a short climb to a low bush saddle then some hasty zig-zags down over a bridge to the open tussock flat where the Iris Burn Hut sits (3 km/1 hour).

With 60 bunks the hut is big, but it has perhaps the nicest setting of any of the huts on the Kepler. Campsite nearby. There is also a worthwhile 20-minute side-track to where the Iris Burn blusters over a waterfall.

From the hut the track is all uphill and steep. For about the first 300-m climb it twists elaborately up through a bush face, then sidles into a discreet side-creek valley. The track crosses the stream, doubles back on itself and crawls steeply up another bush face for 300 m to emerge from the bush just below the crest of the spur (3 km/2–3 hours).

Looking back (after wiping off the sweat) the views are already good. After a short climb you reach a mock saddle, really just a dip in a leading spur, which has a very fine lookout over Lake Manapouri. The views continue to be good as you progress up the laddered and boardwalked spur till you see the Hanging Valley Shelter protruding on the main ridge (2 km/2 hours).

It's great to get there, knowing most of the steep climbing is over with, but the shelter is basic; no water, no mattresses. At about this point you may wish you had brought more water.

The ridge track is well graded and at first undulates along the top before cleverly sidling some rock outcrops and pinnacles to the basic Forest Burn Shelter (3 km/1 hour). There's a steepish climb from this shelter over loose faces of scree, the track zig-zagging up to Luxmore Saddle, at 1270 m the highest point of the track. Worth a short dash up to Luxmore Summit.

Then it's downhill. A gentle rambling lollop as the 'garden path' swings around into a big and pretty tarn-filled basin, turning the flanks of the spurs to reveal more and more fine views of Lake Te Anau and the Murchison Mountains. The 4 km/1 hour from Luxmore Saddle slips by quickly, the complex of Mount Luxmore Hut soon coming into view. With 60 bunks, the hut is rather a wart on the landscape, but it does have fine lounge views.

The descent down to Lake Te Anau is much easier than most downhill tracks. It is well graded, and after crossing the open tops (2 km/1 hour to the bushline) it drops through bush and eases under some limestone bluffs (1 km/30 minutes). Then it's 6 km/2 hours of beech forest down to Brod Bay. You might have arranged a boat pick-up here after a stop for lunch, or you might choose to camp here for the night. There's a toilet, driftwood, picnic tables, and a murderous breed of sandfly.

The track wanders along the shore bays 4 km/1–2 hours to Dock Bay and then a final 1 km/20 minutes to the Control Gates.

It is easy to miss out the last bit of track down the Waiau River, but it's a shame to do so. If you have a car at Rainbow Reach it probably is quicker to walk out along the riverside track. The 11 km/3–4 hours of the river section has a quiet charm of its own. There's mature red beech forest beside the slick and silent river, and the track ambles from river terrace to riverside, where the peacefulness of the day is only occasionally broken by the kingfisher's hoarse 'kek, kek, kek'.

Dusky Sound

Total tramping time: 4–6 days
Total tramping distance: 84 km
Grade: medium
Highest point: 1109 m; Centre Pass
Maps: Fiordland National Park 273/3; Resolution
B44; Manapouri C43; Hunter Mountains C44

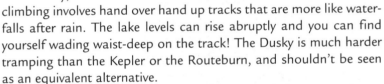

To the heart of Fiordland National Park and the deep fiord of Dusky Sound. Well-marked tracks and plenty of huts, and a range of remote scenery that would be hard to match anywhere in New Zealand. However, this area has among the heaviest rainfalls in the country, and the tracks are slow; sometimes the climbing involves hand over hand up tracks that are more like waterfalls after rain. The lake levels can rise abruptly and you can find yourself wading waist-deep on the track! The Dusky is much harder tramping than the Kepler or the Routeburn, and shouldn't be seen as an equivalent alternative.

At the northern/Manapouri end of the track regular tourist boats provide good access across Lake Manapouri. Access to the southern start of the track is difficult. From Te Anau travel 25 km east to the Key Road junction. Turn down the road 55 km to the Lilburn Valley Road, which leads 35 km to Lake Haluroko. A boat taxi service runs on the lake and should be prebooked.

It's worth considering the use of floatplanes, which though expensive can get you into Dusky Sound where you can walk back, or pick you up from Lake Haluroko. The Fiordland National Park headquarters at Te Anau can supply travel information for the area.

Lake Haluroko is an elongated body of water 30 km in length, twisting in and out of the mountains like a great water snake. From the jetty and Haluroko Burn Hut (12 bunks, wood stove) the track heads upstream in pleasant beech forest 7 km/2 hours to a walkwire. Once across, the track climbs sharply 200 m then sidles 4.5 km/1–2 hours to Halfway Hut (12 bunks).

Easy-going bush travel upvalley past two side-creeks to a 3-wire crossing of the upper Haluroko Burn (3 km/1 hour). The track rises

Climbing up to Centre Pass

100 m or so till it recrosses the Hauroko Burn for the last time (1.5 km/40 minutes) and begins a steady 300-m ascent to Furkert Pass (1.5 km/1 hour).

Lake Laffy is a small gem in the dull tussock, with Lake Roe Hut (12 bunks and wood stove) tucked to one side, a little back and up from the lake. Plenty of scope for exploration in this area, either up to the shining expanse of Lake Roe or further on to the tops of the Merrie Range.

From the hut climb west up 150 m along the poled route till the track slips between Lakes Horizon and Ursula (1 km/30 minutes), then up onto the rolling tops of the Pleasant Range, where the poles wander about many hillocks and delightful tarns, dropping 250 m down to the park-like bushline (3.5 km/1–2 hours). The long finger of Dusky Sound is visible probing the hills to the west, and there are some good dry campsites up here.

The track down is precipitous, hand-over-hand stuff sometimes, 900 m to a very long 3-wire bridge across the Seaforth River (2 km/2 hours). Loch Maree Hut is in a lovely position on a peninsula jutting into the lake; 12 bunks and wood stove.

A side-trip can be taken down to Dusky Sound itself, a long tramp of 14 km/4–5 hours over a sometimes very muddy track which was originally constructed as a 'road' by a Public Works gang in 1903.

The hut at Supper Cove has 12 bunks and a dinghy to fish and sight-see from. This essential side-trip would take at least 2 days return.

From Loch Maree Hut it is a steady 8 km/2–3 hours in beech forest to a walk-wire over the Kenneth Burn. Climbing 250 m the track follows the Seaforth River as it curls around the distinctive Tripod Hill past Gair Loch to Kintail Hut (4 km/1–2 hours).

A footbridge crosses the Seaforth and the track slips into Kintail Stream, then crosses another footbridge, climbing vigorously to the bushline where it sidles more gently to the tussock gap of Centre Pass. All told a 750-m climb over 4 km/2–3 hours from Kintail.

The track over the pass is well poled and there are plenty of tarns. There is a good side-trip from the pass up onto Mt Memphis, and camping is quite possible amid the sprinkling of tarns on the peak, or on the pass itself.

A mild descent of 3 km/1 hour beside the hectic Warren Burn, at first tussock then sidling through the bush. There's a camp right on the bushline but nothing further till the Upper Spey Hut (12 bunks, wood stove), a 600-m descent from the pass.

Immediately downstream from the hut is a wide, spongy clearing, then ribbonwood forest intermingles with beech; 1 km/30 minutes to the first walk-wire, and 5 km/2 hours to the second. There are scattered camping areas on the occasional grass river flats, especially the last 1 km/20 minutes from the second bridge to the Manapouri road. In wet weather this section of track gets surface flooding.

It's 4 km/1 hour down the road to the portal of the power station, the information centre on the foreshore, the jetty where you can pick up the regular tourist boat, and the usual hordes of avaricious sand-flies.

Waitutu Tramway and Port Craig

Total tramping time: 3–4 days (Wairaurahiri River return)
Total tramping distance: 40 km (Wairaurahiri River return)
Grade: easy
Highest point: 60 m; Edwin Burn viaduct
Maps: Fiordland National Park 273/3;
 Port Craig C46

A coastal walk to Port Craig, just about the end of New Zealand's earth, a wet, hard, stubborn place. Yet the coastline is stunning — sandy beaches, sea-stacks, blowholes, rocky headlands, dense lowland forest and an historic tramway with its massive viaducts still standing. Two huts and generally flat, undemanding tramping. Of course it rains a lot.

From Tuatapere turn off Half Mile Road 6 km towards the Waiau Mouth, then take the 8-km road to Rowallan Burn (just past Papatotara) to reach the Blue Cliffs Beach road, and drive 4 km along to the prominent DOC signpost on the beach.

There's a walk of about 6 km/2 hours along the Blue Cliffs Beach to the start of the tramping track, and a low tide is advantageous as it is fast travel on the exposed sand. Even at high tide you can usually get along the beach, but the travel is slow, and a big surf could make it dangerous.

Where the Hump Burn bustles in, follow the road briefly around to some private baches 500 m/10 minutes to where the Waitutu Track starts.

From the track sign walk on a well-graded bush track to Flat Creek (3 km/1 hour). Take the footbridge alternative at the junction and cross over and follow the track as it drops to a small sandy bay, then pick up another track which scurries over the headland to a fine beach known as the Blowholes (1 km/20 minutes).

Walk 1 km/20 minutes along the beach, with its rock stacks and view west to Port Craig. A low tide exposes extensive tidal platforms and with a moderate swell the blowholes operate on the offshore reef at the south end. Two reasonable campsites on the foreshore grass terraces and a tiny rock bivvy at the western end.

Tidal pools

Nip round the headland to Breakneck Creek, where at low- to mid-tide the coast can be followed to Whata Cliff. This way is well worth taking, as the permanent high-tide route is a quagmire, and the log-book at Port Craig is full of discontent and gnashing of teeth.

The low-tide route has some scrambles over rocks (particularly at Breakneck Creek) but generally it is a pleasant tramp round rock headlands and over easy exposed sands. After 3.5 km/1 hour there's a steep climb up from the beach at Whata Cliff and another well-graded track goes 1.5 km/40 minutes into Port Craig and the hut.

Port Craig was the site of a logging mill in 1918, but is now muted with neglect. Wire hawsers, bolts and bricks are scattered randomly, railway sleepers melded to the rock foreshore by rust, wagons perched incongruously by a wharf which is slowly being gnawed to pieces by the sea. The original schoolhouse has been converted into a trampers' hut (12 bunks), and there is also a large sea cave down at the northern end of the beach. Actually, it's a hole in the head-land, but it does provide romantic shelter for 6 people.

From Port Craig the historic tramway starts slicing through deep cuttings as it turns the corner and runs down the southern coast. It's easy walking for 15 km through old embankments, cuttings and regenerating forest almost to the banks of the Wairaurahiri River. It crosses several viaducts, remarkable examples of bush engineering. The track can get a lot of surface flooding, making for sloshy travel.

After 6 km/2 hours from Port Craig you reach the junction with Sand Hill Point, worth the brief 10-minute detour. It's an ancient camp area used by the Maori. Pingao, a rare native sedge, tops the dunes with an orangey cap. You need a permit to visit this point. Excellent views along the coast.

For the next 5 km/1-2 hours beyond Sand Hill Point the tramline crosses four spectacular viaducts. They are certainly the largest wooden viaducts remaining in New Zealand, and some Southlanders claim the world.

The first is after 1 km, the second and biggest is across the Percy Burn after 2 km, spanning the creek by 124 m and raised 34 m above the Burn. Another 1.5 km to the Edwin Burn viaduct, then 1.5 km to the Francis Burn viaduct, where there is an old lineman's hut, still serviceable as a shelter in wet weather.

It's 4 km/1 hour to the end of the tramway, where a very muddy track completes the last 300 m/15 minutes down to the Wairaurahiri River, where there is a 12-bunk hut. Across the footbridge there is some splendid podocarp forest, well worth a wander into.

Coastal route notes

The Waitutu Track does continue for another 26 km to the Waitutu Hut and on to Big River, but it is a rough tramping trail, and a dead-end. Allow at least an extra 3-4 days to get to the end at Big River and back to the Wairaurahiri Hut.

It is also possible to walk back along the coast from the Wairaurahiri Hut to Sand Hill Point, but you need to judge the tides accurately as there is a shortage of escape routes, especially at the start. About 10 km/3-4 hours to Sand Hill Point.

It is possible to scramble round to Port Craig itself from Sand Hill Point, but it is slow going over extensive tidal platforms (8 km/3-4 hours). Again a good low tide is needed, and the inland tramway would be quicker and safer.

Rakiura Track

Total tramping time: 9–12 hours/2–3 days
Total tramping distance: 30 km
Grade: easy/medium
Highest point: 300 m; bush saddle
Maps: Stewart Island 336-10; Ruggedy D48;
  Halfmoon Bay E48/F48
(See *New Zealand's Top Tracks* **by Mark Pickering for**
a more detailed description of this track.)

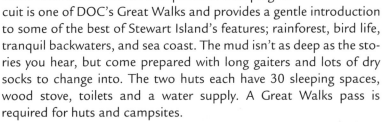

Rakiura or 'land of the glowing skies' is the Maori description of this wilderness island. This far south the skies have a soft, elusive light, constantly changing as rain squalls drift across the low, thickly forested island. This relaxed and pleasant tramping circuit is one of DOC's Great Walks and provides a gentle introduction to some of the best of Stewart Island's features; rainforest, bird life, tranquil backwaters, and sea coast. The mud isn't as deep as the stories you hear, but come prepared with long gaiters and lots of dry socks to change into. The two huts each have 30 sleeping spaces, wood stove, toilets and a water supply. A Great Walks pass is required for huts and campsites.

There are two public transport routes to the island: the Southern Air service from Invercargill airport to Halfmoon Bay (or Oban), a 20-minute hop, or the fast catamaran, the *Foveaux Express*, which takes about an hour to cross the stormy 30-km-wide strait; take a seasick pill. Both services operate all year round, though with reduced services during the winter months. Oban has a general store, tearooms, post office, DOC information base, hotel, pub, backpackers and a lot of charm.

Lee Bay is 5 km from Halfmoon Bay, via the attractive Horseshoe Bay. The Kaipipi road-end is 2 km from Halfmoon Bay. It can be reached by walking to the airport road junction, then taking the right-hand road up the valley for another kilometre. Although there is a taxi service on the island most trampers could walk to either end of the track.

The track to Maori Beach starts from Lee Bay, 5 km/1 hour from Halfmoon Bay. There is some Stewart Island mud, but the track is well-graded, as it was once the main land route to the sawmill settlement at Maori Beach. It pays to keep your camera handy as the light changes quickly and elusively.

The forest is initially cutover, with fuchsia and supplejack, then kamahi and rimu start to dominate, with some tall rimu closer to Maori Beach. There's no beech forest on Stewart Island.

It's about 1 km/30 minutes to Little River, and the track skirts the sand at a lower tide. Upstream from the bridge there is a pleasant picnic site, with a toilet, and some splendid rata and rimu trees.

After Little River the track climbs steeply, and glimpses the bouldery coastline as it cuts across the headland at Peters Point and drops abruptly to Maori Beach (2 km/1 hour). At a lower tide you can cross directly to the beach, but there is a very muddy alternative high-tide track if you get stuck.

Maori Beach is a 1-km/20-minute sweep of sand, golden when the fickle Stewart Island sun emerges. There is a designated camping area at the east end, with cooking shelter and toilet. It's worth visiting the old sawmill relics, where a massive boiler broods in silence.

The track from Maori Beach does a big up and down climb of 150 m (passing the track junction to North Arm) before dropping to Magnetic Beach (where some gold was prospected in 1866), which you can follow around to Port William at low tide. There's an alternative high-tide track (2 km/2 hours).

Port William was the site of a government-sponsored settlement in the 1870s. There is a 30-bunk hut, jetty, picnic and camping areas, and it is a pleasant place to explore.

The track over to North Arm is probably the longest day for most people; it's about 12 km from Port William. Retrace your steps along Port William beach to the North Arm track junction.

After a while the track drops 1 km/20 minutes down to a pretty unnamed stream, which it follows for some distance, first over a side-creek bridge then over a top footbridge (1.5 km/40 minutes). From here the track starts to climb for 3 km/1 hour on well-constructed board-walks as it reaches the bush saddle at a height of about 300 m. A lookout tower gives great views of Paterson Inlet and even the distant South Island.

More boardwalks on the shorter 2-km/40-minute descent as the track drops right down to the roomy North Arm hut. It's worth going down to the shoreline at low tides and exploring the numerous rocky coves and exposed shellfish reef platforms.

From the North Arm hut the main track continues over several headlands for 2 km/40

Fishbait

minutes before dropping down to Sawdust Bay, the site of a sawmill in 1914–18. A sheltered campsite here, with toilet and small shelter. At low tide you can walk out a long way into the bay.

The track dips over a bush saddle for 3 km/1 hour and skirts a little above Prices Inlet, with occasional coastal views, until it drops down into the head of Kaipipi Bay and crosses the inlet over an elegant boardwalk. Shortly afterwards a small side-track goes down to a tiny peninsula in the bay which is a great lunch spot.

From here on you are following the access to the Kaipipi Bay sawmills, which employed over 100 people in the 1860s. Milling continued in this area for 60 years. The 'Kaipipi Road' is quick travel and after 3 km/1 hour reaches the road-end, and it is an easy 2-km/30-minute stroll back to Halfmoon Bay.

The Stewart Island Circuit

Total tramping time: 8–10 days
Total tramping distance: 110 km
Grade: medium
Highest point: 350 m; Thomson Ridge
Maps: Stewart Island 336-10;
  Halfmoon Bay E48/F48; Ruggedy D48

The Stewart Island circuit or north-west circuit is a huge tramping trip, circumnavigating the top half of Stewart Island. It starts from Halfmoon Bay, then goes on to Port William, East Ruggedy, Hellfire Beach and Masons Bay before cutting inland to Freshwater and back to Halfmoon Bay. It is the longest trek in this book and for an average tramper would take at least 8-10 days. That's a lot of food to carry. The birdlife is prolific and vocal, parakeets, tui, bellbirds, kaka are all in excellent voice, and because Stewart Island kiwi uniquely forage during the day you might (with some luck) see one of those.

Although this is a coastal tramp you see precious little of the coast. Out of a 110-km circuit there's only about 15 km on the beaches. However, the tracks are well-marked, with lots of huts, and you certainly feel that you are on your own. To reduce the tramping time some people fly in direct to Masons Bay and walk back around the coast.

For access and route descriptions to Stewart Island and Port William see Rakiura Track, page 297. Halfmoon Bay to Port William is 11 km/5 hours.

From Port William cross over a small saddle and footbridge to the pretty Sawyer's Beach (750 m/15 minutes). Then it's a long thrash 3 km/1-2 hours inland, the track often boggy and invariably twisting in and out of gullies with little in the way of a sea view. This is typical of the coastal travel.

You reach a footbridge and the track skirts Little Bungaree Beach then jumps over a headland and pops out on the golden curve of Big Bungaree Beach (1 km/30 minutes). Follow the beach 1 km/20 minutes round to a 20-bunk hut.

Flat out, Maori Beach

The track now slips and slides 3.5 km/1–2 hours inland over bog, roots and gullies to the fine openness of Murray Beach. After enjoying the shoreline for 1.5 km/30 minutes, the track again turns inland, crosses a footbridge (past a well-preserved steam engine 50 m down a side-track), then follows an old boardwalked tramway.

This easier travel lasts 1 km/20 minutes, then it's back to gully winding for 3 km/1–2 hours until you come to a track junction above Christmas Village Bay, and it's only a few minutes down to the 16-bunk hut. Unfortunately the beach consists only of pebbles, but there are penguin burrows in the scrub backing the beach. The best time to spot the penguins is early morning and late evening.

From the hut a track climbs up to regain the main trail, then drops into a gully, over a footbridge and up the other side; it's a steep 150-m climb to the Mt Anglem junction (1 km/1 hour).

(Note: Mt Anglem is a serious 800-m climb, the highest point on Stewart Island, and only worth doing on a fine day; 10 km/6–7 hours return.)

From Anglem junction it's 5 km/1–2 hours of mostly dry track through rich rimu forest and a constant blanket of crown ferns, then an easy descent via a footbridge to Lucky Beach (again pebbly). The route follows the beach 500 m/10 minutes then sharply climbs some 100 m or so (300 m/15 minutes). Now begins 4 km/1–2 hours of busy bush sidling, passing many little side-streams on the way, till a long descent to the slow, brown-stained Yankee River.

A 20-bunk hut is located 5 minutes downstream. There's some good camping on the foreshore with plenty of driftwood.

It's a big 200-m climb from the hut to a headland covered in kamahi forest, and the same sort of descent through a manuka belt before bursting out onto huge sand dunes at the east end of Smoky Beach (3 km/1–2 hours). There's a reasonable campsite here. Along the far end (2 km/40 minutes) the track turns inland to a footbridge.

It's better to avoid the complicated detour to the footbridge and cross the sinuous Smoky Creek directly to the track, which climbs steeply onto a plateau of kamahi and rata twisted over large rock stumps (1 km/40 minutes). The track now follows five remorseless and deeply etched gullies, which take time, patience and more than a few swearwords to negotiate. It's 2.5 km/1–2 hours overall to the poorly placed Long Harry Hut (6 bunks) where only the toilet has a view, which is a pity because the beach is lovely.

The track sidles 2 km/1 hour inland to a wild boulder coastline, follows that for 1 km/30 minutes, then climbs steadily up through tall coastal scrub to the top where there's a lookout with a superb view over East Ruggedy Beach and islands (2 km/1–2 hours).

Drop 200 m to the river (1 km/20 minutes). If you fancy, you can follow the coast and pick up a short track to a derelict hut which has a good view. Otherwise continue on the main track over Ruggedy Stream (characteristically signposted by brightly coloured buoys), then wander inland through sand dunes and manuka 1 km/30 minutes to the 16-bunk East Ruggedy Hut.

The inland track from here is rather ho-hum some 7 km/2–3 hours to the Waihuna Bay junction. This coastal variation is well worth taking rather than the continual ho-humness of the route via the old Bensons Hut site.

(The old track across the island from Bensons Hut to Freshwater across the swamplands has been discontinued, i.e. not maintained, which is no loss. It was a dreadful scunge.)

Climb up and over the 250-m pass and descend into the remote

Waituna Bay 2.5 km/2 hours, then the track climbs another 200 m and sidles the bush ridge for 4 km/1–2 hours to the dramatic Hellfire Pass Hut (16 bunks). Tremendous views to the sea-stacks and crags of the coastline, and the rata is twisted into strange shapes by the prevailing westerlies.

From the hut the track climbs about 100 m through bush, cruises along at 200-m level for a while, then drops down to the coast over a number of gullies to a short, wild, unnamed beach (5 km/2–3 hours). Campsite here. A further 1.5 km/1 hour of bush travel to the Little Hellfire Biv; good camping here.

It's 1 km/20 minutes along this superb beach then a stiffish climb of 2 km/1–2 hours over Mason Head and down to the lovely arc of Masons Bay. Great sense of space after all the forest travel. They can and do land light aircraft at low tide on this beach. Another 4.5 km/1–2 hours to marker buoys that lead the track inland 1 km/20 minutes through the sandhills to the 24-bunk hut .

It's worth considering doing a day trip down to the other end of Masons Bay to the old Kilbride homestead (private) and The Gutter, a low-tide piece of sand that just manages to join one of the Ernest Islands to the shore. About 20 km/6–8 hours return from the hut.

Masons Bay Hut to Freshwater Hut is surprisingly straight and quick travel, 12 km/3–4 hours following an old vehicle track (there was a farm at Masons Bay once). A generally dry track, passing through belts of coastal scrub and avenues of manuka. The hut has 12 bunks, and sits beside the deep tidal inlet of the Freshwater River. Rocky Mount at 549 m is a possible side-trip, with superb views of Paterson Inlet.

The stretch of track to North Arm Hut is a bit tedious and boggy. From Freshwater, after sidling and climbing above the river for 2 km/40 minutes of reasonable travel, the track gets steep and climbs up to 350 m on the Thompson Ridge (2 km/1–2 hours). Some rather pathetic views for all that effort. Then the track just as promptly descends 2 km/1 hour to a footbridge, and sidles several small bays for 2.5 km/1 hour to the Rakiura Track junction and the 30-bunk hut.

For access and route description down the Kaipipi Road to Halfmoon Bay see Rakiura Track, page 297; 10 km/4 hours to Halfmoon Bay.

OTHER TRAMPING BOOKS FROM REED PUBLISHING (NZ) LTD

New Zealand's Top Tracks
Mark Pickering
$19.95
This book is a practical guide to the eight walking tracks designated
Great Walks by New Zealand's Department of Conservation. Each
track is described in detail; how to get there, how long it will take,
the best time to go and what you will see.

A Tramper's Guide to New Zealand's National Parks
Robbie Burton and Maggie Atkinson
$29.95
This is a succinct but comprehensive guide to all the country's
national parks. Written by two keen and experienced trampers, with
the support of the Department of Conservation, this completely
revised edition provides practical descriptions of every established
walking track or route, as well as up-to-date information on access,
track conditions, huts and campsites, and scenic attractions.